The Counter-Reformation

# Blackwell Essential Readings in History

This series comprises concise collections of key articles on important historical topics. Designed as a complement to standard survey histories, the volumes are intended to help introduce students to the range of scholarly debate in a subject area. Each collection includes a general introduction and brief contextual headnotes to each article, offering a coherent, critical framework for study.

## Published

*The German Reformation: The Essential Readings*
C. Scott Dixon

*The Third Reich: The Essential Readings*
Christian Leitz

*The Counter-Reformation: The Essential Readings*
David M. Luebke

## In Preparation

*The Enlightenment: The Essential Readings*
Martin Fitzpatrick

*The English Civil War: The Essential Readings*
Peter Gaunt

*The Cold War: The Essential Readings*
Klaus Larres and Ann Lane

*The Russian Revolution: The Essential Readings*
Martin Miller

*The French Revolution: The Essential Readings*
Ronald Schechter

# The Counter-Reformation

*The Essential Readings*

Edited by David M. Luebke

BLACKWELL
*Publishers*

Copyright © Blackwell Publishers Ltd 1999. Editorial arrangement and introduction
copyright © David M. Luebke 1999.

First published 1999

2  4  6  8  10  9  7  5  3  1

Blackwell Publishers Inc.
350 Main Street
Malden, Massachusetts 02148
USA

Blackwell Publishers Ltd
108 Cowley Road
Oxford OX4 1JF
UK

*Library of Congress Cataloging-in-Publication Data*

Library of Congress data has been applied for.

ISBN 0–631–21103–9
    0–631–21104–7 (pbk)

*British Library Cataloguing in Publication Data*

A CIP catalogue record for this book is available from the British Library.

Typeset in 10½ on 12 pt Photina
by Best-set Typesetter Ltd., Hong Kong
Printed in Great Britain by MPG Books Ltd, Bodmin, Cornwall

This book is printed on acid-free paper

# Contents

# Acknowledgments

Bossy, John, "The Counter-Reformation and the People of Catholic Europe," *Past and Present*, 97(1970) (Oxford University Press).

Burke, Peter, "How to Become a Counter-Reformation Saint" in Kaspar von Greyerz (ed.), *Religion and Society in Early Modern Europe, 1500–1800* (German Historical Institute/London: Routledge, 1984).

Evennett, H. Outram, "Counter-Reformation Spirituality" from H. Outram Evennett, *The Spirit of the Counter-Reformation* (ed. John Bossy), (Notre Dame: University of Notre Dame Press, 1970).

Forster, Marc R., "The Thirty Years' War and the Failure of Catholicization" in Marc R. Forster, *The Counter-Reformation in the Villages: Religion and Reform in the Bishopric of Speyer, 1560–1720* (Ithaca: Cornell University Press, 1992).

Jedin, Hubert, "Katholische Reformation oder Gegenreformation?" [Catholic Reformation or Counter-Reformation?] from Hubert Jedin, *Katholische Reformation oder Gegenreformation? Ein Versuch zur Klärung der Begriffe nebst einer Jubiläumsbtrachtung über das Trienter Konzil* (Luzern: Verlag Josef Stocker, 1946).

MacCormack, Sabine, "The Heart Has Its Reasons": Predicaments of Missionary Christianity in Early Colonial Peru, *Hispanic American Historical Review* 65 (3) (August 1985), pp. 433–46. Copyright © 1985, Duke University Press. Reprinted with permission.

O'Malley, John W., SJ, "Was Ignatius Loyola a Church Reformer? How to Look at Early Modern Catholicism," *Catholic Historical Review* 77 (April 1991), (Washington D.C.: The Catholic University of America Press).

Reinhard, Wolfgang, "Reformation, Counter-Reformation, and the Early Modern State: A Reassessment," *Catholic Historical Review* 75 (July 1989), (Washington, D.C.: The Catholic University of America Press).

Weber, Alison, "Little Women: Counter-Reformation Misogyny" from Alison Weber, *Teresa of Avila and the Rhetoric of Feminity*. Copyright © 1990 by Princeton University Press. Reprinted by permission of Princeton University Press.

# Editor's Introduction

## I   Battles Over Definitions

Few things seem as confident as book titles; they announce in boldface the volume's topic, as if to suggest that its conceptual boundaries are clear to all and easy to survey. But in fact, few historical topics enjoy that much solidity, and among them the "Counter-Reformation" must rank with the least determinate. For one thing, "Counter-Reformation" is hardly the only possible designation. As long as the historical study of religion in sixteenth- and seventeenth-century Europe remained the intellectual hostage of denominational competition between Catholics and Protestants, the latter used "Counter-Reformation" to imply that the Catholic reforms had been nothing more than the involuntary reflex of a passive and indolent Roman church. Catholic historians, quite naturally, tended to reject the label in favor of other designations that did not describe the event solely as a reaction to the challenge of Protestantism. Instead, Catholic historians preferred terms that emphasized the historical continuities with late medieval reform movements and spiritual revivals, labels such as "Catholic Reform" or "Catholic Reformation." The title of this book, therefore, is a bit misleading, for it implies a degree of consensus among historians that has never existed.

So why this and not some other, more fashionable title? One reason is that the "battle over definitions" has abated in recent decades. To some historians, it had always seemed rather artificial. "Counter-Reformation or Catholic Reformation?" asked the English historian A. G. Dickens in 1969, "Was it not quite obviously both?"[1] Perhaps so, and nowadays

1   A. G. Dickens, *The Counter Reformation* (New York: Harcourt, Brace & World, 1969), 7.

most historians would agree, at least in the abstract if not always in practice. In particular, there is little disagreement about the papacy's central role in the process of reform. But this has not prevented others from proposing a more specific historical terminology. Thus Eric W. Cochrane, a historian of Florence during the "forgotten" seventeenth and eighteenth centuries, recommends using the term "Tridentine Catholicism." This designation refers to the Alpine city of Trent – called "Tridentum" in Latin – where a council of church fathers assembled, in three phases, between 1545 and 1563.[2] Among many other things, the Council of Trent reconfirmed medieval teachings on the authority of tradition, the number and essence of sacraments, the indissolubility of marriage, and the veneration of saints and relics; it clarified doctrines on the Mass, purgatory, penance, and indulgences; it repudiated various Protestant "heresies," such as consubstantiation and the doctrine of justification by faith alone; perhaps most importantly, the Council of Trent adopted institutional reforms meant to intensify the moral discipline of all clergy and to clarify the powers, obligations, and duties of bishops.[3]

By focusing on the Council of Trent and the sweeping impact of its reform decrees on modern Catholicism, Cochrane's term avoids the messy and contentious problem of its historical continuity with the many reform initiatives of the late Middle Ages. Others have proposed more elastic labels that might embrace both "Counter-Reformation" and "Catholic Reform," such as "Early Modern Catholicism," an alternative label John W. O'Malley advocates in the third contribution to this collection. Most recently, R. Po-chia Hsia entitled his overview *The World of Catholic Renewal*, the better to incorporate both "Counter-Reformation" and "Catholic Reform" under "the larger rubric of world history."[4] Each of these designations has both advantages and disadvantages: if "Counter-Reformation" over-emphasizes reactive qualities, it captures better the disruptive force of Protestantism – the first Christian "heresy" in western Europe since the collapse of the Roman Empire to assert itself successfully as a state-supported alternative to the established Catholic faith. Similarly, Cochrane's "Tridentine Catholicism" implies the superior importance of institutional reforms over other kinds of change in

2 Eric W. Cochrane, "Counter-Reformation or Tridentine Reformation? Italy in the Age of Carlo Borromeo," in John M. Headley and John B. Tomaro, eds, *San Carlo Borromeo: Catholic Reform and Ecclesiastical Politics in the Second Half of the Sixteenth Century* (Washington: Folger Books, 1988), 31–46.
3 See Henry J Schroeder, ed., *Canons and Decrees of the Council of Trent* (Rockford: Tan Books and Publishers, 1978).
4 R. Po-chia Hsia, *The World of Catholic Renewal, 1540–1770* (Cambridge: Cambridge University Press, 1998), 7.

sixteenth-century Catholicism, such as the proliferation of new religious orders or the spiritual movements H. Outram Evennett describes in the second contribution to this book. But neither of these phenomena owed their existence directly to the Council of Trent and its decrees. The decision to use "Counter-Reformation" instead of these alternatives reflects a compromise with necessity: no term can serve all purposes fully, and "Counter-Reformation" is still the most widely recognizable designation. Its use here is not meant to preclude the interpretations behind other labels. Still, let the reader beware: no label is fully sufficient or completely free of ideological baggage.

In light of this contentious legacy, it seemed appropriate to divide the essays contained in this book into two groups. The first set – gathered under the rubric "Definitions" – reviews debates over the label "Counter-Reformation" and its alternatives; the second – "Outcomes" – consists of essays that measure the impact of the Catholic reforms on various aspects of social, cultural, and political life during the sixteenth, seventeenth, and eighteenth centuries.

As the three readings in Part I make clear, it is no longer possible to view the Counter-Reformation solely as a reaction to Protestantism. The first of these is an influential essay published shortly after World War II by Hubert Jedin, a Catholic priest and church historian who had been living in exile from Nazi Germany in Rome, on and off, since 1933.[5] Jedin tried to transcend what he considered to be a false opposition between "Counter-Reformation" and "Catholic Reformation." He argued that both terms should be used together: "Counter-Reformation" should refer specifically to Rome's attempts to recover lands and souls lost to Protestantism, while Catholic Reformation should describe the movement of revitalization that had begun within the church prior to Martin Luther. In Jedin's view, the Council of Trent represented both the culmination of "Catholic Reformation" and the onset of "Counter-Reformation." Whether he realized it or not, Jedin's solution also had the effect of moving debates away from politicized and ultimately irresoluble battles over historical essence: the difference between "Catholic Reformation" and "Counter-Reformation" was partly qualitative, but also a matter of historical sequence and causation. Abandoning the search for an all-encompassing historical label freed him to craft chronologically and substantively more precise interpretations. Not long afterwards, H. Outram Evennett delivered six lectures on "The Spirit of the Counter-Reformation" which were meant to integrate

5  Jedin's mother was a Jew who had converted to Catholicism; he therefore counted in the Nazi racial typology as "non-Aryan" and a "First Degree *Mischling*"; see Konrad Repgen, "Hubert Jedin (1900–1980)," *Historisches Jahrbuch* 101 (1981): 325–40.

the history of spirituality with the history of the church as an institution and to reveal "organic similarities in the evolution of ecclesiastical
and secular societies."[6] The second of his lectures is included here. True,
their emphases were different – Jedin focused on institutional change,
while Evennett's analysis was preoccupied with transformations in
Catholic intellectual and spiritual life. But between them, Jedin and
Evennett succeeded in shifting the terms of debate away from the
polemics that had dominated historical debate since the mid-nineteenth
century.

The final contribution to Part I is an address delivered in 1990 by
John W. O'Malley as president of the Catholic Historical Association.
O'Malley reviews the question of definitions as it has evolved since
World War II in order to illustrate the shortcomings of definitions based
on a narrowly institutional definition of reform. To illustrate his
point, O'Malley cites the example of Saint Ignatius Loyola's Society of
Jesus. Among all of the many reform-era religious orders – Theatines,
Capuchins, Somaschi, Barnabites, Angelics, Ursulines, Discalced
Carmelites – Loyola's Jesuits were the order associated most closely
with the militant, missionary zeal of Tridentine Catholicism. But as
O'Malley points out, Ignatius and the first Jesuits concerned themselves
little with institutional reform, even though the spiritual rigor and
worldly activism of their order are central to most definitions of the
Catholic reforms. This discrepancy results from an understanding of
Counter-Reformation that is too focused on the reform of doctrine and
institutions that took place at Trent. As an alternative to "Counter-
Reformation" or "Catholic Reform," O'Malley recommends an alternative label – "Early Modern Catholicism" – that is broader than those of
Jedin or Evennett and can encompass more than the topics of institutional and intellectual history.

His argument also indicates that no clear consensus has formed
around any alternative to "Counter-Reformation." Apart from the lin-
gering effects of confessional polemics, what might explain this lack of
agreement? Beyond all disagreements over analysis and interpretation,
no scholar would question the use of "Reformation" to identify a more
or less agreed-upon set of events and historical processes. What prevents
a similar consensus from forming around "Counter-Reformation"? The
most superficial explanation is that "Counter-Reformation" is a Johnny-
come-lately to the lexicon of European historical periodization. As
Albert Elkan observed long ago, scholars did not invent the term until

6   H. Outram Evennett, *The Spirit of the Counter-Reformation* (Notre Dame: University of Notre Dame Press, 1970), 3.

the 1770s, and not until the 1860s did historians accept it as a term to signify a single phenomenon with global significance.[7] Thus its very existence as an "event" was obscure until relatively recent times. Here, the contrast to the Protestant Reformation could hardly be stronger: as a phrase employed to describe a distinct historical period, it is much older. To be sure, the Latin term *reformatio* pre-dated Luther's movement and in his day meant many things, including a restoration of things to their original true form and essence: to reform was to undo deformity.[8] Similarly, the term "Protestant" initially described princes and estates of the Holy Roman Empire who in 1529 objected to what they perceived as abrogations of their sovereign right to reform religion within their respective territories.[9] As a term of historical periodization, the term "Protestant Reformation" emerged only toward the end of the seventeenth century. Nevertheless, this was a full century before the term "Counter-Reformation" emerged as a historical signifier. Simple chronology ensured that any historical label for the sixteenth-century Catholic reforms would take shape in response to interpretations of Protestantism and its impact on the history of Christian religion – even if these had been free from the polemics of "identity politics."

But they were not. Another, more important reason for the lack of conceptual consensus has to do with the formation of national identities in mid-nineteenth-century Europe. This is a vast topic and can only be touched upon in passing here. Suffice it to say that the "Counter-Reformation" formed as a historical concept at the "high noon of the European nation state," as David Blackbourn calls it, a time when tensions between religious loyalties and nationalist sentiments were becoming more and more acute, especially for Catholics.[10] Confessional rancor, of course, was old as the confessions themselves. New to the nineteenth-century nation-state, however, was the struggle to enlist broad-based, popular participation in certain "myths" of national consciousness, usually rooted in common language and other historical realities, of course, but also political, artificial, and intolerant of alter-

7    Albert Elkan, "Entstehung und Entwicklung des Begriffs 'Gegenreformation,'" *Historische Zeitschrift* 112 (1914): 473–93.
8    See John C. Olin, "Introduction: The Background of Catholic Reform," in his *The Catholic Reformation: From Savonarola to Ignatius: Reform in the Church, 1495–1540* (New York: Harper & Row, 1969), xv–xxvi.
9    See the brief but useful introduction in R. W. Scribner, *The German Reformation* (Atlantic Highlands: Humanities Press, 1986), 1–6.
10    David Blackbourn, *The Long Nineteenth Century: A History of Germany, 1780–1918* (Oxford: Oxford University Press, 1997), 414.

native non-national loyalties. During the second half of the nineteenth century, many European states waged battles against the Catholic church – the principal source of international, non-secular authority – mainly for control over cultural and social institutions such as education and marriage.[11] To varying degrees, Catholics throughout western Europe were compelled to reconcile new, secular loyalties with older and sometimes conflicting obligations to the apostolic authority of the Holy See. The problem of "double loyalty" and the conflicts it generated were most common in predominantly Catholic countries, but they also occurred in states with religiously mixed populations – the Netherlands, Switzerland, and Germany.

Nowhere, indeed, were these tensions so conspicuous as in lands where national unification was most recent and unstable: Italy (1861–70) and Germany (1871). In the German Empire, especially, unification was soon followed by a surge of anti-papal feeling, a ban against the Jesuit Order, and a campaign of official intimidation against the majority of Roman Catholic clerics and schoolteachers who resisted laws requiring state certification of priests and inspections of Catholic parochial schools. This campaign had been meant to unify Germany culturally, but instead it polarized Protestant and Catholics more deeply than at any point, arguably, since the eighteenth century. The polarization left its mark, inevitably, on academic historians. Liberal nationalists described German identity through stories about the historical development of high culture and state power that bound the fate of Protestantism with national destiny – narratives that also associated papal power with political disunity and cultural backwardness. In so doing, they legitimated the unified German nation-state and its actions in their own day. Helmut W. Smith observes that for Protestant historians such as the Prussian patriot, Johannes Gustav Droysen (1808–84), "political Catholicism was synonymous with unfreedom, the rituals of the church with idolatry."[12] Not surprisingly, several of the historians who advocated the concept of "Catholic Reform" were also politically "ultramontane" – that is to say, they supported a strong, conservative papacy and looked for political guidance beyond the Alps to Rome. In Germany during the 1870s, any Catholic who held "ultramontane" views was susceptible to being labeled a *Reichsfeind* – "enemy of the state." Thus it is no coincidence, as O'Malley points out, that the "battle over definitions" was carried out largely among German scholars. But elsewhere in late nineteenth-century Europe, too, the tension between

11   Winfried Becker, "Der Kulturkampf als europäisches und als deutsches Phänomen," *Histroisches Jahrbuch* 101 (1981):422–46.
12   Helmut Walser Smith, *German Nationalism and Religious Conflict: Culture, Ideology, Politics 1870–1914* (Princeton: Princeton University Press, 1995), 28.

secular and confessional commitments often divided historians into "rival camps."[13]

## II  Counter-Reformation Outcomes

A third explanation for the lack of historical consensus is that in certain respects, the "battle over definitions" has not so much abated as changed shape, and continues in new form down to the present. These newer debates are no longer motivated by the confessional struggles of the past; nor are they driven by the need to articulate national consciousness. But as Hsia notes, a distant echo of the old, confessional battles of the nineteenth century can still be heard in contemporary scholarship.[14] Part II of this book – "Outcomes" – contains essays that are meant to convey the thematic variety of this research as it has evolved since the 1960s. They show that certain questions that were central to the "battle over definitions" remain very much alive, even as historians have broadened their research into the domains of social, cultural, gender, and world history. These concern, first, the social bases of spiritual and institutional renewal and second, the question of historical continuity from the sixteenth century on.

As for the first, much of Evennett's argument turned on showing that "the Counter-Reformation was first and foremost a powerful religious movement," more than a mere affirmation of medieval spirituality, certainly not the unnatural imposition of reforms on an unwilling populace. No "stimulus of fear would have guaranteed permanency or success [in the Counter-Reformation] unless there had also been present the necessary spiritual basis."[15] But Evennett begged the social question: if the Counter-Reformation had a social basis, then among whom? How broad was this support? It was one thing to disprove old Protestant canards about an oppressive and top-heavy Catholic hierarchy supported only by the force of Spanish arms, quite another to show that as a "religious movement," the Counter-Reformation had any more than the narrowest social foundation.

By the time Evennett's lectures were published in 1968, social historians were already applying their craft to the study of religion in the sixteenth century. As a useful point of departure, some asked what meaning Protestantism might have had to ordinary Christians.[16] There

13    George P. Gooch, *History and Historians in the Nineteenth Century* (1913; reprint Boston: Beacon, 1959), 510–22.
14    Hsia, *World of Catholic Renewal*, 2.
15    Evennett, *Spirit of the Counter-Reformation*, 24.
16    See, for example, Gerald Strauss, "Success and Failure in the German Reformation," *Past and Present* 67 (1975): 30–63.

was no denying that in many German towns and regions, the Reformation arrived on a wave of popular enthusiasm that often well exceeded the ability of magistrates to control. But in terms of belief, how "Lutheran" was the average denizen of a Saxon town, say, and how long did the transformation take? To get an answer, historians tried to measure the degree to which the powerful and educated in sixteenth-century Europe shared a common religious culture with subject populations – the vast majority of peasants and burghers. Having posed the question in this way, they soon discovered that the Reformation – as a set of theological assertions and educational agendas – was quite different from the religion most nominal Protestants experienced in the conduct of their everyday religious lives. The more historians asked whether Luther, Huldrych Zwingli, Jean Calvin, and their followers achieved what they had hoped to accomplish, the more the Protestant Reformation seemed a failure: even in regions where the Reformation was introduced successfully, the "corrupt" beliefs and practices of the pre-reform days lingered long after the official introduction of Protestantism.[17] Resistance to Protestant moral discipline was lively and persistent also. All this seemed to indicate a deep gulf separating "elite" and "universal" religion, on the one hand, from "popular" and "local" religious practices – not only in regions that had adopted some form of Protestantism, but in those parts of Europe that remained Catholic as well.[18]

Predictably, the Counter-Reformation posed a similar set of questions and answers about the success or failure of reform. Here too, historians began to perceive enormous contrasts between "official" Catholicism, as codified at the Council of Trent, and "popular" Catholicism as it was practiced in Europe's thousands of parishes. Like the Protestant Reformation, the Council of Trent appeared to have been a failure, at least in the short run. Moreover, it was difficult to identify religious movements comparable in size and social diversity to the Protestants' first wave of support. It seemed that initially at least, the social basis of the Counter-Reformation did not extend much beyond educated, aristocratic, and bourgeois circles. Decades, even centuries passed before the great mass of ordinary, rural or working-class Catholics had been "acculturated" so fully that they identified themselves religiously in primarily confessional terms and their beliefs were "orthodox" by the standards set at Trent.

17 The Swiss canton of Bern, for example: see Heinrich Richard Schmidt, *Dorf und Religion: Reformierte Sittenzucht in Berner Landgemeinden der frühen Neuzeit* (Stuttgart: G. Fischer, 1995).
18 See William A. Christian, Jr., *Local Religion in Sixteenth-Century Spain* (Princeton: Princeton University Press, 1981).

This thesis about the "acculturation" of popular religion in sixteenth-and seventeenth-century Europe owed much to the work of the French historian Jean Delumeau, for whom the Counter-Reformation was one episode in a chronologically far longer story of cultural domination.[19] Specifically, he considered the Counter-Reformation part of a broader campaign to Christianize the masses, involving greater discipline of parish priests and chaplains, improved religious instruction, the suppression of pagan holdovers in popular magic and festivity, a stricter code of sexual morality, and more centralized church control over lay religious organizations. Several of the essays in Part II reflect some, if not all of Delumeau's views, and with them a vision of the Counter-Reformation as cultural conflict. In his path-breaking essay on "The Counter-Reformation and the People of Catholic Europe," John Bossy argues that by imposing a regime of ritual conformity on ordinary Catholics, the Counter-Reformation church drove a wedge between the secular and the sacred in parish life. The goal was to eliminate the village as an active participant in religious life and to isolate the individual Catholic as an object of ecclesiastical moral discipline. Bossy considers it mistaken to think that medieval Christians were "passive": rather, the Counter-Reformation excluded laypeople from autonomous religious action – through confraternities, for example. Thus ordinary believers were transformed from active into passive participants. In this sense, his argument corresponds closely to the "acculturation" thesis and its central emphasis on the imposition of conformity. To be sure, resistance to change was often great and progress was therefore slow: winning "hearts and minds" took at least a century to complete. But, Bossy claims, by 1700 or so "it seems fairly clear that the vague injunctions of the Council of Trent had achieved . . . a high degree of practical realization."

One explanation for this is that the church hierarchy was not always quick to implement the reforms. As Peter Burke shows in his essay on "How to Become a Counter-Reformation Saint," official ideals did not form overnight, either. Burke studies the timing and pace of canoniza-tions after Trent and the group characteristics of Counter-Reformation saints; his analysis shows that in Rome, too, several decades were needed to recover "nerve" from the shock of Protestant schism before canon-izations could resume in 1583. After that, canonizations were few and highly regulated. Burke argues that the collective attributes of Counter-Reformation saints indicate the church's emerging priorities and cul-

19    Jean Delumeau, *Catholicism between Luther and Voltaire: A New View of the Counter-Reformation* (London: Burns & Oates, 1977).

tural ideals: the model Counter-Reformation saint was aristocratic, male, self-disciplined, and full of missionary zeal.

The point is simply that the more historians directed their attention to the lower orders of European society, the more "official" Counter-Reformation Catholicism seemed to diverge from the religion of the people. For the same reasons, the rupture between late medieval and Counter-Reformation Catholicism also seemed much larger than it had to Evennett or Jedin. This raises the second persistent aspect of the "battle over definitions" – namely, the matter of historical continuity or discontinuity between movements of Catholic renewal in the fifteenth and sixteenth centuries. Jedin and his followers have been careful to avoid suggesting that "Catholic attempts at reform" in the late Middle Ages "would have led to a general reform [in the sixteenth century] even if there had been no schism [with Protestantism]."[20] Be that as it may, proof of medieval continuities had justified re-characterizing the Counter-Reformation as a "Catholic Reform" having its own historical origins, independent of the Reformation and the specifically German circumstances that produced it. Oddly enough, this hardly settled the question of continuity. Some critics still doubted whether it was possible to identify any Catholic reform that had been separable from the reaction to Protestantism, and argued instead that the Reformation and Counter-Reformation must be understood in combination as a fundamental break with the medieval past.[21] According to this view, both movements helped to cause unprecedented accumulations of power and represented a victory for religious intolerance over the gentler, more humanistic reform movement of the late fifteenth century. The decades of research since Jedin and Evennett have not strengthened the case for continuity much. As Elizabeth Gleason notes, the search for continuities between the reform proposals between the late Middle Ages and the sixteenth century, "far from showing a clear line of development, turns up a bewildering mass of data but no real patterns."[22] For Delumeau and fellow adherents of the "acculturation" thesis, too, the Counter-Reformation represented a fundamental break with medieval Christianity as practiced by the large majority.

Discontinuity was also central to new perspectives on the historical evolution of relationships between church and state power. This was the

20   Olin, ed., *The Catholic Reformation*, xiii.
21   Gottfried Maron, "Das Schicksal der katholischen Reform im 16. Jahrhundert: Zur Frage nach der Kontinuität in der Kirchengeschichte," *Zeitschrift für Kirchengeschichte* 88 (1977): 218–29.
22   Elizabeth G. Gleason, "Catholic Reformation, Counter-Reformation, and Papal Reform in the Sixteenth Century," in Thomas A. Brady, Jr. et al., eds, *Handbook of European History 1400–1600*, vol. 2, *Visions, Programs, and Outcomes* (Leiden: E. J. Brill, 1995), 318.

"confessionalization" thesis, first articulated by the German historian, Ernst Walter Zeeden, and summarized for this collection by Wolfgang Reinhard in his essay, "Reformation, Counter-Reformation, and the Early Modern State."[23] According to Reinhard, both the Catholic and Protestant reforms fundamentally rearranged the relationship between church and state. Since the reformers' ambitions far exceeded the resources of any church, Protestant and Catholic leaders alike turned increasingly to the state for aid in enforcing change; hostile competition between the confessions also encouraged the formation of close alliances with the secular authorities. For kings and princes, the reform of lay morality promised to yield a more pliant subject population and a more integrated social order. Thus absolutism and religious intolerance remained inextricably until the late eighteenth century – a finding that contradicts the older view that the centralization of state power in early modern Europe went hand in glove with the neutralization of religious conflicts. Contrary to the nineteenth-century stereotype of Catholicism as backward, one outcome of this conservative and authoritarian symbiosis between secular power and the confessions was to modernize the state and the relationship between individual and society. Together, both Reformations helped bring about the indispensable prerequisite of absolutism: the transformation of subjects into the willing objects of state domination.

Finally, research into the role of women and gender in the Counter-Reformation has tended to strengthen the case for discontinuity. This, too, is a vast topic and remains badly under-researched; moreover, as with the social history of Counter-Reformation, historians of the Protestant reform have posed the guiding questions. During the 1970s and 1980s, a lively debate unfolded over the emancipating effects of Protestantism for sixteenth-century women. One school of thought held that the Protestant reformers elevated women's status by treating women as spiritual equals, by rejecting celibacy and female monasticism, by legalizing divorce, and by sanctifying marriage and the family. Another view was that the Reformation constituted a "crisis in gender relations" that ultimately re-defined power and social status as functions of male control over female sexuality: closing convents, for example, was part of an uncoordinated but widespread effort to exclude women from autonomous participation in economy and politics that included the suppression of prostitution.[24] The ideal outcome

---

23    Ernst Walter Zeeden, "Grundlagen und Wege der Konfessionsbildung in Deutschland im Zeitalter der Glaubenskämpfe," *Historische Zeitschrift* 185 (1958): 249–99.
24    See the opposing views of Steven E. Ozment, *When Fathers Ruled: Family Life in Reformation Europe* (Cambridge, Mass.: Harvard University Press, 1983) and Lyndal Roper, *The Holy Household: Women and Morals in Reformation Augsburg* (Oxford: Clarendon Press, 1989).

was to be a masculine "republic of households" in which convents and autonomous women had no place. For different reasons, both positions underscored discontinuity with the late medieval precedents. So, too, has most research on women in the Counter-Reformation, especially with regard to women in religious orders.[25] Most notably, the Council of Trent mandated that "no nun shall . . . be permitted to go out of the monastery, even for a brief period under any pretext whatever," an innovation that threatened to exclude women entirely from the worldly activism of most reform-era orders.[26] For lay women, similarly, the Council's reaffirmation of clerical celibacy and the indissolubility of marriage spelled greater suspicion of female religiosity and increased anxiety over female sexuality. Religious activism among women seemed to contradict the masculine essence of Counter-Reformation Catholicism.[27]

Can debates over continuity relate the full complexity of these relationships? Merry Wiesner recently revived Jedin's distinction between an inward-looking Catholic Reformation and the extroverted Counter-Reformation and has redrawn it along the lines of gender, stressing aspects of both continuity and discontinuity. As in the Middle Ages, she suggests, women continued to involve themselves actively in movements to reform abuse *within* the established church without necessarily violating prescribed gender roles. But even more than in medieval crusades against heresy and "the Saracen," the Counter-Reformation's militant struggles to retrieve Protestant souls and to convert non-Christians were to be a masculine undertaking.[28] In her essay entitled "Little Women: Counter-Reformation Misogyny," Alison Weber describes how these contradictory sensibilities interacted during the life and times of Saint Teresa of Ávila, the best known of female Counter-Reformation saints. Weber shows that Spanish humanists began the sixteenth century rejecting the Pauline doctrine of women's spiritual inferiority, just as Martin Luther and his followers did. Weber shows how holy women (*beatas*) flourished under Cardinal Ximénez de Cisneros – a key figure in the Catholic Reformation – and the spiritual "democratization" he promoted. Teresa of Ávila's fame as a mystic and reformer of the Carmelite order preceded the Counter-Reformation's return to the doctrine of

25    Kathryn Norberg, "Women: Religious and Lay," in John W. O'Malley, ed., *Catholicism in Early Modern History: A Guide to Research* (St. Louis: Center for Reformation Research, 1988), 133–46.

26    Twenty-fifth session, ch. 5 (December 4 1563); Schroeder, ed., *Canons and Decrees*, 220–1, 488–9.

27    Elizabeth Rapley, *The Dévotes: Women and Church in Seventeenth-Century France* (Kingston: McGill-Queen's University Press, 1990).

28    Merry Wiesner, *Women and Gender in Early Modern Europe* (Cambridge: Cambridge University Press, 1993), 195.

inherent feminine inferiority. Increasingly, church officials ridiculed Teresa as a "little" or "silly woman" (*mujercilla*); later on, the documents of her canonization employed such phrases as "virile woman" and "manly soul" to re-assign her gender altogether. But Teresa was also able to adopt the misogynist label "*mujercilla*," disarm it, and turn it to her own defense against accusations of heresy. The implications are several: on the one hand, the new misogyny of a militant and masculine Counter-Reformation is unmistakable. On the other hand, Teresa's self-defense preserved her right to claim an authoritative voice. Teresa was canonized in 1622 and proclaimed patron saint of Spain. Not even Spain of the Inquisition was a "monolithic and unremittingly repressive society."[29]

The implications go beyond disproving partisan stereotypes of the Counter-Reformation as a violent imposition of Catholic orthodoxy, "Spanish-style." If Spain was not monolithic, was there *any* region in which the Counter-Reformation could be described as a process of cultural domination that ruptured continuities with medieval Christianity in order to produce subservient and self-disciplined underlings for the Age of Absolutism? To pose the question this way is, admittedly, to caricature the Counter-Reformation's role in "acculturation" and "confessionalization": both of these arguments about historical interactions between culture and power are more complex than that. Still, some questionable assumptions underlie both theses. Both, for example, tend to simplify the history of cultural interactions into binary conflicts between powerful "elites" and the weak "people," in which the mighty possess the initiative as historical actors. This, in turn, reflects a deep-seated "statist" tendency to view "the people" as passive, which can blind one to the practical dependence of church- and state-sponsored religious and moral reforms on local needs and interests. Is it accurate to view the Counter-Reformation as a binary and conflictual interaction? How might we view it differently? As far as "parochial discipline" is concerned, Heinrich R. Schmidt argues that typically, a variety of statue- and gender-groups within village society enacted "parochial discipline," but selectively and in accord with their group's own interests.[30] Similarly, Joel Harrington has revealed the persistence of custom against the attempts of both Protestants and Catholics to reform marriage and family life. This, in turn, casts doubt on the explanatory power of "con-

29  Alison Weber, "Between Ecstasy and Exorcism: Religious Negotiation in Sixteenth-Century Spain," *Journal of Medieval and Renaissance Studies* 23 (1993): 221–34.
30  Heinrich Richard Schmidt, "Sozialidisziplinierung? Ein Plädoyer für das Ende des Etatismus in der Konfessionalisierungsforschung," *Historische Zeitschrift* 265 (1997): 639–82.

fessionalization" and on the notion of a sixteenth-century "crisis in gender relations."[31]

But are such criticisms applicable to the harsher, more obviously state-driven manifestations of Counter-Reformation? Systematic efforts to re-convert lost territories to Catholicism were easily the most aggressive form of confessional struggle, but as Marc R. Forster shows in his contribution to this volume, its success or failure depended heavily on the local balance of powers and interests. In the German prince-bishopric of Speyer, for example, Forster shows how the local church aristocracy supported Catholicization in a general way, but resisted any threat it might pose to the customary rights and privileges its members enjoyed. Many had an interest – not shared by Jesuit missionaries – in maintaining the peace with Protestants, especially after the devastating Thirty Years' War. At the local level, Catholicization campaigns met with fierce resistance from villagers for whom Protestantism had become the traditional religion. Among Catholic villagers, moreover, Forster argues that "parochial discipline" failed because of the ongoing vitality of popular Catholicism.[32] Forster's data may not be typical – the prince-bishopric of Speyer was a weak state, and Catholicization campaigns were more successful in the politically stronger Bavaria, Austria, and in eastern Europe generally. Still, his investigations *do* expose the enormous complexity of social and political interests involved, wherever Catholicization was attempted. Gradually, a picture is emerging of the Counter-Reformation as a highly complex interaction with many players – a process, in other words, that cannot be reduced to the tidy social and political dichotomies implicit in "acculturation" and "confessionalization."

Outside Europe, of course, circumstances were radically different. Nevertheless, the dynamics of conversion in America bear certain similarities to Catholicization in Europe. A great limitation of debates over continuity and discontinuity was their excessive focus on Europe – but this was to ignore the truly global dimensions of Counter-Reformation as a cultural phenomenon. It coincided, roughly, with the consolidation of Spanish political control over much of North and South America, not to mention the extension of European commercial imperialism to much of Africa and Asia. Yet even in the "new" lands of America, the process of converting indigenous populations to Catholicism was not simply a

31   Joel Harrington, *Reordering Marriage and Society in Reformation Germany* (Cambridge: Cambridge University Press, 1995).
32   Marc R. Forster, "The Élite and Popular Foundations of German Catholicism in the Age of Confessionalism: The *Reichskirche*," *Central European History* 26 (1994): 311–26.

one-sided process of domination. In her contribution entitled "The Heart Has Its Reasons: Predicaments of Missionary Christianity in Early Colonial Peru," Sabine MacCormack shows how the dilemmas of proselytization within a culture totally alien to the Europeans' reduced doctrinal diversity among the missionaries. Initially, some of them had endorsed a method of conversion that would take cognizance of indigenous Quechua language and culture. With the encouragement of the viceregal colonial government, however, the colonial church gradually shifted towards a policy of conversion by force. The Andeans' diverse responses ranged from outright rejection – including rebellion – to various forms of syncretism and cultural adaptation. Ironically, therefore, a policy of forcible conversion *increased* religious diversity among the target population – as it had in the prince-bishopric of Speyer, as well.

No anthology is free of intellectual biases, and this collection no exception. Every article included here implies a decision to exclude others, a process necessarily guided by certain general goals and criteria. Accessibility ranked high among the latter, as did the historiographical impact of a particular text. Some of these essays count as *bona fide* classics in the historical literature on Counter-Reformation – Jedin's especially, but also the contributions by Evennett, Bossy, and Reinhard.

More important than the influence of a particular text, however, have been a series of substantive objectives. First and foremost, I have hoped to cover a wide variety of themes, from the more traditional concerns of institutional and religious history contained in the essays by Jedin and Evennett, to the Counter-Reformation's consequences for "high" or "official" religious culture (Burke) and the early modern state (Reinhard), its impact on the moral discipline of laypeople (Bossy), on relations between the confessions (Forster), and on women (Weber), as well as its effects on non-Europeans (MacCormack). Second, I have hoped to include a variety of historiographical approaches and interpretive frameworks. Evennett's analysis reflects the training of a historian steeped in the assumptions of intellectual history as it was practiced in the first half of this century; the work of Bossy and Reinhard reflect the theories of "acculturation" and "confessionalization," respectively; Sabine MacCormack's article combines intellectual history with anthropology, for example, while Weber's analysis is feminist and her focus literary; and so on. A related concern, which reflects perhaps a social historian's bias, was to select essays containing a primary emphasis on process and implementation – how the Catholic reforms were carried out and the practical limits on their execution, not to mention the reverse effects of implementation on the church and its operations. Thus the majority contextualize the Counter-Reformation in local or regional cultural transactions.

This leads to third and final goal, which is to present the Counter-Reformation as it unfolded in a wide variety of political and cultural landscapes. Anyone who scans my footnotes can detect the effects of my training in German history, but hopefully this has not skewed the choice of contributions geographically. Still, certain lands are left out: there was Counter-Reformation in eastern Europe, among English Catholics, and throughout the Americas, not just Peru. Instead, the geographical emphasis here is on central and western Europe – France, Spain, and territories of the Holy Roman Empire. What goes for landscapes, finally, goes for themes as well, and there are necessarily many substantive gaps in this collection. There is, for example, little here on the complex relationship between Counter-Reformation and religious art and architecture, on the important role of the Spanish or Roman Inquisitions, or on the work of Counter-Reformation missionaries in Asia. As with the choice of titles, therefore, let the reader beware: the essays collected here are not the final word.

# Part I   Definitions

# 1

# Catholic Reformation or Counter-Reformation?

## *Hubert Jedin*

Originally appeared as Jedin, Hubert, "Katholische Reformation oder Gegenreformation?" in Hubert Jedin, *Katholische Reformation oder Gegenreformation? Ein Versuch zur Klärung der Begriffe nebst einer Jubiläumsbetrachtung über das Trienter Konzil* (Luzern: Verlag Josef Stocker, 1946), pp. 7–38.

### Editor's Introduction

Perhaps more than anyone else, Hubert Jedin (1900–80) changed the way scholars think about the reform of Catholicism in early modern Europe. He published the following essay while preparing for publication the first volume of his life's work, a multi-volume history of the Council of Trent (1545–63). Until it appeared in 1946, defining the "Counter-Reformation" conceptually was still largely a matter of engaging in ancient confessional polemics, especially in Jedin's native Germany. Protestant scholars typically described the sixteenth-century reforms of Roman Catholicism as little more than an "anti-movement," a reaction of the Reformation that Luther had initiated. Predictably, Catholic historians tended to describe them positively as a creative renewal with independent sources in the vigorous piety and "grass-roots" reform movements of the late Middle Ages. Jedin's essay was arguably the first systematic attempt to transcend these religiously charged oppositions. After tracing the conceptual genealogy of both "Counter-Reformation" and "Catholic Reformation," he tries to reconcile the two notions, arguing that neither label is complete without the other. The sixteenth-century reform *was* a "reformation" with its own pious origins, he argues; but the shock of religious schism was still needed to mobilize the Church Militant. The papacy stood at the intersection of "Catholic Reformation" and "Counter-Reformation," and the Council of Trent expressed their union. To be sure, Jedin's approach has limits: it pays scant attention to relationships between elite and popular religiosity; his understanding of cause, effect, and historical significance was primarily institutional; its scope is strictly European; and the role of gender in defining orthodoxy appears not at all. Still, most historical writing about the "Counter-Reformation" since 1950 presupposes his fundamental synthesis of definitions.

# Catholic Reformation or Counter-Reformation?

*Hubert Jedin*

Historical concepts are like coins. Usually, one allows them to pass through one's fingers without examining the quality of their minting. But when one inspects them under illumination, it often turns out that they have not been stamped or molded with the precision one expects of legal tender. That is no accident. As the study of human society in the past, the essence of history is such that its concepts cannot be delineated so sharply as those, say, of the law, let alone mathematics. History has it relatively easy when it is merely describing sets of similar historical facts, such as the "migrations of peoples" [and the end of the Roman Empire]. But the task is harder when it involves the phenomena of cultural life, as with "scholasticism," "Renaissance," or "Enlightenment." The most difficult conceptualizations involve events that proceed directly from upheavals in spiritual life, as with the "investiture conflict," the "Reformation," or the "Risorgimento."[1]

The concepts "Catholic Reformation" and "Counter-Reformation" belong to this last group. Both terms presuppose the "Reformation," which we are accustomed to define as the doctrinal and institutional schism in Christianity during the sixteenth century. Yet these labels are most problematic in just this connection to the Reformation. When one examines their use in the historical literature, it quickly becomes apparent that non-Catholic historians typically avoid the first concept ("Catholic Reformation") and replace it with some other descriptor, such as the "the renewal of the Catholic church." Catholics, by contrast, either do not use the concept of "Counter-Reformation" at all or employ it only with reservations.

Fundamentally divergent metahistorical viewpoints stand behind the different uses of both terms. In somewhat simplified form, these viewpoints can be characterized in the following way: Catholic historians are concerned to explain the sixteenth-century renewal of the Catholic church – before, during, and after the Council of Trent – as an expression

---

1  Editor's note: The "migration of peoples" refers to the period during the fourth and fifth centuries when Germanic tribes invaded the Roman Empire, causing its downfall; the "investiture conflict" refers to the high medieval struggle between popes and Holy Roman Emperors over the right to invest bishops with the spiritual and secular authorities of their office (1085–1122); *Risorgimento* refers to the nineteenth-century movement for Italian unification.

of the profound vitality of Catholic piety. They therefore dispute the influence of religious schism on this process of renewal, or at least minimize it. For them, the Catholic Reformation was the "true" Reformation. They resist the term "Counter-Reformation" because they suspect that behind it lurks the idea that the regeneration of the church was only a reaction to the religious division, a mere "anti-movement" without an internal dynamic of its own, burdened by the application of force in matters of conscience and representing the triumph of the political over the religious . . . a host of things that are repellent to modern people.

The Protestants and the majority of scholars who do not share in the Catholic worldview regard their Reformation either as the true restoration of the church to its aboriginal form, or at least as the breakthrough to a modern, personal religiosity. They measure the efforts that were aimed at renewing the church from within according to their success or (more often) their failure, both before the religious schism and after its eruption. They regard the Counter-Reformation, as it established itself after the middle of the [sixteenth] century, as the triumph of a politically and militarily superior Pope over the non-political Lutherans and the politically isolated Calvinists. In their eyes, the Counter-Reformation is responsible for almost everything that they find objectionable in modern Catholicism.

The task of my inquiry is not to take issue with these viewpoints, lying as they do beyond history in the ideological domain of assumptions and prejudices. Rather, it merely attempts to reach some understanding of the meaning of the concepts in question, operating from generally recognized historical facts, and to rid historical terminology of misunderstandings. In order to achieve this goal, I will investigate:

1   the history of the origins and diffusion of the two concepts ("Counter-Reformation" and "Catholic Reformation"); then, I will attempt
2   to identify their meaning and internal coherence;
3   to define them against other commonly used terms and to suggest their value for the periodization of church history; and finally
4   to make these insights useful for an interpretation of the Council of Trent and its place in church history.

## I   Origins and Diffusion of the Concepts "Counter-Reformation" and "Catholic Reformation"

The term "Counter-Reformation" is older by far than "Catholic Reformation." Its origins have been investigated already [in 1914].[2] I can

2   Albert Elkan, "Entstehung und Entwicklung des Begriffes Gegenreformation," *Historische Zeitschrift* 112 (1914): 473–93.

therefore be brief. Ever since the Göttingen jurist Johann Stephan Pütter (1725–1807) coined the term in 1776, "Counter-Reformation" was used to describe the forcible re-conversion of a Protestant region to the Catholic observance. Used originally in the plural, "Counter-Reformations" referred not to a coherent movement, but to individual re-conversion campaigns. Catholics experienced this meaning – and its association with the use of violent force in religious affairs – as a reproach. But this was not its only, or to be more precise, not its whole meaning. Soon, the search for historical causes and motivations behind these "individual campaigns" led to the discovery of a powerful movement. But the end of the sixteenth and at the beginning of the seventeenth century, this movement was in a position not only to repair the severely damaged state of the church, but to recover lost ground as well. At length, it was discovered that this movement had been founded on an inner regeneration of the church, and that the Council of Trent and the Jesuit Order were the decisive factors in it.

Leopold von Ranke characterized this "restoration, which also implanted Catholicism anew," as the original source of a Counter-Reformation movement. He also grasped the importance of the papacy for its implementation. In his *History of the Popes* and even in his *History of the Reformation in Germany*, Ranke still spoke of "Counter-Reformations" (*Gegenreformationen*) in the plural. But he recognized the movement's homogenous character and thus took a decisive step toward forming a concept of "Counter-Reformation" (*Gegenreformation*). This term became generally accepted in the historical literature during the 1860s and 1870s. Moriz Ritter was the first history professor to hold a university lecture series on the Counter-Reformation (1876); his *German History in the Reformation Era* played a key role in establishing the concept.[3] As *contre-réforme* and *controriforma*, the idea soon passed into the historical writing of other European peoples, although it did not become the basis for historical periodization, as it had in Germany. Elsewhere, historians spoke of the "Age of Religious Wars," the "Elizabethan Era," the "Age of Henry IV," Philip II, and the like.

In time, Eberhard Gothein's book *Ignatius Loyola and the Counter-Reformation* (1895) became the definitive assessment of the Counter-Reformation's cultural and religious roots. Gothein located the movement's origins in Spain: for him, Loyola and his Jesuit Order were the instruments by which "Golden Age" Spain rescued the church and simultaneously seized predominance in the West. But in his quest for Spanish origins and in the evaluation of Spanish archives, Gothein had been preceded by Wilhelm Maurenbrecher, a student of Heinrich von

---

3  Moriz Ritter (1840–1923), *Deutsche Geschichte im Zeitalter der Gegenreformation und des Dreissigjährigen Krieges, 1555–1648*, 3 vols. (Stuttgart: J. G. Cotta, 1889–95; reprint Darmstadt: Wissenschaftliche Buchgesellschaft, 1974).

Sybel. Through the rigorous investigation of historical origins, he arrived at another concept that concerns us, the "Catholic Reformation." The first and only volume of his *History of the Catholic Reformation* appeared in 1880.

Originally, Maurenbrecher had intended to write a history of the "Counter-Reformation." But in the course of his studies, he recognized that "in order to establish a secure understanding of those events and of the people who lived with the consequences of Reformation," not to mention reciprocal influences between the conflicting religious parties, he would need to expand his research beyond the period of religious schism itself. Indeed, "it became apparent that the roots of the Counter-Reformation extended back to the earliest period of the Reformation, and that some of its seeds were planted in the generation before the German religious upheaval. In addition to the Evangelical or Protestant Reformation, it became necessary to recognize a Catholic Reformation."[4] In his first volume, consequently, the author described the reform of the Spanish church during the time of Queen Isabella and Cardinal Ximénez de Cisneros, the rise of Savonarola in Florence, the Brethren of the Common Life, the Windesheim congregation and of early humanism in Germany, not to mention the Fifth Lateran Council and the reform initiatives of Erasmus of Rotterdam. His was an overview of reformist impulses within the medieval church like no other historian had offered before.

No less fruitful was the historical agenda that Maurenbrecher had intended for the two subsequent volumes of his work: to trace the mutual, spiritual influences between old believers and renovators – not their political interactions – until the death of pope Clement VII (1523–34). At the risk of exaggeration, one can assert that Maurenbrecher traced the path that a generation of historians would follow: studies on the pre-Reformation era and on the efforts that ultimately led to the formation of the *Corpus Catholicorum* and to the decrees of the Council of Trent.[5]

Catholics quickly sensed that Maurenbrecher's book was of major importance for revising the interpretation of the Reformation and the Counter-Reformation then dominant among professional historians. The two leading professional publications, the *Historisch-Politische Blätter* and the *Historisches Jahrbuch*, devoted long and for the most part benevolent reviews to it, while of course noting also its gaps and weak-

---

4 Wilhelm Maurenbrecher (1838–92), *Geschichte der katholischen Reformation* (Nördlingen: Beck, 1880), preface.
5 On the achievements of German Catholicism in this area see Hubert Jedin, *Die Erforschung der kirchlichen Reformationsgeschichte seit 1876: Leistungen und Aufgaben der deutschen Katholiken* (Münster: Aschendorff, 1931).

nesses.[6] Thus Franz Dittrich, who at the time was busy preparing his work on Contarini, objected that Maurenbrecher had not adequately appreciated the Italian roots of the Catholic Reformation, and that he had overlooked the findings of a book published two years earlier, Constantin von Höfler's *The Latin World and its Relationship to Reform Ideas of the Middle Ages.*[7]

In his analysis of medieval reform efforts among the Latin peoples, Höfler chose a formulation closely akin to Maurenbrecher's, namely "The Latin Reformation" (*Die romanische Reformation*). By this Höfler meant a continuation of reform ideas that had emerged throughout the fifteenth century within the mendicant orders and among a few exceptionally saintly personalities. He also examined the reform attempts of Pope Alexander VI (1492–1503) and the subsequent Spanish efforts. Although he was operating from the standpoint of medieval history, Höfler's guiding idea was clearly similar to Maurenbrecher's: he wanted to portray the internal reform attempts of the waning Middle Ages as a counterpoint to the German schism, in order to demonstrate the continuity of ecclesiastical development from the Middle Ages to the Counter-Reformation.

Already twenty years before Höfler, a Swabian priest named Joseph Kerker had been working along the same lines. In an article entitled "Church Reform in Italy Immediately Prior to the Council of Trent,"[8] Kerker referred to the Oratory of Divine Love as a "hopeful sign" of renewal within the church and lauded Pope Paul III (1534–49) for recruiting humanists to the "cause of Catholic reform" by means of his famous cardinal nominations between 1535 and 1539. From now on, according to Kerker, to include humanists in the College of Cardinals became a matter of "good form." If we overlook this last exaggeration, the fact remains that Kerker, too, drew a contrast between the confessional schism and an early sixteenth-century internal reform movement – which he described as a "Catholic Reform." He sought the roots of the Tridentine reforms mainly in Italy, within the humanist reform movement prevalent there. Ultimately, Kerker concluded that "no region of Europe in those times had a more influential prelacy than Italy."

Let us pause to summarize! We have seen that from the beginning of its formation, the term "Catholic Reformation" had been motivated by the

6   *Historisch-Politische Blätter* 88 (1881): 608–22; *Historisches Jahrbuch* 2 (1881): 602–17.

7   Karl Adolf Constantin von Höfler (1811–97), *Die romanische Welt und ihr Verhältnis zu den Reformideen des Mittelaters* [Sitzungsberichte der Wiener Akademie, Philosophisch-Historische Klasse, vol. 91] (1878), 257–538, esp. 460ff.

8   Joseph Kerker, "Die kirchliche Reform in Italien unmittelbar vor dem Tridentinum," *Tübinger Theologischer Quartalschrift* 41 (1859): 3–56.

concern to draw a contrast between a predominantly Latin movement of Catholic renewal and the German schism. This antithetical opposition was latent already in Kerker's notion of a "Catholic Reform"; it appeared more clearly in Höfler's "Latin Reformation"; and was explicit in Maurenbrecher's notion of "Catholic Reformation." Maurenbrecher coined this term because he realized that the forces responsible for the Counter-Reformation had origins in the period before the religious schism, so that it was no longer possible to see it only as a reaction. Here he encountered Kerker's thinking, developed on the narrower basis of Italian evidence. Höfler, by contrast, came at the problem from the perspective of the Middle Ages. He, too, noticed that the late medieval reform efforts of the Latin peoples eventuated in the Tridentine reforms, so that a continuity existed which one could contrast with the German Reformation.

This antithetical aspect of "Catholic Reformation" soon elicited a repudiation from Protestant historians. The biographer of Emperor Charles V, Hermann Baumgartner, asked whether "we are in fact justified to speak of a Catholic Reformation?"[9] The Spanish reform, he observed, obstructed its own path because it did not abandon the fundamental principles of the church or seek to alter its essence. It was therefore no "Reformation," but only a restoration! Eberhard Gothein expressed a similar view.[10] He called the term "Catholic Reformation" downright misleading, because the reform efforts during Queen Isabella's reign were "only the latest revival of ecclesiastical life on the basis of asceticism and practical activism" that had occurred throughout the Middle Ages.

Here, Gothein had hit on the crucial point. Both he and Baumgartner assumed a definition that the originally Latin term "Reformation" had acquired in German usage – to refer specifically to the movement begun by Martin Luther and which led to the religious division. But they ignored the original, broader meaning of the word *reformatio* as it was used in ecclesiastical circles from the late Middle Ages until well into the sixteenth century: renewal of the church "in head and members," but without alteration of its essence in dogma, liturgy, or discipline. Originally, Luther himself and – to an even greater extent – Philip Melanchthon wanted nothing more than an internal reform of the Catholic church. Much time elapsed before the realization took hold on both sides that Luther's was no work of renewal, but one of radical reconstruction, and that this would lead to lasting division within the church. Early on, the movement called itself a "Reformation," a defensive artifice that disguised its revolutionary character. Consequently there is no reason to reject the term "Catholic Reformation" as mis-

9   *Historische Zeitschrift* 46 (1881): 154–64.
10   Eberhard Gothein (1853–1923), *Ignatius von Loyola und die Gegenreformation* (Halle: Niemeyer, 1985), 40.

leading. Indeed, Maurenbrecher chose it in order to place the beginning of the German Reformation in its original historical context; this was his sense of the antithesis. One may admit that Kerker's "Catholic Reform" excluded such misunderstandings more effectively; on the other hand, the distinction between "Reform" and "Reformation" does not exist in the Italian and French renditions of the term (*riforma cattolica* and *réforme catholique*).

But on the Catholic side, too, there were qualms about adopting the concept. The preeminent textbooks on church history excluded it. Franz Xavier Kraus described the internal renewal leading up to the Council of Trent as the "Catholic Restoration," but subsumed it under the conventional periodization term "Counter-Reformation."[11] Jakob Marx spoke of it as the "true Reformation."[12] In the third, revised edition of his *Handbook of General Church History*, Cardinal Joseph Hergenröther wrote that "the church accomplished a Catholic Reformation against the Protestant" and pushed its origins back to the fifteenth century.[13]

Only Franz Dittrich fully appropriated the term Maurenbrecher that had coined.[14] Taking Kerker's lead, he gave the concept greater historical depth by exposing the Italian, in addition to the Spanish, roots of the renewal movement, for example, in the reform congregation of St. Justina, the reform initiatives that emerged during the Fifth Lateran Council and under Pope Clement VII, and in the shining example of Gian Matteo Giberti, Bishop of Verona. In this direction he was followed by that historian who would establish firmly the notion of a "Catholic Reformation," at least in the Catholic historiography: Ludwig von Pastor, author of a sixteen-volume *History of the Popes since the End of the Middle Ages*.[15]

Actually, Pastor did nothing more than finished what his teacher, Johannes Janssen, had begun.[16] No doubt Janssen's *History of the*

---

11    Franz Xaver Kraus (1840–1901), *Lehrbuch der Kirchengeschichte für Studierende*, 3rd rev. edn. (Trier: F. Lintz, 1887), 558ff.

12    Jakob Marx (1855–1924), *Lehrbuch der Kirchengeschichte* (Trier: Paulinus, 1903), 585.

13    Cardinal Joseph Hergenröther (1824–90), *Handbuch der allgemeinen Kirchengeschichte*, 3rd rev. edn. (Freiburg im Breisgau: Herder, 1884), 230.

14    Franz Dittrich, "Beiträge zur Geschichte der katholischen Reformation im ersten Drittel des 16. Jahrhunderts," *Historisches Jahrbuch* 5 (1884): 318–98; 7 (1886): 1–50.

15    Ludwig von Pastor (1854–1928), *Geschichte der Päpste seit dem Ausgang des Mittelalters, mit Benutzung des Päpstlichen Geheimarchives und vieler anderer Archive*, 16 vols. in 21 (Freiburg im Breisgau: Herder, 1899–1933); translated and published in 40 volumes as *The History of the Popes, from the Close of the Middle Ages, Drawn from the Secret Archives of the Vatican and Other Original Sources* (London: Kegan Paul, 1923–53).

16    Editor's note: Johannes Janssen (1829–91) was author of an eight-volume *History of the German People since the End of the Middle Ages* (*Geschichte des deutschen Volkes seit dem Ausgang des Mittelaters* [Freiburg im Breisgau: Herder, 1881–94]).

*German People since the End of the Middle Ages* had popularized the idea of a spiritual and religious flowering in Germany before the Reformation, which in turn prepared the way for a broader conception of an internal Church renewal that had both preceded and ran parallel to the Reformation. But Pastor himself was responsible for this, too: by carefully collecting all the papal initiatives for reform of the Church, and especially of the curia, he merely followed Janssen's example in the first three volumes of *History of the Popes*. For Pastor, these initiatives demonstrated the accuracy of Janssen's portrayal of pre-Reformation Germany. But in the fourth volume, which treated the history of the two Medici popes, Pastor went a step further. The founding of the Oratory of Divine Love in Rome in 1517 proved to Pastor that an internal movement of ecclesiastical renewal had arisen independently of the German schism, though it took root only in the reign of Pope Paul III and pervaded the Roman Church only as a result of the Council of Trent. It could not, therefore, be understood as a reaction to religious division. Pastor saw the famous inaugural speech at the Fifth Lateran Council, given by the General of the Augustinian Order, Egidio da Viterbo (1469–1532), as a manifesto of reform; in Cardinal Ximénez, Ludwig von Pastor saw the movement's prophet.

In Italy, historians such as Pietro Tacchi Venturi, Alfred Bianconi, and Pio Paschini gave greater depth and complexity to Pastor's observations on the Oratory of Divine Love. Venturi discovered that the Oratory in Genoa had served as a model for the Roman one; it was founded in 1497, twenty years before Luther's "Ninety-Five Theses."[17] In his saintly humility and his active charity, the Oratory's founder, the layman Ettore Vernazza (ca. 1470–1524), seemed the very opposite of Giorlamo Savonarola (1452–98), the Dominican monk who had descended into politics. Alfred Bianconi interpreted the Company of Saint Girolamo – founded in Vincenza by Cajetan de Thiene (1480–1547) – in a similar light and traced Ettore Vernazza's influence as far as Naples.[18] Pio Paschini, finally, pointed to similar foundations in Bologna, Brescia, Florence and elsewhere as evidence of a "great spiritual vigor" in Italy at the beginning of the sixteenth century.[19]

Beginning with volume seven of his *History*, Pastor appended the subtitle "History of the Popes in the Era of Catholic Reformation and

---

17   Pietro Tacchi Venturi (1861–1956), *Storia della Compagnia di Gesù in Italia* (Rome: Civiltà cattolica, 1910).
18   Alfred Bianconi, *L'opera delle Compagnie del "Divino amore" nella riforma cattolica* (Città di Castello: S. Lapi, 1914).
19   Pio Paschini (1878–1962), *La beneficenza in Italia e le Compagnie del Divino Amore nei primi decenni del Cinquecento* (Rome, 1925); the quote is from Paschini's *S. Gaetano Thiene, Gian Pietro Carafa, e le origini dei chierici regolari teatini* (Roma: Scuola tipografica Pio X, 1926), 5.

Restoration." As he explained in a separate essay, the first of these two concepts should signify the inner regeneration of Catholicism, while the second referred to its institutional restoration in areas that were endangered by or lost to Protestantism. Volumes seven through eleven carry this subtitle; from volume twelve on, it is replaced by a new one, "History of the Popes in the Era of Catholic Restoration and the Thirty Years' War." In his recapitulating introduction to volume thirteen, we learn that Pastor saw the pontificate of Gregory VIII (1572–85) as a decisive turning point from Catholic Reformation to Restoration and counterattack. The pontificates of Sixtus V (1585–90) and his successors down to Paul V (1605–1621) were characterized by the both tendencies simultaneously, then dominated by Restoration, which reached a high point under Pope Gregory XV (1621–3).

Thus Pastor adopted the concept of "Catholic Reformation" as his own and replaced the term "Counter-Reformation" with "Catholic Restoration." Numerous Catholic historians followed his lead, but so did a few Protestant historians in the German-speaking countries; the translation of his *History* into Italian, Spanish, French, and English, extended Pastor's influence into all the western European countries. Still, a number of revealing differences are apparent.

While Italian historians eagerly seized the task of investigating their country's role in the ecclesiastical renewal, applying the term "Catholic Reformation" far beyond the realm of church history, they also retained the concept of "Counter-Reformation" and for a long time used the two terms synonymously. In 1901, Tacchi Venturi characterized the Vittoria Colonna's patronage of the Capuchins as a "riforma cattolica."[20] Bianconi thought he might devote an entire volume to tracing the renewal movement's Italian origins. He did not fulfill this plan, perhaps because in the meantime Tacchi Venturi had anticipated the topic in the first volume of his *History of the Society of Jesus in Italy*.[21] In an instructive 1927 essay on "The Catholic Reform in Italy," Filippo Masucci summarized the results of research to that date and distinguished between two phases: an earlier period, which began well before the Protestant split in the fifteenth century with reforms of the Dominican and Franciscan orders and the founding of the Oratory of Divine Love; and a second phase characterized by the founding of the Theatine and Barnabite orders.[22] Giuseppe Toffanin thought he could discern the influence of these orders in Italian literature produced under the papacy of Julius II (1550–5) and the Medici popes. According to Toffanin, old-style

20  Tacchi Venturi in *Studi di Storia e Diritto* 22 (1901): 149–79.
21  Tacchi Venturi, *Storia della Compagnia di Gesù*.
22  Filippo Masucci, "Sulla riforma cattolica in Italia," *Archivo della Società Romana di Storia Partia* 50 (1927): 189–201.

humanism was already dead before the religious schism cast its shadow;
in Zaccaria Ferreri's re-writing of the Brevier hymns, he saw the
influences of Catholic Reformation.[23]

But the concept of "Catholic Reformation" did not always retain its
original meaning. Guido de Ruggiero (1888–1948) adopted the term
in his *History of Philosophy*, but gave it an entirely new meaning.[24] He
admitted the church's attempt to contain the spread of Protestant Reformation had been accompanied by a process of internal reform (*operosità
autoriformatrice*). But de Ruggiero dismissed the pre-Tridentine roots of
the movement and questioned their autonomous religious strength. For
him, the movement was merely one aspect of a struggle imposed upon
the church from without, a piece of Counter-Reformation (*riforma nella
controriforma*). Like Benedetto Croce, de Ruggiero saw only a reaction
that could not be equated, say, with the Renaissance and the Protestant
Reformation. It was a dead end in the history of ideas. Apparently, the
concept of "Catholic Reformation" by no means succeeded in establishing the continuity of renewal efforts from the late Middle Ages into the
seventeenth century. Many authors still use it as a synonym for the
"Counter-Reformation." Thus it was possible for a reviewer of Antonio
Corsano's *Italian Religious Thought* – which described the Platonist
Marsilio Ficino as one of the most prominent precursors of the Catholic
Reformation – to exchange "Catholic Reformation" with "Counter-
Reformation," apparently without noticing the error.[25]

Italian historians were even less receptive to Pastor's proposal to
replace the concept of "Counter-Reformation" with "Catholic Restoration." Arturo Carlo Jemolo (1891–1981) assigned equal value to both.[26]
But in his contribution to the Görres Society's *Staatslexikon*, he defined
"Catholic Restoration" as epitomizing the attempts to contain the
Protestant Reformation and to win back lost territories and placed its
beginnings in the first years after the religious division. By the same
token, that highly influential church historian, Pio Paschini, clung to
the term "Counter-Reformation" in all of his many studies.[27]

The historians of Spain – whose "Golden Age" had given Maurenbrecher the inspiration for his *History of the Catholic Reformation* –

23   Giuseppe Toffanin, *Il Cinquecento* (Milan: Villardo, 1929).
24   Guido de Ruggiero, *Storia della filosofia*, 4 vols. in 13 (Bari: Laterza & figli,
1943–8).
25   Antonio Corsano, *Il pensiero religiose italiano: Dall'umanesimo al giurisdizional-
ismo* (Bari: Laterza, 1937); review in *La Rinascita* 3 (1941): 72. Paolo Cherubelli also
used "riforma cattolica" and "restaurazione cattolica" synonymously in his "Storia
religiosa della Rinascita," *La Rinascita* 5 (1942): 313ff.
26   *Enciclopedia italiana*, 36 vols. (Rome: Istituto Giovanni Treccani, 1929–39), 11:
260–3.
27   See, for example, Pio Paschini, "Riforma e controriforma al confine nordori-
entale d'Italia," *Arcadia* 4 (1923): 321–90.

adopted the term rather hesitantly. As far as I can tell, this may have been because they thought Pastor had not done justice to the Spanish contribution to the movement for church renewal.[28] As a result, Spanish historians were eager to give the term more content and to uncover the continuity of developments in Spain from the end of the anti-Morisco campaigns into the age of Philip II.[29] But they also preferred other terms, such as "Spanish Renaissance"; in their hands also, the movement for internal church reform gets clustered together with a reaction against Protestantism under the rubric of "Catholic Restoration."

French scholarship further enriched the content of "Catholic Reformation." One of the most egregious gaps in Maurenbrecher's presentation was his failure to recognize reform efforts in France at the beginning of the sixteenth century. Nor did Pastor address their importance adequately. Had France – the most populous country in Europe, this intellectual leader of the Church, whose internal vitality enabled it to recover so quickly from the storms of the Hundred Years' War – had France really contributed nothing to the renewal of the Church?

Pierre Imbart de la Tour's masterpiece closed this gap.[30] He analyzed the ecclesiastical reforms at the time of Charles VIII and Cardinal Georges d'Amboise, men like Standonck and Raulin, the circle of humanist reformers at Meaux, "this grand, most original, most profound movement of Catholic reform, which most historians have viewed as nothing more than a kind of inconsequent Protestantism." By calling this movement "Evangelism," Imbart de la Tour introduced an entirely new tenor to history of sixteenth-century church reform and more than any other author demanded a deeper understanding of it. But he avoided the term "Catholic Reformation," as did Augustin Renaudet in his studies on French humanism.[31] Joseph Roserot de Melin emphasized the spontaneity of French reforms before the Council of Trent, but nevertheless characterized them as a "contre-réforme."[32] Relatively speaking, the term "réforme catholique" was seldom used. Gabriel Monod, who had adopted the term directly from the German historiography

28   See Bernardino Llorca, *Manual de Historia ecclesiastica* (Barcelona: Labor, 1942) 569ff: "Principios de la reforma católica."
29   See above all Marcel Batallion, *Erasme en Espagne: Recherches sur l'histoire spirituelle du XVI<sup>e</sup> siècle* (Paris: Droz, 1937), and the numerous works of the Dominican Vicente Beltrán de Heredia, *Historia de la reforma de la provincia de España (1450–1550)* (Rome: S. Sabinae, 1939) and *Las corrientes de espiritualidad entre los dominicos de Castilla durante la primera mitad del siglo XVI* (Salamanca: [s.n.], 1941).
30   Pierre Imbart de La Tour (1860–1925), *Les origines de la réforme*, 3 vols. (Paris: Firmin-Didot, 1905–14), esp. vols. 2–3.
31   Augustin Renaudet (1880–1958), *Préréforme et humanisme à Paris pendant les premières guerres d'Italie (1494–1517)* (Paris: Champion, 1916).
32   Joseph Roserot de Melin, "L'établissement du Protestantisme en France," *Revue d'histoire de l'église de France* 17 (1931): 26–81, 180–219.

before Ludwig von Pastor, had several followers, but there was little interest in the question of continuity. Rather, French historians tended to use "Catholic Reformation" to refer to reforms during the second half of the sixteenth century.

In England, historians treated the term with even more caution, although not the events it described. There, the work of Cardinal Francis Aiden Gasquet on English monasteries and his book on *The Eve of the Reformation* had an impact similar to Janssen's in Germany, with the difference that Gasquet's value judgments were more carefully balanced and made better headway than those of the German historian.[33] Under the neutral title "Catholic Europe" in volume one of the *Cambridge Modern History* (1902), William Barry evaluated the humanist reform efforts associated with John Colet and the reforms of Cardinal Thomas Wolsey (1475–1530) together with the initiatives in Spain and Italy. In volume two (1903), R. V. Lawrence treated the phenomena characterized since Ludwig von Pastor as the "Catholic Reformation," from the Oratory of Divine Love to the Council of Trent. He also used the term "Catholic Reform," though not to designate the whole movement, but only a "part of mediation" (Pastor's "Expectants"), whom he contrasted to the "Counter-Reformation." The old meaning of this term has dominated the English historiography since Ranke to the present day. J. H. Pollen acknowledged the concerns that Catholics have about this term in his article on "Counter-Reformation" for *The Catholic Encyclopedia*.[34] But he declared his satisfaction with the term, as long as it was clear that it referred to more than a mere reaction and that the Reformation did not govern it.

In 1930, H. Outram Evennet voiced his opinion on the concept of "Counter-Reformation" in the conclusion to his book on Cardinal Guise.[35] Evenett correctly noted that it was a much more complex phenomenon than one normally assumes. He distinguished between positive and negative elements: on the positive side, it was "a phase in the long chain of Catholic expansion and development" and therefore independent of the Reformation. Its negative element consisted in the defense of medieval Christianity and finally the counter-attack against the revolution in the church. Both elements influenced and pervaded

33   Editor's note: Cardinal Francis Aidan Gasquet (1846–1929), *English Monastic Life* (London: Methuen, 1904), and *The Eve of the Reformation: Studies in the Religious Life and Thought of the English People in the Period Preceding the Rejection of the Roman Jurisdiction by Henry VIII* (London: John C. Nimmo, 1900).

34   J. H. Pollen, "The Counter-Reformation," *The Catholic Encyclopedia* 4: 437ff.

35   H. Outram Evenett, *The Cardinal of Lorraine and the Council of Trent* (Cambridge: Cambridge University Press, 1930), 465ff. Editor's note: Charles de Lorraine, Cardinal Guise (1524–74) was among the most influential French representatives at the Council of Trent.

each other mutually. The years between the Treaty of Cateau-Cambrésis (1559) and the Council of Trent (1563) were crucial for the consolidation of the whole movement.[36] In France and Germany, the "Party of
Moderation" – an unorganized group of moderates sharing similar
political views – was subdued and the idea of continuity prevailed. Evennett articulated an extraordinarily important idea: that in fact the years
between 1559 and 1563 were crucial not only for the fate of moderates
and mediators, but in every other respect as well. Although he did not
appropriate the expression "Catholic Reformation," Evennett accurately
appreciated its essence, its complexity, and its inner connection to the
"Counter-Reformation."

It is time to end this conceptual tour, which was never meant to be a
comprehensive survey, and attempt to summarize the results in a few
sentences:

1   As investigation into the "Counter-Reformation" deepened, scholars
    generated the concept of a "Catholic Reformation." The originator
    of this term was the Protestant historian, Wilhelm Maurenbrecher,
    and its main popularizer was Ludwig von Pastor.
2   While the older term describes the church's reaction to religious
    schism, the newer concept emphasizes the continuity of internal
    developments within the church.
3   Spain and Italy were primarily, but not solely responsible for it; the
    origins of "Catholic Reformation" must be sought in these countries.
4   Since Pastor, historians (especially Catholics) have been
    inclined to replace the term "Counter-Reformation" with "Catholic
    Restoration."
5   The numerous uncertainties surrounding the use of these and
    related terms makes a sharper distinction among their meanings all
    the more desirable. To this task I now turn.

## II  The Meaning and Relationship Between
"Catholic Reformation" and "Counter-Reformation"

During the age of the great reform councils of Constance and Basel,
many believed that a reform of the church "in head and members" could
not be accomplished unless the power of popes was limited by a regularly convening General Council of the Church. Conciliarist theory
vested supreme authority in matters of faith and reform in the General

---

36   Editor's note: The Treaty of Cateau-Cambrésis (April 3 1559) ended a long, 65-
year period of intermittent warfare between France and Spain for control over
Italy.

Council. For its adherents, an institutional reconstruction of the church – involving severe restrictions on the existing system of benefice reservations and annates,[37] if not its abolition, as well as an institutional strengthening of the College of Cardinals – was the *sine qua non* of ecclesiastical reform. The end of the conciliarist schism at Basel destroyed hopes for these reformers. The papacy assumed the task of church reform, but did not solve it. Many adherents of the conciliar movement became convinced that the work of reform should not begin at the top, with constitutional and administrative adjustments, but from below, amongst themselves and in the reform of individual human beings and small congregations.

A dialogue written during the Council of Basel expressed this persuasion. In it, a man named Jacob addresses his interlocutor, Johannes: "Where, do you think, should the Reform begin?" And Johannes answers: "With itself, naturally! The hand that would wash another must itself be clean."[38] That was the path of self-reform among the "members" of the church, the program that Egidio da Viterbo summarized at the inauguration of the Fifth Lateran Council: "men must be changed by religion, not religion by men." The "Catholic Reformation" commenced with this "grass-roots" reform during the fifteenth century.

It was not limited to *one* country. Rather, its traces can be found throughout western Europe. It encompassed all the reform efforts of the secular clergy and within the religious orders, the reforms of zealous bishops such as Antoninus of Florence and Barozzi of Padua, Cardinal Ximénez and Archbishop Talavera in Grenada, the bishops Johann von Eich of Eichstätt and Friedrich von Zollern of Augsburg, not to mention the founders of observantine branches of the mendicant orders and the reform congregations within the monastic orders. It embraced the great popular preachers Bernardino da Feltre, Giovanni da Capistrano, Olivier Maillard, Daniel von Soest, and Geiler von Kaisersberg, as well as the mystical piety of the Carthusian monks and the "Modern Devotion" movement (*devotio moderna*) in the Netherlands. All those who earnestly strove for the cure of their own and their neighbor's souls were active in our sense of grass-roots reform.

---

37   Editor's note: Papal benefices were church offices dispensed from Rome, including all episcopal offices; these could be "reserved" for a sum of money, pending the death of an incumbent office-holder. Annates were a tax on the first year's income from the proceeds of a benefice given to the pope.

38   Johannes Haller (1865–1947) et al., eds, *Concilium Basiliense: Studien und Quellen zur Geschichte des Concils von Basel*, 8 vols. (Basel: Helbing & Lichtenhahn, 1896–1936), 1: 184.

The Oratories of Divine Love and the charitable brotherhoods of Saint Hieronymus in Italy must also be understood in this connection. But to characterize them as the sole origin of the "Catholic Reformation" would be an enormous exaggeration of their importance. For they were not alone. One can find similar phenomena in all the countries of Europe, at least by the turn of the sixteenth century. In Italy, the group that gathered in Venice around Paolo Giustiniani, Vincenzo Quirini, and Casparo Contarini was certainly no less influential than the others. But the lay quality that distinguishes them can also be found in the "Modern Devotion." And what was the knight Iñigo Loyola doing, when he hung up his sword in Montserrat, other than reforming himself? In seeking refuge within himself, he, too, heeded the call of God and the spirit of his times.

This reform from below had one great weakness. It consisted of many rivulets, each flowing in its own direction, at times seeping into the riverbed, at other times reinforcing each other, but never converging in a powerful torrent. Nor was such a convergence brought on by the new religious ideals that had emerged from redaction of the original text of Holy Scripture, the works of the Church Fathers, and a deepened knowledge of the ancient church that had been emerging since the turn of the century. Humanistic reformism was encumbered by the skeptical criticism that Erasmus of Rotterdam had inflicted upon church institutions and practices. For a moment, in 1515–16, it appeared as though humanism might take hold of the other reform movements and create something new. But the outbreak of religious schism destroyed this illusion.

Grass-roots reform could only affect the whole church only if it conquered the papacy. It did not succeed in this soon enough. On more than one occasion, the Renaissance popes initiated reforms, but never pursued them seriously, not even at the Fifth Lateran Council, whose convocation had been forced by the schismatic Council of Pisa.[39]

Thus arrived that other "Reformation," which was founded on a doctrinal heresy and whose religiosity rejected essential aspects of the Catholic faith, which discarded the papacy in raw fashion and tore apart the unity of the church. By its bold claims to reestablish the true and original Christianity, the Protestant Reformation sapped valuable energies from the Catholic Reformation in northern Europe, energies that in the south continued to promote grass-roots reforms and the establishment of new religious orders, especially that most important and successful among them, the Society of Jesus.

39   Editor's note: Pope Julius II convened the Fifth Lateran council after several cardinals, with the support of French king Louis XII, assembled what purported to be a general council of the church at Pisa, thus threatening another schism. The first action of Fifth Lateran was to condemn the council at Pisa.

The papacy did not observe these developments passively, but it continued to use the antiquated techniques that had enabled it to contain opposition throughout the fifteenth century. Now, however, papal legates and nuncios accomplished little, and the Edict of Worms proved every bit as ineffective as the Bull *Exsurge Domine.*[40] Pope Clement VII recoiled from summoning another ecumenical council because he considered such an adventure too dangerous. It remained for his successor, Paul III, to include a council in his program of action; through his renovation of the College of Cardinals, he began to expose the centers of church power to Catholic Reformation's energies.

For in the meantime, the ideas of the German schism had made their way across the Alps and the Pyrenees. At first, only individual preachers and small groups gathered around them; most among them belonged to the upper strata of society. But events like the fall of Bernardino Ochino gave pause for concern.[41] The spiritualism of Juan Valdés and the Meaux circle, the translations into Spanish of Erasmus' *Enchiridion* and booklets like *Beneficio di Cristo* (1543) came to be seen as threats to orthodox piety.[42] In their *Consilium de emendanda ecclesia,* a group of earnest, zealous reformers whom Pope Paul III had summoned for consultations argued that a series of decidedly radical reforms in all areas of church life were inescapable.[43] Clearly: the path taken thus far could lead no further. The papacy and the curia would have to reform itself as well.

The dreadful catastrophe of religious schism in Germany swept away the embankments that had inhibited a confluence of streams in the reform movement. It opened the eyes of decision-makers to the presence of a new spirit in the church's midst and to the realization that new methods and new men were needed to save it. The crust of habit was too rigid for a breakthrough entirely from within; an impetus from without was necessary. The fate of Pope Adrian VI (1522–3) teaches

40   Editor's note: The bull *Exsurge domine* of Pope Leo X (June 15 1529) condemned Luther's ideas as heretical.

41   Editor's note: Bernardino Ochino (1487–1564), a Franciscan monk, joined the stricter Capuchin order in 1534 and became its vicar-general in 1538. Accused of teaching Lutheran ideas, Ochino fled Rome to Geneva in 1542. He subsequently fled to Augsburg, England, and Zürich; he died of plague in 1563 while travelling in his native Moravia.

42   Editor's note: An English-language translation of the *Beneficio di Cristo* (1543) may be found in Elisabeth G. Gleason, ed., *Reform Thought in Sixteeth-Century Italy* (Ann Arbor: American Academy of Religion, 1981), 103–62.

43   Editor's note: Gasparo Contarini (1483–1542) et al., *Consilium delectorum Cardinalium, & aliorum praelatorum, de emendanda ecclesia* (1538). An English translation may be found in John C. Olin, ed., *The Catholic Reform: From Cardinal Ximenes to the Council of Trent, 1495–1563* (New York: Fordham University Press, 1990), 65–79.

that no single individual – not even someone situated at the pinnacle of authority – was able to prevail. The external impetus did not create the forces of renewal, but liberated them, so that they could flourish, unite, and effect change throughout the church as whole.

This irruption of Catholic Reformation into the church's center was the *second* and decisive stage in its development. It did not occur in an instant, but was a slow process checked by many setbacks, even as the dimensions of the catastrophe continued to increase. Papal confirmation of the Society of Jesus (1540) and calling of the Council of Trent (1545) were milestones of progress. The decisive victory was achieved in 1555, when popes Marcellus II (April–May 1555) and Paul IV (1555–9) – both representatives of the new spirit, despite their many differences – ascended the throne of St. Peter at the moment when the defections from the church had reached their greatest magnitude, when Catholic restoration in England had failed and the advance of Calvinism in France had reduced the extent of uncontested Catholic terrain to the two southern peninsulas of the European continent.

Serious historians should not dispute that the breakthrough of Catholic Reformation in the period between 1534 and 1555 occurred under pressure from the religious schism. But in the very next breath one must add that this pressure activated and liberated energies that were already present in essence, and that they had emerged, with the ideas and the people who realized them, prior to the religious schism during the era of "grass-roots" reform.

If only one compares the many reform memoranda of the sixteenth century with those of the fifteenth, a congruity of fundamental ideas immediately leaps into view. No book of Luther's is so unoriginal as his letter to the nobility.[44] Nearly all the recommendations made before and during the Council of Trent for amending the College of Cardinals were already contained in the reform literature of the fifteenth century. Naturally so! The remedies applied at Trent resembled cures attempted earlier, because the diseases had remained the same.

The French reform proposals put before the Council of Siena (1423) complained of the devastation that resulted in monasteries when abbots received their office as an ecclesiastical benefice (*commenda*) with no less vigor than the grievances of Nürnberg, presented exactly a century later. Dominico Soto spoke no less urgently on the moral obligation of bishops to reside in their diocese than had Ludolf of Saxony (d. 1377).

---

44 Editor's note: Jedin refers to Luther's tract, *An den christlichen Adel deutscher Nation von des christlichen Standes Besserung* (1520), translated as *An Open Letter to The Christian Nobility of the German Nation Concerning the Reform of the Christian Estate*, by C. M. Jacobs, in *Works of Martin Luther* (Philadelphia: Holman, 1915), vol. 2.

In light of the abuses he saw before him, Ramón Llull spoke so forcefully on the need for priests to reside in their parishes that some historians believe the delegates to Council of Trent must have known about his observations. But did the delegates even need to read about such things in old books, when the bishop of Clermont was telling them in 1546 that only sixty priests were actually resident in a large French diocese with 800 parishes?

The history of the religious orders offers multiple examples for the continuity not only of ideas, but also of actual reform efforts. Within the Augustinian order, Giorlamo Seripando continued the reforms begun by his predecessor and benefactor, Edigio da Viterbo. The Dominicans attached themselves to Cardinal Cajetan; their Spanish observance, which achieved its greatest historical impact at the University of Salamanca, reflected the influence of Savonarola's spiritual doctrines. The Prior General of the Carmelite Order, Nicholas Audet (d. 1562) continued the work of his predecessor, John Soreth (1394–1471).

The observantine orders and the older reformist circles produced the men on whom the papacy drew to revitalize the church. Among the authors of the *Consilium de emendanda ecclesia* was Gregorio Cortese, member of the Benedictine congregation of St. Justina. Contarini, who emerged from the Giustiniani's circle in Venice, became the driving force behind curial reform in the late 1530s. Ignatius Loyola read the *Life of Christ* by Ludolf the Carthusian, Peter Canisius received his first inspiration at the Charterhouse of St. Barbara in Cologne. A. M. Zaccaria and Juan de Avila proposed the idea of an apostolic mission among the young and the forgotten. Giberti showed the way to a modern, systematic cure of souls in his diocese of Verona.

There had always been apostolic missions and pastoral care. What was new was that in the centers of power, the cure of souls gradually came to be conceived as the church's highest unwritten law. The lesson was learned that one should not distribute bishoprics and benefices in order to provide incomes for dependents, but that one must seek out pastors and leaders for the Catholic people. A new ideal of priests and bishops emerged. The mere prebendary – who spent his episcopal incomes in Rome, Venice, or at some court – gradually became a nuisance. Bishops now required an education in theology; they were expected to be pious, to set an example for the clergy, and to lead his diocese in person, not through a pastoral vicar – hence the growing importance of absenteeism in the reform literature surrounding the debates at the Council of Trent. This was perhaps the most decisive aspect of the breakthrough of Catholic Reformation: at the centers of

power within the church, the standards imposed on the moral and professional behavior of the clergy, especially the higher clergy, became
stricter. At the end of the century one pope (Clement VIII) even conducted a visitation of his Roman parishes in person.

These new standards and demands were given legislative form in the
reform decrees of the Council of Trent, especially its final session (1561-
3). For the most part, these reflected proposals submitted by the
Spaniards, Portuguese, French, and by the Emperor. Council President
Morone's great merit was to have achieved a compromise despite both
opposition within the Council and still-strong resistance from the curia.
The *third* stage of Catholic Reformation had been achieved.

In contrast to the conclusions of a superficial, purely panegyric historiography, it cannot be emphasized enough that the reform decrees of
the Council of Trent were by no means the sole cause of Catholic Reformation. Rather, they were at least as much its expression and effect. The
Council was summoned because the outcry for reform could no longer
be ignored. Its reform decrees are the legislative version of ideas that
already pushed to the surface for a new balance between needs and
experiences of the nations and the curial tradition. The decrees are not
the ideal itself, but their accommodation to circumstances in reality.
They were a compromise.

Only implementation still remained. This *fourth* and final phase of
the Catholic Reformation was the longest. It includes not only the
implementation of the reform decrees, under the auspices of newly-
founded Council congregations, papal nuncios, numerous visitations,
and synods by which the gold of general laws were exchanged into the
small coin of daily life, the founding of seminaries for the education of
a new clergy, but also the measures of popes, such as the renovation of
liturgical texts under Pius V, of the calendar under Gregory XIII, and the
reorganization of curial administration under Sixtus V. Of course, the
best aspects of Catholic Reformation at this stage lay not in the merely
mechanical execution of laws, but in the new spirit that animated them.
Carlo Borromeo meant more to the Catholic Reformation than any law.
The decisive thing was that the papacy retained firm leadership and
control over the whole process. In this connection, the pontificate of
Gregory XIII was without doubt a climactic period, but by no means an
end point. Reform of the church's internal condition continued, here
and there, throughout the seventeenth and even into the eighteenth
century.

Up to this point, I have characterized this process of renewal as a
"Catholic Reformation." Surely it would conduce to mutual understanding among historians if we could resolve to replace this term with

"Catholic Reform," a term that Kerker once proposed and more recently endorsed by Joseph Greven[45] and Joseph Lortz.[46] It says essentially the same thing, but diminishes the secondary, antithetical implications contained in the other expression, while leaving the precise and well-established meaning of "Reformation" untouched. One might be justified to speak in the plural of "Catholic Reforms" during the first phase, simply because they had not yet become unified. Nevertheless, it strikes me as necessary to retain the singular term "Catholic Reform" to describe the phenomenon as a whole, because it better expresses the continuity of development from the fifteenth to the sixteenth century.

The church drew strength from the Catholic Reform to defend itself against Protestant innovations. It was the precondition of Counter-Reformation. Everything it accomplished contributed indirectly to this defense, but the reform was not in itself defensive in nature; rather it developed from the inner vitality of the church. To ward off the enemy, the church devised new methods and weapons, with which it finally went over to the attack, in order to regain that which had been lost. "Counter-Reformation" is a concept that epitomizes the qualities and deeds the church assumed in the course of this reaction.

It encompasses, first of all, the doctrinal conflict with Protestantism, i.e., the literature of theological controversy. Beginning with the simple polemics against specific doctrinal errors practiced by Luther's first opponents Johann Eck, Emser, Fabri, Cochläus, it developed into manuals for theological controversy such as Eck's *Enchiridion*,[47] which was distributed in 82 printings, and Albertus Pighius's *Controversianum*.[48] But it soon became clear that the best defense was a positive exposition of church teachings on the disputed points. Cardinal Johannes Gropper (1503–59) had already shown the way, and the Council of Trent did not limit itself to condemning errors as anathema. Instead, in its chapters on doctrine – especially that concerning justification – the Council produced a positive exposition of Catholic dogma. Numerous tracts on justification, the church, primacy, and the sacraments then enriched this theology. At the same time, a new discipline – controversial theology – entered literature and university

45  Joseph Greven, *Die Kölner Kartause und die Anfänge der katholischen Reform in Deutschland* (Münster: Aschendorff, 1935).
46  Joseph Lortz, *Die Reformation in Deutschland*, 3rd edn., 2 vols. (Freiburg: Herder, 1949).
47  Editor's note: Johann Eck (1486–1543), *Enchiridion locorum communium aduersus Lutteranos* (1525).
48  Editor's note: Albertus Pighius (ca. 1490–1542), *Controuersiarum Praecipuarum in comitijs Ratisponensibus tractatarum, & quibus nunc potissimum exagitatur Christi fides & religio, diligens, & luculenta explicatio* (1541).

curricula. Cardinal Bellarmino's *Controversies* were the greatest achievement of this genre.[49]

Not only theologians went to battle; the whole church was filled with a militant spirit. The warrior Ignatius Loyola gave his company both the structure and spirit of a Christian soldiery; through his *Spiritual Exercises*, this spirit disseminated widely. Just as St Augustine saw world history as a great struggle between the Two Cities, Ignatius presented everyone the choice of fighting with one or the other army. There could be no passive bystanders!

Hence the elimination of Erasmus and the irenic theology associated with him. Ignatius and Gianpietro Caraffa, though vocal enemies of one another, were of one mind about him. As a matter of principle, Catholic reforms might well have followed the model of early Christianity and cast off many medieval trappings. But there could be no break with the immediate past; rather, it was necessary to maintain an organizational continuity with the existing order. In any case, the outbreak of revolution within the church struck the humanist reform movement too soon, before it had outgrown the radicalism of youth and achieved maturity in Saints John Fisher and Thomas More. It was their undoing. The Protestant reformers had adopted their critique of scholasticism and certain forms of religious practice from the humanists' example. The retreat to tradition that now set in swept humanism aside. There remained much to be said for an irenic solution until the schism hardened into organized counter-churches and as long as the hope remained that a well-timed ecumenical council might retain a large number of undecided people within the church. But by 1541, when Julius von Pflug and Gasparo Contarini attempted to achieve reunification at the Colloquy of Regensburg, the moment had passed. In Spain, the battle against Erasmus was joined already in the 1530s; in the following decade, Evangelism was suppressed in Italy; and at the Colloquy of Poissy (1561) the "moderates" of France were defeated. The final stage was the defeat of humanist reformers in the battle over residency requirements, fought out at Trent in 1562.

Jesuits and Capuchins are usually thought of as the exponents of this pugnacious Counter-Reformation spirit, and so they were. But we must not forget that the same spirit filled the nuncios whom Pius V and Gregory XIII dispatched into endangered regions, the preachers who disputed with the Protestants from their pulpits, even the artists represented the victorious struggles of orthodoxy against heresy on the walls and ceilings of newly-built Baroque churches.

49   Editor's note: Cardinal Roberto Francesco Romolo Bellarmino (1542–1621), author of *Disputationes de controversiis Christianae fidei adversus huius temporis haereticos* (1586–93).

In this battle, the papacy availed itself of both ecclesiastical and secular means of coercion without hesitation. There had been local inquisitions already in the Middle Ages. Spain had shown how effective and fearsome a weapon a centrally organized inquisition could be. So now a Roman Inquisition was founded (1542) and sent into battle against heresy. The press was the most important instrument of heretical propaganda. The attackers' broadsheets were more appealing than the Catholics' well-reasoned refutations. Local book-bans and lists of forbidden texts – such as those of the Sorbonne (1544), the faculty at Louvain (1549), and the index of Giovanni della Casa in Venice (1549) – were all in vain. Pope Paul IV replaced them all with the first general index of prohibited books. When it proved impracticable, it was replaced with the improved, Tridentine index of Pope Pius IV.

Deploying the arm of secular power against heresy was also nothing new. The medieval state regarded the heretic as a revolutionary who threatened the very foundation of social life and with it his own. Already at the end of 1520, the papal Nuncio Hieronymus Aleander had obtained an official edict from Emperor Charles V against Luther's writings for the Habsburg Netherlands. In May 1521, the Edict of Worms applied the ban throughout the Empire. Already by 1530, Cardinal Campeggio was firmly convinced that only the use of force – a war of religion – could suppress Lutheranism. This was in fact attempted in the War of Schmalkalden (1544–7), but it backfired. The reasons for this failure were many; for our purposes, it is important to note that the Empire was no longer a state, properly speaking. The axiom of religious peach achieved at Augsburg (1555) – *cuius regio, eius religio*: "he who governs the territory determines its religion" – showed where the modern state lived: in the Empire's constituent territories.

Only the modern, bureaucratic, territorial states could carry out the Counter-Reformation, not the Empire. Only they possessed the necessary political means; indeed, their very survival depended on such tools. The Protestant princes had greatly increased their power by confiscating church properties and by erecting central church governments in their territories. If they did not wish to remain behind forever, the Catholic princes had to assert rights of dispensation over episcopal nominations and the taxation authorities of bishoprics, monasteries, and parishes within their territories. By dismantling innovations and the territorial estates that protected them, the princes strove to restore the homogeneity of state power. The papacy assisted by converting the opponents of *cuius regio, eius religio*. But it could not prevent a gradual reversal of roles as the Catholic Restoration was carried out. In the end, it was not the state that gave support to an endangered church, but the church that aided the nascent absolutist state. The Liechtenstein Dragoons that "re-Catholicized" Silesia tended the affairs of the House of Habsburg, not those of Catholic religion. In fact, the church had not desired this brutal compulsion, but did nothing to stop it. Naturally, it took most of the blame.

To sum up: defending against Protestant innovations impressed upon the church certain characteristics, whose embodiment we call the Counter-Reformation. The origins of reaction go back to the first days of the religious schism. The Catholic polemics, which evolved into a literature of theological controversy, began with Johann Eck's *Obelisks*. Harnessing the power of state to the struggle against heresy began with Aleander's first nunciature; the Society of Jesus received its confirmation in 1540, the first indexes of prohibited books were in the 1540s, the Roman Inquisition was founded in 1542. But these defensive measures only became fully effective after Catholic Reform had conquered the papacy and the popes assumed central leadership in the struggle, during the decisive years between 1555 and 1564. Only then did reaction transform into victorious self-assertion. The cowardice and pessimism that had lamed many fighters for the church diminished. In a few years, the time had come for the church to strike back and to focus on the recovery of lost terrain. The "German Congregation," founded in 1568, expanded its activities under Pope Gregory XIII; under his reign, nuncios transformed from mere diplomatic representatives into protagonists of Catholic interests in the endangered areas. The missions of Ninguarda and Porzia and the Cologne nunciature served this purpose exclusively. Later on, the Congregation for the Propagation of the Faith assumed some of these duties.

The doctrinal and political disunity of its original opponent, Lutheranism, stood the church in good stead. Already by the 1550s, Calvinism was proving itself to be a far more dangerous enemy; it too was centrally organized and filled with a mighty will to power. Only in later phases did the Lutheran king Gustavus Adolphus of Sweden emerge as the recognized leader of Protestantism in its struggle for survival.

The inner relationship between Catholic Reform and Counter-Reformation should now be clear enough. It resided in the central role of the papacy. A papacy inwardly renewed by Catholic Reformation became the standard-bearer of Counter-Reformation. In its counterattack on Protestant innovation, the papacy deployed existing religious energies and power-political tools. For the popes, the reform decrees of the Council of Trent were a means to an end, and the Society of Jesus was certainly a powerful instrument in their hands.

The much-noted Latin character of the Counter-Reformation explains this inner connection between the two phenomena. The forces of Catholic renewal that facilitated and fulfilled the breakthrough of Catholic Reformation to the heart of the church had originated for the most part in Spain and Italy. Some were present north of the Alps, but most of these were so engulfed in the religious schism that only a few islets remained, such as the Cologne Charterhouse and several north German Dominican monasteries. The terrible dearth of priests in Germany rendered impossible an unaided reconstruction of Catholicism. Help would have to come from outside, and those who provided it – above all in the form of new religious orders – were the papacy, in the first place, and second the House of Habsburg.

In light of the close, inner contiguity between Catholic Reform and Counter-Reformation, one might ask whether it is even necessary to divide the whole phenomenon between *two rubrics?* Isn't one enough, such as "Catholic Restoration" or "Catholic Counter-Reformation"?

To be sure, both phenomena converged in concrete reality, in individual people and events. The Council of Trent and the Jesuit Order belong to both the history of Catholic Reform as well as the history of the Counter-Reformation. We would arrive at an impasse if we tried to decide whether particular personalities belonged in one or the other line of development. Perhaps it is possible to ascribe Giberti, Seripando, Filippo Neri, Juan and Teresa de Avila to the Catholic Reform; but it is altogether impossible to regard Ignatius Loyola, Carlo Borromeo, and Francis de Sales simply as Counter-Reformation figures, because they bore within themselves aspects of both.

Still it strikes me as necessary to retain the duality of these terms. Church history needs it in order to distinguish between two lines of historical development that differ both in origins and essence: a spontaneous movement grounded in the continuities of spiritual life versus a dialectical process that emerged from a reaction against Protestantism. With respect to Catholic Reform, the religious division performed merely an activating function; with respect to Counter-Reformation, it acted as a driving force. The term "Catholic Restoration" does not adequately capture the first of these two, because the parallelism to Protestant Reformation is lacking; still less with the second, because it wholly ignores the reciprocal effects that existed between religious division and the development of the Catholic church. The concept "Counter-Reformation" emphasized this aspect, but suppresses the element of continuity. If we want to comprehend the development of the church during the sixteenth century, we must remain mindful of two fundamental elements: the element of continuity contained in the concept of "Catholic Reform," and the element of reaction contained in the concept of "Counter-Reformation."

We are now in a position to answer the question posed in the title of this investigation. It is impossible to speak of Catholic Reform *or* Counter-Reformation; rather one must speak of Catholic Reform *and*

Counter-Reformation. It is not a matter of *either or*, but one of *both and. The Catholic Reform was the church's reorientation toward Catholic ideals of living through an internal process of renewal, while Counter-Reformation was the self-assertion of the church in the struggle against Protestantism.* The Catholic Reform was based on a grass-roots reform that emerged under the pressure of decline among the individual institutions within the church during the late Middle Ages; it achieved victory with the conquest of the papacy, the convening of the Council of Trent and its implementation. If Catholic Reform was the soul of a reviving church, its body was the Counter-Reformation. During the Catholic Reform, energies built up which were later released in the Counter-Reformation. At the point of intersection between them was the papacy. The religious schism deprived the church of valuable energies and diverted them in other direction; but it also awakened the remaining energies, increased them, and deployed them fully in the field of battle. Religious division was an evil, but one from which many positive things developed. We can see their effects in the twin concepts of "Catholic Reform" and "Counter-Reformation."

Translation © David M. Luebke 1998

# 2

# Counter-Reformation Spirituality

## *H. Outram Evennett*

Originally appeared as Evennett, H. Outram, "Counter-Reformation Spirituality," in his *The Spirit of the Counter-Reformation*, ed. John Bossy (Notre Dame: University of Notre Dame Press, 1970), 23–42.

### Editor's Introduction

If Hubert Jedin's contribution was to reorient historical definitions, that of H. Outram Evennett (1901–64) was to focus them on culture and to describe more precisely the changing nature and effects of Catholic religiosity. In a series of lectures delivered at the University of Cambridge in 1951 and first published in 1968, Evennett argued that a new kind of spirituality lay at the heart of the Counter-Reformation, a spirituality epitomized by the *Spiritual Exercises* (1541) of Ignatius Loyola, founder of the Society of Jesus. More than Jedin, Evennett emphasizes that the sixteenth-century Catholic reforms were unthinkable without the stimulus of a "new and competing" form of Christianity in Europe; by the same token, however, he stresses that without the equal impetus of spiritual renewal, these reforms would have remained as ephemeral as their fifteenth-century predecessors. For Evennett, the Counter-Reformation was "first and foremost a powerful religious movement," only secondarily a set of institutional reforms; indeed he managed, in John Bossy's words, "to construct a convincing and at least reasonably comprehensive plan of the Counter-Reformation almost without mentioning the Council of Trent." In this, the second of his six lectures, Evennett outlines in general terms what he considers the essential elements of Counter-Reformation spirituality: a departure from the contemplative mysticism of the late Middle Ages; a turn toward more rigorous and self-disciplined meditation and prayer; greater emphasis on zealous, worldly activism in the form of charity and labor for the salvation of souls; a revival of the sacraments, especially confession and communion; and even a kind of individualism.

# Counter-Reformation Spirituality

*H. Outram Evennett*

At the end of my first lecture, I suggested a formula for a possible definition of our subject, namely that in the largest view what we were dealing with was the whole process of adaptation to the post-medieval world of Catholicism – by which expression I mean the religion and organization of the western medieval Church remaining under Rome. This formula is not intended as a subtle attempt to take the "counter" out of "Counter-Reformation" but rather to embrace it within a wider grasp. In stressing the positive, even perhaps, *pace* Croce, the creative side of the movement, we cannot allow ourselves to forget – and indeed it would be flying in the face of history to do so – how vigorously the Counter-Reformation was stimulated in all its aspects and how profoundly it was conditioned by the challenge of Protestantism. The coming into existence of new and competing forms of established Christianity in Europe was one of the things to which adaptation of outlook and policy was needed, and while this brought a new and modernized efficiency in catechismal and controversial methods, and a new impulse to the serious study of Church history, it also served to intensify those habits of caution, suspicion, intransigence, and the appeal to force which are the hallmarks of an anxious defensive, involved in the elaboration and safeguarding of more rigorous definitions. Such traits, indeed, characterized not merely the public relations (as it were) of the Church but also her own internal workings. The inquisitorial principle with all its practical applications – whether in the development of new inquisitorial tribunals proper, or in efforts to control reading, or in other ways – so far from declining towards an ultimate vestigial condition, appropriate to a free community, was strongly felt by authority to be a religious as well as a social necessity. The effect produced on the ecclesiastical attitude towards new intellectual or scientific ideas not in themselves directly concerned with or resulting from religious heresy, could not but be constrictive, and the quasi-tolerance of philosophic and other novelties which marked the Church of the Italian Renaissance came necessarily to be heavily modified. The Church of the Counter-Reformation, indeed, was sufficiently in tune with the age to become and remain acutely conscious that the Catholic conception of Christianity was challenged not merely by the revolutionary, yet still Christian, dogmas of Luther and Calvin, but also by the seeping into the European

mind of something more subtle, more deeply burrowing under foundations – a general philosophical scepticism and the nascent ideas of free
thought and rationalism.

Against the attractions which the doctrine of Justification by Faith
alone, with all its radical presuppositions and practical consequences,
undoubtedly held out for some; against the pull, for the more worldly,
of scepticism and hedonism, what had the old Church to offer? The
Counter-Reformation could hardly have occurred had it been no more
than "the hastily improvised defence of the vested interests of an archaic
ecclesiastical corporation bereft of contemporary or future spiritual
significance."[1] I return with renewed conviction to this sentence written
more than fifteen years ago. The Counter-Reformation was first and foremost a powerful religious movement, and it is only by recognizing this,
not as an afterthought, but as the first condition of a fruitful approach
to its study, that we can hope to reduce it to unity and to arrive eventually at some reasonable appraisal. It involved, however, more than the
simple reaffirmation of medieval spiritual teachings, and it eventually
created a mature spirituality with clear characteristics of its own, on
which the impress of the new times and their atmosphere was in many
ways clearly discernible.

Yet the spiritual arms and the apostolic technique of the medieval
Church in the fifteenth century had not been negligible: preaching
abounded in great quantity, though often doubtless of questionable
quality, and perhaps of sporadic incidence; the invention of printing cut
both ways – it helped the propagation of Catholic piety and devotion and
the preparation for the Counter-Reformation, as well as assisting Protestant propagandists; new devotions and religious practices multiplied
rapidly to stimulate the religious feelings of the faithful. Across the
century passes a long procession of saints and revivalists, holy women,
visionaries, prophets, monastic reformers, and the often sincere efforts
for ecclesiastical betterment of politicians. The fifteenth century – so full
of contradictions – was full of reforms and reformers who between them
could not make a Reformation; either in the Catholic or in the Protestant sense. It is not enough, in explanation, to point to the frustrating
influence of the papal court whence came a flood of dispensations
and exemptions cutting across the efforts of the reformers, a worldly
outlook, all the obstructions and disappointments inevitable in a highly
organized administrative central machine, and a preoccupation with
culture, politics, and finance. The essential sterility and ephemerality –
in the long view – of all reform movements between the Council of Constance and the pontificate of Paul III proceeded in the last analysis from

1    Evennett, *The Counter-Reformation* (Catholic Truth Society, London, 1935), p. 1.

the tiredness of generations which seemed to have lost the art of creation, or re-creation, in so many spheres of human activity; which could
produce neither a Loyola nor a Luther; which could not summon the
strength of will to deal radically with the condition of affairs which the
embedding of all ecclesiastical offices, from the highest to the lowest, in
the social, financial, and economic structure of society had led to. It is
as if the more virile psychology and willpower of a new, less worn-out
generation of men was required for the seeds of reform, already so
widely present in the fifteenth century, to strike deep roots and acquire
a true power of effective and lasting growth. If religion is an essential
ingredient in men's lives, it is perhaps no surprise that stronger purpose
and a more lasting staying-power should have appeared in their spiritual strivings simultaneously with the manifestation of a new
masterfulness and freedom in their politics and other secular activities.
Without questioning the practical abilities of many fifteenth-century
characters, new ability and determination seem nonetheless to have
come into the blood of the generation born in the later years of
the fifteenth century – for what reason, history by itself can perhaps
hardly determine. And with men of the stamp of the Cortes, the
Michaelangelos, the Ferdinands of Aragon, the Henry VIIIs, there
appeared also the Luthers and Zwinglis, the Cajetans, Carafas and
Loyolas. Contemporaneously with the discovery of America and the
sea route to the East, with the quick conquests of the new political spirit
in the European states, with the gradual evolution in Luther's mind of
his new religious outlook, there were also being formed, among the
many possible seedbeds of a more powerful Catholic religious revival,
certain germinating centers of a new spiritual urgency and compelling
example, which would supply the first spear-heads of the "Counter-
Reformation."

If we scan the period from Columbus's first voyages to the sack of
Rome – after which the Roman court first began to apply itself in seriousness to the question of reform – several such centers can be noted.
In Italy many associations, or oratories, half lay, half clerical, had been
formed in a number of cities, not only for the cultivation of a more
intense and lasting piety among their members, but also for the perfor-
mance of urgent charitable works, the care of orphans, the education
of the poor, and most of all the institution of hospitals, principally
for sufferers from the new disease of syphilis, regarded as incurable,
brought in, it was said, by the French, and which most ordinary hospitals would not deal with. Here much was due to the influence of St
Catherine of Genoa,[2] a lay woman, and her disciple and biographer

---

2   See *Enciclopedia cattolica*, III, 1145–8; and more generally Pastor, *History of the
Popes*, X, chs 12–13; XI, ch. 13; Evennett, *New Cambridge Modern History*, II, 285–90.

Ettore Vernazza, and from Genoa derived the Oratory of Divine Love in Rome which ran a hospital for *incurabili* and whence came the four founders of the Theatine Congregation of reformed priests and their first novice. Similar circles existed in many other centers. Those in Brescia and the surrounding district have recently been studied by Cistellini;[3] from this group came St Angela Merici. In Venice the group represented by Contarini and his friends is held to have had a continuous existence stretching back to Ludovico Barbo, the early fifteenth-century reformer of the Italian Benedictines and the founder of the Congregation of Sta Justina of Padua.[4] The rather freer Naples group is well known. The cult and influence, too, of Savonarola were strong and persistent, long after his death, producing notable effects – if we are to believe Marcel Bataillon and Fr Beltrán de Heredia[5] – on both the Spanish and the north Italian Dominicans, especially the latter: from these came a remarkable spiritual leader, John Baptist Carioni, better known as Fra Battista da Crema, author of the widely read *Vittoria di se stesso* and spiritual director of some of the men who made the earliest foundations of clerks regular in Italy.[6] Thus, though lay was mixed with clerical inspiration in these numerous Italian circles, the traditional inspiration of friars and monks was by no means lacking; and side by side with the work, so lay in original concept, of St Angela Merici, there was the remarkable influence of enclosed contemplative nuns such as Laura Mignani, the Augustinian canoness, the confidant of St Cajetan; the Dominican Blessed Stefana Quinzani; and others. It was into the cloisters of Camaldoli that the earliest Venetian friends of Contarini went; while the primitive Franciscan spirit – never wholly dead at any time in Italy – was germinating again in Mateo da Bascia and his followers who canalized his aspirations into the renewed apostolic and ascetical fervor of the Capuchin order. In Spain and France and Germany as well as Italy the observant branches of Franciscans and Dominicans and other friars were making headway, and there are some remarkable chapters in the history of the reformed Preachers in Spain related by Fr Beltrán de Heredia.[7] Luther came from a strictly observant, not a lax, branch of the Augustinians. More powerful in the north was the influence of the

3  A. Cistellini, *Figure della riforma pretridentina* (Brescia, 1948).
4  On Barbo, *Enciclopedia cattolica*, II, 830–1.
5  [Editor's note: Vicente Beltrán de Heredia, *Las corrientes de espiritualidad entre los Dominicos de Castilla durante la primera mitad del siglo XVI* (Salamanca, 1941); and Marcel Bataillon, *Érasme et l'Espagne: Recherches sur l'histoire spirituelle du XVIe siècle* (Paris, E. Droz, 1937; reprint Geneva: Droz, 1998).]
6  *Enciclopedia cattolica*, II, 1049–50, referring to O. Premoli, *Fra Battista da Crema secondo documenti inediti* (Rome, 1910), etc.
7  *Historia de la reforma de la Provincia de España* (? Madrid, 1939). General accounts in H. Jedin, *History of the Council of Trent* I (London, 1957), 139–45, with bibliography p. 140; Aubenas and Ricard, *L'Eglise et la Renaissance*, pp. 275–311.

German Carthusians, especially the Charterhouse of Cologne, which kept alive the spirit of northern Catholic piety that owed so much to the Canons of Windesheim and the Brethren of the Common Life, with their traditions of new devotion and regular meditative prayer.[8] Even in the south, where Valladolid and Montserrat, Chezal-Benoît and Subiaco had led or were leading Benedictine revivals, these northern influences were powerful. Spanish translations of Ludolph, the Saxon Carthusian, of Thomas à Kempis, and others of the northerners, were abroad in Spain before 1500 and certainly in the early decades of the sixteenth century, when the Basque gentleman Iñigo de Loyola was beginning his extraordinary career.

In all these quarters, and no doubt others, we find, not self-conscious and ambitious programs for the reform of the Church as a whole but, what was more necessary for that reform, the taking up, refertilizing and modernizing by men of outstanding spiritual fibre, of the disciplines of prayer, self-control, and charitable activity, whether as individuals or in community life, in the personal search for the Kingdom of God, and for the good of their neighbors. No doubt, however, these were as yet small oases, in an enormous area where the most lamentable deficiencies and abuses existed. None of these groups or individuals whom I have mentioned seems to have been conscious of being influenced by what was happening in Germany and Switzerland, the import and permanence of which were for long misunderstood and underestimated in Italy. And yet all their efforts might have been as ephemeral as those of their fifteenth-century predecessors had they not become caught up in a more general organized movement of urgency and enthusiasm; and for the formation and correlation of this, under the aegis of the papacy, the fear of what was occurring in Germany was indeed, ultimately, largely responsible. The Counter-Reformation, helping to give self-conscious unified shape to the Catholic reform, may perhaps be said to have properly come into existence under the pontificate of Paul III. And yet no amount of unity of control or direction, or stimulus of fear, would have guaranteed permanency or success unless there had also been present the necessary spiritual basis. The spirituality of the Counter-Reformation Church, its roots deep in the past, developed nevertheless under the pressure of outward circumstances.

In its gradual formation, against the evolving background of the Protestant revolution, the spiritual revival and transformation of Catholicism took, inevitably, more rigid forms than might otherwise have been the case, or than might have been anticipated in the earlier

---

8    Jedin, *History of the Council of Trent*, I, 143–5; L. Cognet, *De la dévotion moderne à la spiritualité française*, (Paris, 1958), ch. 1.

stages, before the humanist ways of thought had become suspect and Lutheranism had crystallized. Books and teachings accepted as valuable in the 1520s found themselves condemned in the more cautious and harsher 1550s, when certain spiritual issues had become fundamentally clearer. The powerful attractions of the idea of Justification by Faith alone, of the new conception of Faith itself, and of the view of Justification as – broadly speaking – imputed rather than actually attained, were not limited to those who ultimately followed the lead of Martin Luther. To many, a comfortable feeling of absolute assurance in God alone, a relief from the continuous strain of effort and conflict in the spiritual life, the removal of all the complicated paraphernalia of Church obligations and the artificial multiplication of sins *quia prohibita*, may well have appeared, in the conditions of the early sixteenth century, as the revelation of a new and purely spiritual religion. But even among certain men of intellectual eminence and real spiritual maturity, who saw the full implications of Fra Martin's revolutionary theology, a stronger emphasis on the part played in man's salvation by freely given divine Grace, as contrasted with his own feeble strivings, was regarded as desirable for a better balanced Catholic spiritual life. Six years before the outbreak of the Indulgence controversy made Luther's theology a subject of public debate, Gasparo Contarini, the eminent Venetian man of affairs (who had not followed his friends Giustiniani, Quirini and Georgi into the cloister of Camaldoli) underwent at his Easter Confession of 1511 a spiritual experience which impressed upon him a new and enduring illumination of the meaning of God's Justice, and which so responsible a Catholic historian as Professor Jedin has recently compared to the famous, if perhaps somewhat elusive, "experience" of Luther, while reminding us, however, that in Contarini's case the experience was one in connection with a sacrament and not in implied hostility to the sacramental principle.[9] The attitude of soul for which Contarini stood and which was shared by many eminent and sincere Catholics, such as Morone, Seripando, Pole, Flaminio, Gropper[10] – to take a few eminent names – and by a penumbra of more freely speculating believers like Juan de Valdés[11] and his circle, may be regarded as an attempt to provide, within the framework of traditional

9   "Ein 'Turmerlebnis' des jungen Contarini," *Historisches Jahrbuch*, LXX (1951), 115–30.
10   For Seripando, H. Jedin, *Girolamo Seripando: Sein Leben und Denken im Geisteskampf des 16. Jahrhunderts* (2 vols, Würzburg, 1937). English translation, omitting studies in vol. II, F. C. Eckhott, *Papal legate at the Council of Trent: Cardinal Seripando* (St Lovis/London, 1947). For others, see *Enciclopedia cattolica*, under names.
11   Ibid. XII, 964, with references.

Catholicism, for some reasonable element of the new religious attitude to which Luther's odyssey and the popularity of his doctrine bore witness.

Fine-spun speculations about the nature of God's Justice and the operation of his Grace in relation to individual men freely seeking him, may well, when reduced to the dry expressions of theological terminology, seem academic and unreal. But behind the various complicated theories of Justification which were flung at each other in the many conferences and controversies of the early sixteenth century, there lay – as later there lay behind the terminology of casuistry which Pascal ridiculed – matters known and felt to be of vital importance for the spiritual life of Christians and the salvation of immortal souls. Professor Jedin, in the first volume of his new *History of the Council of Trent*, has emphasized the extreme importance, in regard to the eventual drafting in 1547 of the Tridentine decrees on Justification, of the exhaustive controversies of the previous thirty years, in which the root theological issue that divided Protestantism from Catholicism had been brought out.[12] In that decree the various half-way houses towards Lutheranism put forward by Contarini, Seripando, Gropper, and others who felt the pull towards a more Augustinian theology were rejected. This fact, vital for the history of Counter-Reformation theology, is of necessity equally vital for the formation of its spirituality, for spirituality must be based on theological correctness if it is to avoid the disaster of mere self-illusion. Even before 1547 – while it could still be maintained that uncertainty about orthodoxy existed – the authorities were much concerned to detect and check any apparent tendencies towards the false mysticism that they felt would be involved in any kind of approach towards the principle of the rejection of works as an essential ingredient in the attainment of salvation. After 1547, however, uncertainty was at an end, and one of the foundation-stones of Counter-Reformation spirituality was irrevocably laid.

The theological definitions of the Council of Trent in regard to Grace, while not rendering impossible such later phenomena as Baianism, the Molina-Bañez controversy "de Auxiliis," or Jansenism, were nevertheless sufficiently clear and comprehensive to provide both a basis and a framework for the development of the new devotional movements and spiritual techniques of the hour. They afforded no true grounds for that hostility towards contemplative prayer and mysticism which the related fears of Lutheranism and Illuminism implanted, justifiably or unjustifiably, so deeply in the minds of many of the ablest and most

12  Jedin, *History of the Council of Trent*, I, 409, n. 7, and in general 355–409; for Tridentine debates and decree, ibid. II (London, 1961), book iii, chs 5, 7 and 8; *Seripando*, chs 5, 20–2.

devoted Catholic reformers. Nevertheless, the view that Justification by Faith alone must logically lead to Illuminism or quasi-mystical aberrations was widely held, especially in Spain. It may well have done an injustice to the essentially unmystical Martin Luther, who, we are told by Mr Rupp, "drove himself nearly daft . . . trying to follow the mystic counsels of St Bonaventura, until his own commonsense bade him desist."[13] In these circumstances, the effect of the Tridentine decrees was to make doubly sure in practice that the spirituality of the Counter-Reformation would be one in which activity of all kinds was to play a very large part; in which active striving after self-control and the acquisition of virtues would be vital; in which zeal for good works of mercy and charity, and labour for the salvation of souls, were to predominate: a spirituality which was to reflect the bustle and energy and determination of sixteenth-century man, feeling at last that he had a power over himself and over things, to be applied, in the Counter-Reformation, for the greater glory of God and the revival of his Church. The spirituality of the Counter-Reformation sprang from a triple alliance, as it were, between the Tridentine clarifications of the orthodox teaching on Grace and Justification, the practical urge of the day towards active works, and certain new developments in ascetical teaching and practice which promoted this outlook. These developments had been taking place slowly during the previous hundred and fifty years, but were now brought to a head and popularized according to the practical needs of the time and the particular religious climate generated by the necessities of the Counter-Reformation struggles. I am referring here chiefly to the systematization of the meditative form of mental prayer, which was much cultivated in the fifteenth century, in the first instance as a way towards the reform of monastic and clerical life. Thence it was adapted progressively to the requirements of the devout layman, to become eventually, through the agency of the great spiritual masters of the sixteenth and seventeenth centuries – Ignatius, Scupoli, François de Sales, Bérulle, Vincent de Paul – one of the cornerstones of the new and reinvigorated spirituality that was gradually diffused, by means of all the new apostolic techniques of the Counter-Reformation, throughout the whole Catholic Church.

The late Henri Watrigant, of the Society of Jesus, in a series of articles designed as a chapter in a projected history of meditation, examined very fully the history of the development of the art and practice of meditation in the late fourteenth and the fifteenth centuries.[14] He dis-

13   Gordon Rupp, *Luther's progress to the Diet of Worms* (London, 1951), p. 28.
14   "La méditation méthodique et l'école des Frères de la Vie Commune," and "La méditation méthodique et Jean Mauburnus," *Revue d'ascétique et de mystique*, III (1922), 134ff and IV (1923), 13ff; "La genèse des Exercices de Saint Ignace de Loyola," *Etudes*, LXXI (1897), 506ff; LXXII, 195ff; LXXIII, 199ff.

tinguished between two main sources of the movement: first, the writers and teachers of the *devotio moderna* in the Low Countries and north-western Germany; and, secondly, the Franciscan and Carthusian traditions, behind which lay, of course, a long earlier history of doctrines and practices of prayer, partly meditative, partly mystical in nature. It is a great injustice to suppose – as some seem to[15] – that there was nothing more to the spirituality of the *devotio moderna* than sensible, or superficial, devotion based, consciously or unconsciously, on a nominalist intellectual agnosticism. The series of writings and influences that from 1370 onwards emanated from the Brethren of the Common Life and the Canons of Windesheim, and those under their influence, and which formed an important source of Counter-Reformation Catholicism, were far from being concerned exclusively with the promotion of sensible devotion – with merely "affective" religion, as the spiritual authors say. It is worthwhile recalling the names of some of these men whose collective, cumulative influence was so widespread and so lasting: Gerard Groote himself, founder of the Brethren of the Common Life; Florent Radewijns, his disciple; Lubert Berner; Peter Gerlach; Gerard of Zutphen; Jan Goossens Vos van Heusden, prior of Windesheim; Henry of Mande; Thomas à Kempis; Jan Mombaer – the *catena* stretches from the last decades of the fourteenth century to the death of Mombaer in Paris in 1520.[16] Of the writers mentioned, Père Watrigant picks out three who were specially prominent by the didactic and systematic nature of their writings and the way in which they developed the whole art of meditation, systematically setting out in orderly method the manner of meditation, arranging meditations in groups, or set exercises, or for periods of time, by the day, the week, or the month; or in ascending grades – ladders of ascent, *scalae*. These three were Radewijns, Gerard of Zutphen, and Jan Mombaer, whose bulky *Rosetum* is an enormous compendium of various treatises on prayer of different types. These three, incidentally, were all men with a university training.

Closely connected with these, and other representatives of the *devotio moderna*, who figure in Johannes Busch's contemporary history of the devotion and of the monastic reformers associated with it, were influences deriving from older traditions – principally Carthusian and Franciscan: Henry of Kalkar, the Carthusian teacher of Groote himself, Henry of Hesse, Denys, Ludolph the Saxon, and other Carthusians; among the Franciscans, the traditions derived from St Bonaventure were carried on by Otto of Passau, David of Augsburg, Ubertino of Casale,

15   I am not sure who is intended here, though it is possibly Hugo Rahner; cf. also Jedin, *History of the Council of Trent*, I, 145.
16   See Jedin, ibid., with bibliography; R. R. Post, *De moderne devotie* (Amsterdam, 1940), esp. pp. 132–47. A. Hyma, *The Christian Renaissance: A history of the "Devotio Moderna"* (New York, 1925), seems undiscriminating.

Henry Herp – "Harpius" – who died at Malines in 1478 and whose work became suspect in the more astringent atmosphere of the middle sixteenth century.[17] Other more individualistic writers added their contributions, such as Pierre d'Ailly and Gerson, Tauler and Ruysbroeck the mystics, Johann de Rode, the German Benedictine reformer.

There emerged from all these writings, among other things, the elaboration and gradual popularization of a systematic method of private, meditative prayer which exercised a wide and profound influence. A "science" of meditation came into being with its own rules and principles, which if regularly and systematically observed, was eminently calculated to strengthen, in each individual, habits of self-control, perseverance in the struggle for virtue, and the maintenance of that sense of continuous self-dedication so essential to monasticism. This method of personal self-improvement was much cultivated in the monastic, and especially the Benedictine, reforms of the fifteenth century, not indeed in opposition to liturgical or corporate acts of worship such as the recitation of the divine office in choir, or the general ceremonial of the Church, but in a complementary though in a certain sense also a contradistinctive way. Italy and Spain, as well as Germany, felt the impulse of this northern spiritual influence which brought order and staying-power, as well as a new devotional warmth and what the Germans call *Innerlichkeit*, into monastic spirituality. It is highly probable that Netherland influences were at work in the early fifteenth century in Venice, among the reformed canons of St George of Alga, whence there came to Padua Ludovico Barbo, founder of the Benedictine congregation of Sta Justina, and author of the *Modus meditandi et orandi*.[18] Centers of Benedictine reform so far apart as Subiaco, Valladolid, Bursfeld and Melk are said, on more or less circumstantial evidence, to have been influenced in a similar way, and, in spite of Benedictine authors who take a different view, it would appear that even so eminent a Spanish work as the Book of Exercises for the Spiritual Life – the *Ejercitatorio de la Vida Espiritual* – of Abbot García Cisneros of Montserrat, though in form and purpose no doubt a true original work, was in its substance almost entirely taken from the northern authors of the previous hundred years.[19] A more subtle problem of derivation, as

17    Accounts of most of these will be found in Cognet, *De la dévotion moderne à la spiritualité française*, ch. 1.
18    Post, *De modcrne devotie*, p. 137, remarks the parallel, but is not clear who influences whom.
19    *Dictionnaire de spiritualité*, II (Paris, 1953), 910–21; A. Albareda, "Intorno alla scuola di orazione metodica stabilita a Monserrato dall'Abate Garsias Jimenez de Cisneros," *Archivum historicum Societatis Jesu*, XXV (1956), 254–316. I have not seen G. M. Colombás, *Un reformador benedictino en tiempo de los Reyes Católicos: García Jiménez de Cisneros, abad de Montserrat* (Montserrat, 1955), who (Albareda, p. 316) suggests a meeting between Cisneros and Standonck and Mombaer in Paris in 1496.

we shall see later, is raised by the other great Spanish work in which the systematic elaboration of formal meditation comes, in some respects, to its climax – the *Spiritual Exercises* of St Ignatius.

Barbo, Cisneros, and most of the authors of the *devotio moderna* wrote specifically for monks. Their works presuppose the monastic routine. But the self-control, attention to prayer, perseverance in virtue, and sense of dedication that are underlined in the religious life, apply in some degree to all Christians, and it was eventually the wider task and destiny of this movement of ordered, meditative prayer, woven into the traditional doctrine of the three ways or stages of the spiritual life – purgative, illuminative, and unitive – and logically expounded by recognized masters, to become one of the most important spiritual arms of the Counter-Reformation to the reform of laity and clergy alike. We should notice here, however, that in the eyes of its greatest exponents in the fifteenth and early sixteenth centuries, the cultivation of systematic, mental-image-forming meditation no more excluded the possibility for some souls of a higher type of contemplative mystical prayer than it condemned, either for monks or for laymen, vocal prayer either private or communal.

All this technique of regular mental prayer with its demands on the powers of the mind and its requirements in the way of preparatory and concomitant asceticism, was conceived and practiced in highly individualistic terms, to the diminution of stress on communal or liturgical values. Surely, we see here the individualism of the age taking its appropriate form in Catholic spirituality – something, perhaps, not wholly unconnected with the process by which, as medieval society dissolved, the mystic interpenetration of Church and society faded and the individual was left to face by itself the problem raised by the mutual confrontation of Church and state as separate perfect societies. The loyalty to the Church which the Counter-Reformation demanded does not seem to have inspired a clear reaffirmation of the doctrine of the Church as the mystical body of Christ in such a way as to make this the basis of a new corporate "mystic." The central position of the individual in the practice of Counter-Reformation spirituality was, admittedly, radically different both from the moral view of his position in the purely humanist ideology and from the theological view of his position in the Protestant scheme of things. Less Pelagian on the one hand than the extreme humanist concepts which exalted the complete self-sufficiency and self-responsibility of the independent human being, it nevertheless rejected the Protestant doctrine of the nature and results of original sin which to some, at any rate, seemed to make nonsense of humanist principles. The Counter-Reformation doctrine of Christian struggle and effort, laborious, long, chequered, perilous, but aided, fostered, and eased by systematic precepts and counsels representing accumulated wisdom and experience, announced that Man – even in face of his Almighty Creator – carried, to some extent, his own fate in his own hands.

But this was, however, only half the story. God would respond to man if man responded to him; the process was mutual and cumulative (I am not using technical theological terms). If the great achievements of the Counter-Reformation, in the spirit as well as in action, rest to a large extent upon the doctrine of ceaseless effort and combat against self; over against this, in necessary complementation, stands the conviction that in another sense it is God who does all, and that in the ultimate analysis his glory is all that matters. Not for nothing was the motto of the Society of Jesus – for all its perhaps sometimes exaggerated stress on action – *Ad Majorem Dei Gloriam*. Hence, the spiritual leaders of the Counter-Reformation, without exception, turned back zealously to the covenanted channels of God's Grace, as an essential factor in the new bursting of spiritual energy – the sacramental system which the doctrine of Justification by Faith alone had so deeply undermined. A more than annual Confession and Communion for serious lay people, a more nearly daily celebration of Mass for priests and bishops, became a note of the reformers in all Catholic countries.[20] The sacrament of Confession was henceforth to be not merely the annual preparation for the reception of Easter Communion, but a regular occurrence in the devout life and in the spiritual combat, linked closely with the technique of regular examination of conscience and the practice of fruitful pious meditation on the life of Christ or other biblical or devotional themes. The confessional became more and more a regular rather than an exceptional resource, and inevitably there came a great advance in the science of confessors, in the whole role of the spiritual director, and therefore also in the development of moral theology, of cases of conscience – in a word, of casuistry. This was an inevitable part of the process, regrettable only when abused. Such a doctrine as probabilism, with all its variations and intricacies, serves to show the length to which a zeal to help Christians by a careful definition of sin, admittedly in a perhaps somewhat legalistic manner, could be carried, in the attempts to clarify and compose consciences.

And if the sacrament of Confession held in Catholic religious life of 1600 or 1650 a place totally different from that which it had held in 1400, similar great changes had come over eucharistic piety. The Middle Ages adored the host at Mass, but outside the liturgy did not pray to it,

20  On frequent Communion, see *Dictionnaire de théologie catholique*, III, 515–52, esp. 531ff: note approval of Zaccaria, Gaetano da Thiene and Ignatius; strong reserve of Domingo de Soto, Azpilcueta. I have found nothing very helpful on Confession.

when reserved, the outward reverence paid in Catholic churches today, nor was it made the center of non-liturgical devotions. The non-liturgical worship of the host in the service of benediction, in the forty hours' exposition,[21] and by practices such as modern "visits" is a Counter-Reformation development. Much popularized by the Capuchins and Jesuits, the forty hours' exposition was first performed in 1527, in Milan, in order to invoke divine aid during a time of war and plague; and the growth of devotions to the blessed sacrament as the abiding sacramental presence of Christ in his Church is wholly a characteristic of modern Catholicism. But it is equally true and certainly no less important that the spirituality of the Counter-Reformation also restored to a much more central place in Christian life the prime purpose of the Eucharist as a divine food in which Christ is given to each individual. It is extremely difficult to form an overall picture of the frequency of Communion in about the year 1500. While many bishops and priests, especially those without care of souls, said Mass only very infrequently, daily Mass, or Mass several times a week, was generally the mark of the reformed monastic communities of the age, or even of the normally observant; it certainly became a mark of the new sixteenth-century congregations. Among the laity, and clergy other than priests, reception of the holy eucharist was much less frequent. The exhortations of theologians do not seem to have been much implemented by the efforts of parochial pastors. But pious circles even in the fifteenth century practiced a more frequent recourse than the obligatory annual. At the Collège de Montaigu in the University of Paris, which had felt the influence of the Flemish reformers Standonck and Mombaer – and every reader of the *Imitation of Christ*, in full, knows Thomas à Kempis's views! – fortnightly Communion was practiced at the time of St Ignatius's stay there about 1530. St Ignatius in his early days communicated, and counselled pious souls to communicate, weekly. Two or three times weekly was laid down for Jesuit scholastics, and was probably the norm among fervent unordained clerics. But the precise frequency with which a man or woman might presume with fruit and without fear of sacrilege to approach the holy table was a matter for direction; and the views of directors might differ, as indeed the practice in convents and lay confraternities varied. Though the Counter-Reformation saw the restoration of Holy Communion as a more integral part of regular Christian life and spiritual "technique," nothing like the free daily Communion of the twentieth century was either advised or practiced, in general, so far

---

21   See articles, "Quarantore," in *Enciclopedia cattolica*, x, 376–8, and "Forty Hours' Devotion" (Thurston), in *Catholic Encyclopedia*, vi, 151–3.

as laymen were concerned.[22] So far as generalization can be hazarded, the daily celebration of Mass by priests probably became very widespread throughout the Church in the sixteenth and seventeenth centuries – the gradual spread and perfection of seminary training would probably bring this about – while monthly or weekly Communion was frequently permitted to lay people who took the practice of religion with regular seriousness, who had embarked on the devout life.[23] In all Catholic countries, especially Italy, eucharistic societies and brotherhoods sprang up. Yet there may have been some falling back in the late seventeenth century, perhaps as the indirect influence of Jansenism, which tended to regard the act of Communion – and indeed the celebration of Mass itself – more as a kind of recognition of merit acquired than as a help towards acquiring it. Early in the seventeenth century, however, the Spanish Carmelite nun, Anne of Jesus, was surprised at the extent of frequent Communion in Paris, and records the surprise of Parisians that the Spanish Carmelite nuns who introduced Carmel into France did not communicate more frequently. But in his account of the great abbesses who reformed so many of the French Benedictine nunneries about the turn of the sixteenth century, Bremond points out the significance of the fact that it was often the introduction of mental prayer which led the nuns to greater frequentation of the sacraments.[24] There was in fact a necessary and close connection between the personal discipline involved in regular periods of daily mental prayer and the new fervour for the sacraments of Confession and Communion. These two aspects of Counter-Reformation piety – the efforts of personal *ascèse*, the "disciplined life of religious regularity," and the recourse to the covenanted channels whence flowed divine Grace *ex opere operato* – are seen once more to come together.

The revival of the sacramental life, the spread and development of powerful new techniques of meditative prayer and eucharistic devotions, the driving urge towards outward activity and good works as a factor in personal sanctification, all deployed, as it were, within the framework of Tridentine doctrine; here I suggest are the essential ele-

22   But cf. Ignatius to Teresa Rejadella, November 15 1543, in H. Rahner, *St. Ignatius Loyola: Letters to Women* (Freiburg/Edinburgh, 1960), pp. 338ff, where he approves the suggestion, admittedly of a nun, that she should receive Communion daily.

23   G. le Bras, *Introduction à l'histoire de la pratique religieuse en France*, I (Paris, 1942), 96, does not suggest any sign of a general eucharistic piety in France in the seventeenth and eighteenth centuries; he is chiefly concerned with rural Catholicism.

24   *Histoire littéraire du sentiment religieux*, II (1921), 440; pp. 436–41 were clearly very important for Evennett here.

ments of Counter-Reformation spirituality, as formulated and taught by a succession of spiritual geniuses of the highest order throughout the sixteenth and seventeenth centuries, transforming and enormously quickening the spiritual life-blood of Catholicism, eventuating in a new creative efflorescence of institutions, and new reorganizations of the practical working and administration of the Church, in a word the beginnings of modern Catholicism. Within this formula we see, of course, ebbs and flows, variations of emphasis, a variety of spirits, according to nation, tradition, religious order, precise period, or play of circumstances. It would be as much out of touch with reality to suggest the early attainment of a rigid uniformity as it would be to forget that for long the new intensification of devotion was seen and felt only in limited circles and that the name of *chietini* for the new class of *dévots* (revealing the impression made by the Theatines) persisted for decades in Italy and Spain. Again, the whole French spirituality of the seventeenth century, for example, in so far as it derived from Bérulle, had a distinctive Christocentric character;[25] while the intensive and exclusive concentration on formal discursive meditation with its mental efforts, and on the principle of activity and struggle – of which the Jesuits were the supreme and the extreme champions – was questioned in a running undertone of dissatisfaction by upholders of a more contemplative doctrine of prayer, not only in Spain, but elsewhere too. In Italy the severe ascetic spirit of St Charles Borromeo, and of the influential *Combattimento Spirituale* of the Theatine Lorenzo Scupoli was in full accord with the new tide; St Philip Neri and the warmer spirit of the Oratorians – not indeed indulgent but somehow modishly Franciscan – represented a variation that found a wide response in the Rome of Sixtus V, Clement VIII, and Paul V which St Philip did so much to convert. The Dominican spiritual influence, widespread and powerful everywhere in the sixteenth century, was not wholly in step with that of the Society of Jesus; the soon ubiquitous Capuchins had a way of their own; the methods of St François de Sales were distinctive.

Nevertheless, it is not invalid to recognize in the dominant spirituality of the Counter-Reformation certain powerful and distinctive traits. Broadly speaking, its genius took individual rather than corporate or liturgical expressions. It was highly sacramental; not biblical, in the Protestant sense of a personal formation based primarily on direct reading of Scripture, its great masters were all impregnated with the Bible and its meditative practices were largely focused on the life and passion of Christ; while the humanity of Christ, which fifteenth-century

---

25   H. Outram Evennett, *The Spirit of the Counter-Reformation* (Notre Dame: University of Notre Dame Press, 1970), 139–41.

devotions such as the rosary and the cult of St Anne had emphasized, was the object of increased veneration. It was exacting, in that it demanded continuous heroic effort at prayer and self-control and self-improvement and good works; practical, in that it closely linked active good works and self-improvement, and assumed the placing of a high value on the former in the sight of God for Justification, and also in that, at any rate with the Jesuits, asceticism was kept within reasonable bounds. It may be rated humanistic in that it proceeded on the belief that each man's destiny for all eternity was partly in his own power to make or mar. The whole trend – even, as Professor Jedin has remarked, among the Carthusians[26] – was away from contemplation towards apostolate. And for many of those traits there can be no doubt that the conditions of the time were in a sense partly responsible: all that was implied in the challenge of the Reformation, in the challenge of the discovery of new races of men to be evangelized, the challenge where it occurred of a hostile state, even perhaps the less obvious but in the long run more far-reaching challenge to the whole Christian concept latent in the germs of secularism and free thought.

Such was, in its main characteristics, I think, the spirituality on which was based the religious formation given in the Tridentine seminaries, especially those under Jesuit management, prevalent among many of the new congregations and the reformed older orders, and given to thousands of devout laity under spiritual directors in the sixteenth and seventeenth centuries. Of this active, virile, exacting religious outlook of Counter-Reformation Catholicism, with all its strengths as well as with what it had of weakness and insufficiency, the Jesuits were the outstanding representatives. It was because they were so fully representative of all its main characteristics, so fully aware of all the supreme urgent necessities of the new epoch and its new climate – so far as the preservation and expansion of Catholicism were concerned – that they became the outstanding force in the whole Counter-Reformation movement; that they became its modernizers (to avoid the overtones of the word modernist) to the extent even of incurring the charge of opportunism, in so many spheres; and that, lastly, the Society of Jesus, while retaining its own peculiar exclusiveness of spirit as a "close corporation," paradoxically enough succeeded in impressing so much of its own principles, outlook and ethos on so many sides and parts of Catholic life and organization.

26   *History of the Council of Trent*, I, 144.

# 3

# Was Ignatius Loyola a Church Reformer? How to Look at Early Modern Catholicism

## John W. O'Malley, SJ

Originally appeared as O'Malley, John W., SJ, "Was Ignatius Loyola a Church Reformer?: How to Look at Early Modern Catholicism," *Catholic Historical Review* 77 (1991): 177–93.

### Editor's Introduction

In his 1990 presidential address to the American Catholic Historical Society, the Jesuit scholar John O'Malley surveyed the development of historical approaches since 1946, when Hubert Jedin posed the question of definitions, "Catholic Reformation or Counter-Reformation?" Like his predecessor, O'Malley seeks to transcend earlier debates, only this time Jedin's own limitations are at issue. Specifically, O'Malley notes the limits of historical definitions and approaches that focus too narrowly on the reform of institutions in a European context. To illustrate the point, he invokes the example of Ignatius Loyola, the Counter-Reformation saint *par excellence*. In what sense, he asks, was Loyola a *reformer* of the Catholic church? Loyola and the first Jesuits worried little about institutional reform; rather, their primary concern was with the "help of souls." Similarly, the Jesuits' missionary activity outside Europe had little direct connection to the Council to Trent, even though its impact was arguably just as great. In place of "Counter-Reformation" and "Catholic Reformation" – with their implicit references to Protestantism and the notion of a decadent fifteenth century – O'Malley recommends using "Early Modern Catholicism," a more elastic, less judgmental term, that encompasses both Jedin's meanings and the many, complex aspects and dimensions overlooked.

# Was Ignatius Loyola a Church Reformer? How to Look at Early Modern Catholicism

*John W. O'Malley, SJ*

Almost fifty years ago, Hubert Jedin published his highly influential essay entitled *Katholische Reformation oder Gegenreformation?*[1] In it he reviewed in masterful fashion the tangled historiography concerning the Catholicism of the fifteenth through the seventeenth centuries and especially the efforts of historians to invent designations that would adequately indicate its character. When I recently reread the essay, I was again impressed with the subtlety, sensitivity, and breadth of information of surely one of the greatest historians of the Catholic Church in this century, then still a relatively young man with thirty-four of his most productive years still ahead of him. To reduce the essay to a few generalities distorts it badly, but to provide a *mise en scène* for what I have to say in relatively few pages about Saint Ignatius and its implications for Jedin's thesis I am compelled to do precisely that.

Although Jedin recognized some validity in terms like "Catholic Restoration" and even "Catholic Renaissance," he ultimately rejected them. He rejected "Counter-Reformation" even more emphatically, because it implied that whatever of importance happened in Catholicism during the period postdated the Protestant Reformation, was reactive to it, and consisted to a large extent in efforts to repress it through force and intimidation. His solution to the problem is well known and has today become normative among historians of almost every persuasion. It is enshrined in textbooks around the world, sometimes in ways that do not do full justice to Jedin.

In any case, Jedin answered the question he posed in the title of the essay by substituting an "and" for the "or" (*oder*), so that according to him the proper way to designate the phenomenon was "Catholic Reform *and* Counter-Reformation." He thus recognized the valid elements in the latter term, but emphasized by the former an earlier, originally independent, and continuing reality, for which he gave many examples. Subsequent historians have greatly amplified these examples, with the result that there can be no possible doubt about the existence of "Catholic Reform" as Jedin described it. In fact, historians today confirm

1 (Lucerne, 1946).

this aspect of Jedin's thesis by inclining to see both the Protestant Reformation and its Catholic counterpart as two different expressions of the same reforming impulses that ante-date 1517. Sometimes in fact they designate every aspect of the Catholic phenomenon simply as "Catholic Reformation."

Despite its widespread acceptance, however, Jedin's thesis has not been without its critics, sometimes explicit, sometimes implicit. In the former category, for instance, in Gottfried Maron, who argues that Jedin failed to take account of the repressive impulses in "Counter-Reformation" that after about 1542 gave even "Catholic Reform" its character.[2] Among the latter we might place Jean Delumeau, as indicated by the title of his *Le Catholicisme entre Luther et Voltaire*, in which he eschews both "Catholic Reform" and "Counter-Reformation" and extends forward the chronological limits beyond what Jedin seems to suggest as valid.[3] In his more recent books Delumeau again implicitly challenges Jedin's chronology by dealing with the thirteenth to the eighteenth century as a cohesive unit.[4]

Wolfgang Reinhard, following the lead of Ernst Walter Zeeden, has taken a different tack for the period after about 1550 by insisting on the similarities between Catholicism and Protestantism in what he calls the "confessional age."[5] In that age Reinhard sees the churches as expressions of the "modern world" and of forces within it toward what he calls "*Modernisierung*." It must be mentioned that Jedin himself intimates the possibility of such an interpretation, for he sees the age of "Catholic Reform and Counter-Reformation" as essentially transitional, already manifesting some of the characteristics of the "modern church."[6] It must also be mentioned that Reinhard sees the Jesuits as manifesting aspects of modernity.[7]

What these examples and the many others that could be adduced indicate is that, whereas nobody questions the aptness of the des-

---

2   "Das Schicksal der katholischen Reform im 16. Jahrhundert," *Zeitschrift für Kirchengeschichte*, 88 (1977), 218–29.
3   (Paris, 1971). The subtitle, *A New View of the Counter-Reformation*, was added to the English-language edition (London and Philadelphia, 1977).
4   See, e.g., *La peur en Occident, XIV<sup>e</sup>–XVIII<sup>e</sup> siècles* (Paris, 1978), and *Le péché et la peur: La culpabilisation en Occident, XIII<sup>e</sup>–XVIII<sup>e</sup> siècles* (Paris, 1983).
5   See, e.g., "Zwang zur Konfessionalisierung? Prolegomena zu einer Theorie des konfessionellen Zeitalters," *Zeitschrift für historische Forschung*, 10 (1983), 257–77; "Reformation, Counter-Reformation, and the Early Modern State," *The Catholic Historical Review*, 75 (July, 1989), 383–404; and the discussion by Robert Bireley, "Germany," in *Catholicism in Early Modern History: A Guide to Research*, ed. John W. O'Malley (St. Louis, 1988), esp. pp. 11–13.
6   *Katholische Reformation*, pp. 44–9.
7   "Reformation, Counter-Reformation," pp. 386–9.

ignation "Reformation" for the phenomena that began with Martin
Luther in 1517, despite the great diversity among them, some historians still find themselves uncomfortable with Jedin's designations, even
while they recognize that they captured something important and
basic.[8]

It is at this point that I should like to introduce Saint Ignatius and
with him the early Society of Jesus. Jedin mentions the official founding
of the Society in 1540 as among the first events of the Counter-
Reformation, and at another point describes the spirit of battle with
which Ignatius, the former soldier, imbued the Society especially
through the *Spiritual Exercises*.[9] He correctly cautions, however, that
Ignatius and the Society must also be seen as part of Catholic Reform,
reminding us that our categories of interpretation convey a neatness
that does not perfectly correspond to the complexity of historical
reality.[10] His treatment thus indicates that Ignatius and the early Jesuits
are best understood as some combination of Catholic Reform and
Counter-Reformation.

Jedin's analysis is confirmed by the treatment other historians accord
the early Society. It is exemplified, for instance, by the entry under
"Jesuits" of the *Oxford Dictionary of the Christian Church* (2nd edition),
which specifies the purpose of the order as "to foster reform within the
Church, especially in the face of the acute problems posed by the Reformation." The diptych is familiar: on the Protestant panel is Lucas
Cranach's portrait of Luther and on the Catholic is Jacopino del Conte's
portrait of Ignatius.

An immense amount has been written about Luther's evolution that
finally brought him in 1520 to publish his "Appeal to the German Nobility," the document that more than any other signaled he was ready to
assume leadership in a program of disciplinary, ritual, and structural
changes in the Church that, while based ultimately on his doctrinal
positions, had ecclesial and ecclesiastical repercussions certainly not
foreseen by him or others in 1517. With the "Appeal" he dramatically
entered center stage to begin his career as among the two or three most
influential church reformers of all times. Few historical personages have
been subjected to more searching and systematic scrutiny than Luther
or undergone more revisionist interpretations, yet no scholar has ever

---

8    See, e.g., Eric Cochrane, "Counter-Reformation or Tridentine Reformation?
Italy in the Age of Carlo Borromeo," in *San Carlo Borromeo: Catholic Reform and Eccle-
siastical Politics in the Second Half of the Sixteenth Century*, ed. John M. Headley and
John B. Tomaro (Washington, D.C., 1988), pp. 31–46.

9    *Katholische Reformation*, pp. 33, 34, 35–6.

10   Ibid., p. 37.

challenged that Luther was a reformer of the Church or that at a certain point he claimed that role for himself.

Ignatius Loyola has not benefited – or suffered – from the same quantity and quality of historical analysis. This situation is part and parcel of the stagnant condition in which scholarship on his side of the situation languished until quite recently. For the past two decades French and Italian historians have been turning their attention to this field with new zeal and new methods, but have applied curiously little of their zeal and methods to the Jesuits and their founder. True, reliable and helpful works on the subject appear with regularity, but they tend to be long on information, short on analysis; they concentrate on leaders like Ignatius, Francis Xavier, Diego Laínez, and Peter Canisius; they tend to interpret these figures and the Society in familiar categories without giving them the more precise definitions that contemporary scholarship makes possible and demands. Among these familiar categories for Ignatius is "reformer of the Church."

I do not know precisely when or how historians first began to speak of Ignatius and the Jesuits of his generation as concerned with that issue. One thing is certain: the expression appears with surprising infrequency in the immense amount of documentation that has come down to us from those Jesuits and, as far as I know, never do they apply the term to themselves, certainly not in the way it was understood in the sixteenth century. That fact should itself give us pause.

How was the expression understood? The sixteenth century was heir to ideas about the reform of the Church first articulated during the Investiture Controversy of the eleventh and twelfth centuries that centered on the disciplinary and moral reform of the episcopacy by means of a thoroughgoing implementation of the ancient canons, authentic and forged. Once formulated, these ideas took on a powerful life of their own, contributing greatly to the bitter controversy among lay and clerical leaders of the Church that marked the high and late Middle Ages. By a curious historical twist in the fifteenth century, they were turned against the papacy, which had originally created them, so that reform of the Church sometimes meant first and foremost reform of the papacy and papal curia. From that reform would follow the reform of the rest of the episcopacy, from which would follow reform of the pastors of parishes and parochial ministry.

You will note that reform of the Church centered on *offices* in the Church – papacy, episcopate, pastorates – and hoped to accomplish its moral and pastoral goals principally through canonical discipline. This understanding of the term is attested to by the legislation of the councils of Constance and Basel, by the numerous other synods of the fifteenth and sixteenth centuries, and most obviously and forcefully by the massive legislation of Trent *de reformatione.*

This definition of reform already suggests why Saint Ignatius and his fellow Jesuits used the term so infrequently. They did, however, occasionally employ it. In Ignatius' correspondence it recurs with unaccustomed frequency at the time of the election of Pope Marcellus II in 1555. As Cardinal Marcello Cervini, that Pope had showed himself friendly to the Jesuits in many circumstances. Ignatius and his collaborators knew him well, and therefore their hopes for "reform of the Church" were high.

The issue seems to have come up in informal conversations at the Jesuit *casa professa* after the election. Ignatius is reported to have said that the Pope should reform himself, the papal "household" or curia, and the cardinals of Rome; if he does that, everything else will fall into place.[11] The sentiment was hardly original, but it indicates a significant strand of thinking in the Society about reform of the Church not confined to Ignatius.

When Marcellus after a pontificate of less than a month was succeeded by Paul IV, the Jesuits tried to look on the bright side of that volatile fanatic, which was the zeal for the reform of the Church for which he had been known for decades. The new Pope initiated a flurry of activities to reform the Roman curia. In private correspondence the next year Juan de Polanco, Ignatius' talented secretary and *alter ego*, showed himself realistic: "They are beginning to deal with reform [of the curia], and it seems in earnest, even if the procrastinations of the past prove that we should not easily believe these things until we see them accomplished."[12]

Despite the concern that these statements indicate, they are more remarkable as exceptions in Jesuit documentation from the period. The reasons are clear. The Jesuits deliberately forswore for themselves the very offices with which reform was concerned – papacy, espiscopacy, pastorate. Such reform did not concern them directly or touch the way they wanted to live their lives or do their ministries. Moreover, the "humility" that they saw as distinguishing their vocation made them loathe to program juridical changes for these venerable offices. More basically, such reform was not what they were about.

What were they about? Although the first Jesuits rarely indeed spoke about reform of the Church, they with some regularity used the term *reformatio.* By it they meant two things. Sometimes it referred to their work in helping convents elect better superiors and otherwise deal with

11  *Monumenta Ignatiana: Fontes Narrativi,* Monumenta Historica Societatis Jesu (henceforth cited as MHSJ) (Madrid and Rome, 1894– ), I, 719.
12  *Monumenta Ignatiana: Epistolae,* MHSJ, XI, 245, X, 665.

their morale and religious observance. Much more often it referred to the change of heart effected in individuals through the *Spiritual Exercises* and the other ministries in which the Jesuits were engaged. It meant conversion. It was thus closer to the biblical and patristic sense than that of church reformers since the eleventh century.[13] It was at the heart of the *Exercises* and therefore of their mission.

Another term that comes close to encapsulating that mission is *christianismum* or *christianitas*, the object of Jesuit catechesis as specified in the papal bull approving the new order, September 27, 1540. *Christianitas* was a term in wide usage and of immense significance in the Middle Ages, as John Van Engen showed in his brilliant article in the *American Historical Review* four years ago.[14] What it means is the making of a Christian, and that is certainly what the Jesuits hoped to accomplish by teaching catechism. *Christianitas* did not consist in memorizing abstract orthodoxies but in introducing the individual to the essential and traditional practices of the Christian religion and to the social responsibilities and opportunities of the believer especially through the spiritual and corporal works of mercy. It was a patristic and medieval idea. Although not quite the same thing as *reformatio*, *christianitas* is related to it as its framework. The more I study the first Jesuits the clearer it becomes to me how the teaching of catechism was emblematic of all their ministries and why they attached such importance to it.

To some extent the Humanists of the fifteenth and sixteenth centuries were simply updating the term *christianitas* when they spoke of *pietas* as the object of their educational program. While that program insisted on the acquisition of information and skills, its true object was what the Germans call *Bildung* – the formation of character – in this case the formation of Christian character.

True, *pietas* had important classical resonances that *christianitas* did not, but these ideas resembled each other in the importance they attached to the appropriation of right sentiments and the necessity of living according to them. I believe that this correlation was probably the principal reason the first Jesuits so easily made the humanistic program of education their own. The Jesuit schools were not, of course, merely schools of catechism – far from it! – but *christianitas* in the broad sense was what they wanted them to accomplish in their students.

In 1551 Polanco wrote an important letter to Antonio Araoz, the provincial of Spain. He encouraged him to open colleges similar to the ones just beginning in Italy. He also listed fifteen "benefits" to be derived

13   See Gerhart B. Ladner, *The Idea of Reform: Its Impact on Christian Thought and Action in the Age of the Fathers* (Cambridge, Massachusetts, 1959).
14   "The Christian Middle Ages as an Historiographical Problem," *American Historical Review*, 91 (June, 1986), 519–52.

from the enterprise – a list as important for what it does not say as for what it does. Nowhere, for instance, is the problem of the Reformation alluded to. In general the "benefits" do not admit interpretation related to reform as we generally understand the term.

The last one comes closest to it when it states: "Those who are now only students will grow up to be pastors, civic officials, administrators of justice, and to fill other important posts to everyone's profit and advantage."[15] In a broad way this benefit can be taken as an aspect of "Catholic Reform." The Jesuits occasionally referred to it as *reformatio*, but understood the term as an articulation of what the Humanists hoped to accomplish by their educational program, more or less independent of the agitated religious issues of the day. The Jesuits seem to have understood the "benefit" as one of the ways they could work toward the medieval goal of the "common good," as the bull of papal approval enjoined upon them, and as an effective way "to help souls" through what they saw as this means that had exponential effects.

In my opinion the expression that best captures the self-definition of the first Jesuits was, in fact, "the help of souls." It is only a slight exaggeration to say that it or its equivalent occurs on almost every page of the voluminous correspondence they left behind. It occurs with telling frequency in Ignatius' so-called *Autobiography*, importuned from him by his colleagues toward the end of his life as a kind of testament or "mirror" in which they would discover the true meaning of their vocation.

Curious about the *Autobiography* from our viewpoint is that, even as late as 1555, when Ignatius finished dictating the text, the year before his death, he scarcely mentions the Reformation, although he had ample opportunity to do so. As he looks back and interprets his life at this late date, moreover, nowhere does he speak about reform or suggest that he or the Society has anything to do with it. The text is remarkable, in fact, for its detachment from all the urgent issues facing the Church, more than suggesting that they had little or nothing to do with his vocation. The military imagery so often attributed to the founder of the Society is almost entirely absent. It occurs, of course, at several key points in the *Exercises*, but, *pace* Jedin, is less pervasive, for instance, than in Erasmus' *Handbook of the Christian Soldier*.

The *Autobiography*, of course, does not tell all. In the Empire after about 1550 and then in other localities especially in northern Europe, the Society took up the struggle against the Reformation with special earnestness, and it did this with Ignatius' blessing.[16] Even before that

15   *Monumenta Ignatiana: Epistolae*, MHSJ, IV, 7–9.
16   See my "Attitudes of the Early Jesuits towards Misbelievers," *The Ways*, Supplement 68 (Summer, 1990), pp. 62–73.

date Ignatius and his colleagues showed themselves eager to stop the advance of "Lutheranism" in Italy and elsewhere. Ignatius supported the establishment of the Roman Inquisition in 1542 and founded the German College in Rome a decade later. In 1554 through Peter Canisius he urged King Ferdinand to repressive measures against "the heretics" in his domains.[17]

Ignatius and his fellow Jesuits came to believe, furthermore, that some of their ideals and practices could be powerful stimuli to needed changes in Catholic ministry. Their adamant refusal to accept alms for the hearing of confessions, for instance, surely helped banish in certain localities the persuasion that a confession was not valid unless one "paid" for it. They knew well the power of example in effecting change. In religious practice their advocacy of more frequent Communion grew out of their conviction that such was the way of the "primitive Church."

When all is said and done, therefore, did not the pursuit of personal *reformatio*, of *Christianitas*, of *pietas*, of "the help of souls" by Ignatius and the first Jesuits contribute enormously to the betterment of Catholicism and therefore to its reform, making them church reformers after all? Have we not merely been splitting hairs, engaging in a *lis verborum*, and making distinctions of no real import if the result was the same in any case? I reply that if we wish to make reform synonymous with renewal, religious revival, "great awakening," "new flowering," and a host of similar terms, that may well be true, but I think we generally want to denote something different when we speak of reform.

What is in a name, you still urge, for a reform by any other name would smell as sweet? In response I would simply quote Alfred North Whitehead: ". . . definitions – though in form they remain the mere assignment of names – are at once seen to be the most important part of the subject. The act of assigning names is in fact the act of choosing the various complex ideas which are to be the special object of study. The whole subject depends on such a choice."[18]

My contention is that our habitual way of naming what happened in Catholicism in the sixteenth and seventeenth centuries is often inexact and therefore obscures what we otherwise know to be true. It has derived to a large extent from German – and, more broadly, northern European – historiography. Thus the Reformation and Catholic efforts to counter it have rendered other aspects of the story secondary. The Society of Jesus, we must realize, was more strongly based in Italy and the Iberian peninsula, and directed much of its attention to India, Japan, and Brazil. True, we cannot understand what happened in all those ter-

17  *Monumenta Ignatiana: Epistolae*, MHSJ, VII, 398–404.
18  *The Axioms of Projective Geometry* (Cambridge, 1906), p. 2, as quoted in Ladner, *The Idea of Reform*, pp. 427–8.

ritories apart from the controversies aroused by the Reformation, but we need to look at it with other lenses as well.

For instance, the intense study of the Renaissance in the past thirty years has taught us that, unlike what earlier scholars assumed, "Renaissance" and "Humanism" are not interchangeable terms, even though neither can be understood without the other. We need to apply somewhat the same kind of rigorous analysis to what I choose to call Early Modern Catholicism, on the one hand, and "Catholic Reform and Counter-Reformation" on the other. As in the example I adduced, they cannot be understood without each other, but they are not precisely the same thing. The first is broader, and helps us take account of important elements that only with difficulty can be forced under the umbrella of the latter. The latter does not capture the full reality and, indeed, in significant measure sometimes distorts it. It forces us despite ourselves into a somewhat narrowly conceived ecclesiastical history and inclines us to slight considerations of the more general shifts in culture that affected religion.

I believe that Saint Ignatius and the Society of Jesus are most appropriately placed under the former rubric, and only then should they be related, as they must be, to "Catholic Reform and Counter-Reformation." But they are not thus unique phenomena. Two others are outstanding.

For the future of Catholicism, first of all, few enterprises in the fifteenth and sixteenth century had greater ultimate impact than the missions in newly discovered lands. The motivation of the explorers, missioners, and their patrons was complex, and in some cases not devoid of eschatological dreams of an end-time of "one flock under one shepherd" or of relationship to the cataclysmic politico-religious situation in Europe.[19] Nonetheless, this enterprise would have gone forward pretty much as we know it, independent of such motivation – even when it existed. It seems, in any case, to have played practically no role with the Jesuits in their ventures overseas. We must recall, moreover, that the missionary activities of the period are not even mentioned in all the decrees of Trent, and, almost as a consequence, not mentioned in any significant way in Jedin's essay.[20]

---

19   See Pauline Moffitt Watts, "Prophecy and Discovery: On the Spiritual Origins of Christopher Columbus's 'Enterprise of the Indies,'" *American Historical Review*, 90 (February, 1985), 73–102, and my "The Discovery of America and Reform Thought at the Papal Court in the Early Cinquecento," in *First Images of America: The Impact of the New World on the Old*, ed. Fredi Chiappelli et al. (2 vols.; Berkeley, Los Angeles, London, 1976), I, 185–200.
20   See the passing observations, *Katholische Reformation*, pp. 72–3.

The papacy provides the second example. While "reform of the papacy" was a crucial issue, well treated by Jedin in his volumes on Trent, that reform never eventuated in ways that were generally desired and foreseen, as is more than suggested in Barbara Hallman's recent book.[21] Paolo Prodi argues, however, that the institution underwent significant changes in the functioning and understanding of papal political authority and that these changes were due not to "Catholic Reform" but to other forces operative in the great shift in culture from the Middle Ages into what we call Early Modern Europe.[22]

One might question, moreover, just how closely "reform" was related to the Thomistic revival, to the development of casuistry, to the development of social ethics, and to similar phenomena of the era.[23] While there undoubtedly was such a thing as what is called "Counter-Reformation Art," there was also much religious art done under Catholic patronage that does not fit what that category would seem to designate. To what degree and in what precise ways, for example, were Caravaggio and Bernini "Counter-Reformation (or Catholic Reform) artists"?

Taking my cue, therefore, from Erwin Panofsky and other historians who have tried to analyze what distinguishes those historical phenomena we properly designate as "renaissances" from other cultural peaks that we do not,[24] I would say that for "reform" some intentionality is required, some self-conscious *intention* not merely to reanimate existing institutions but to reorganize them according to some clear pattern or to displace them with new ones. As I have been suggesting, such intentionality was not absent from Saint Ignatius and his disciples, especially in certain particulars and with the passing of the years, but it was neither their starting point nor their center.

Of course, if we wish to apply the term "reformer" to every religious figure of great intensity who had social or cultural impact, it applies to Ignatius (and to Philip Neri, Jeanne Françoise de Chantal, Joseph Calasanctius) – just as it would apply to Saint Benedict and Saint Francis. In a somewhat different way, it would apply to Thomas Aquinas and the whole enterprise of Scholastic theology – rarely has such a revolution been effected in the traditional pattern of thinking and behaving, which

21  *Italian Cardinals, Reform, and the Church as Property, 1492–1563* (Berkeley, Los Angeles, London, 1985).
22  *The Papal Prince: One Body and Two Souls: The Papal Monarchy in Early Modern Europe*, trans. Susan Haskins (Cambridge, 1987).
23  See, e.g., Jared Wicks, "Doctrine and Theology," in *Catholicism in Early Modern History*, especially pp. 237–41.
24  *Renaissance and Renascences in Western Art* (New York, 1960).

resulted in the creation of a new institution, the university. But we do not generally apply "reformer" or "reform" to these figures or movements because they never declared reform as their intention. Changes like these, even changes supposedly for the better, are not the same thing as reform.

Such changes are quite different from Reformation and from "Catholic Reform and Counter-Reformation" – from Luther and Calvin, from Gasparo Contarini, from Marcello Cervini, from Pope Paul IV, from Carlo Borromeo. They are to some extent different from Teresa of Avila, for she was a late expression of the observantist reform movement of the mendicant orders. Although it is different from the Capuchins, their motivations for a reformed observance were strongly influenced by the "spiritualist" movement in the Franciscan order that had roots back almost to the beginning of the order.[25]

What I am trying to say can perhaps be clarified by an example that has nothing to do with the Church. Perhaps no one in history has had greater impact on the rehabilitation of alcoholics than Bill Wilson and "Doctor Bob," the founders of Alcoholics Anonymous. Nonetheless, we do not generally speak of them as reformers in that field because they never set out on such a crusade or conceived of themselves in such a role. Their object was "to help souls," in this case drunken souls. Alcoholics Anonymous, of course, became incorporated into the institutional treatment of those suffering from the dread disease, but it did so without losing its independence or its original intention, philosophy, and methods.

I suggest that "reformer" came to be applied to Saint Ignatius largely through osmosis. Since so many leading figures of the age defined their principal concern as reform, he must have done the same. But he did not. Since he lived in an age of aberrant or lax religious practice and of the loose morals of the Renaissance (so the argument goes), he must have been aware of this situation and set out to rectify it. But historians of our generation question this assessment of the religious situation, and, in any case, Ignatius manifests little awareness in the main that he lived in a particularly irreligious or immoral age.

Since he lived in the Tridentine age, he might even be described as a Tridentine reformer. But he – and the vast majority of his colleagues – seem remarkably detached from the doings of the Council. That assertion needs amplification and analysis.

A pervasive but unexamined assumption in much that is written about sixteenth-century Catholicism is that the Council of Trent set the

---

25   See Thaddeus MacVicar, *The Franciscan Spirituals and the Capuchin Reform*, ed. Charles McCarron (St. Bonaventure, 1986).

agenda and that all fervent Catholics, including the Jesuits, fell to in implementing it. I have even heard the Jesuits described as essentially agents for the implementation of Trent. While they undoubtedly supported the Council and a few of them were directly involved in it, they had an agenda of their own, generically related to the agenda of the Council but specifically independent of it and different from it.

Within the framework of personal *reformatio, Christianitas*, and so forth, the Jesuits' agenda consisted in their ministries. If we examine those ministries, those efforts "to help souls," the discrepancies with Trent emerge. Trent was concerned with providing the traditional rhythm of Word and Sacrament by the *pastor* to the *faithful* in their *parishes* on Sundays and holydays, reinforced by canonical penalties.

Jesuits ministered to the faithful by Word and Sacrament, but relied on persuasion and operated outside the parochial structure. Moreover, they had an array of other ministries that Trent altogether ignores or at best barely mentions – elaborate programs of adult education in Scripture and moral issues through their so-called "sacred lectures"; preaching programs in the streets, shipyards, hospitals, and barracks; engaging volunteer crops of adults and children in the teaching of *Christianitas*; fostering confraternities under lay management for the spiritual and corporal works of mercy; promoting so-called "ministries of interiority" like retreats and spiritual direction; evangelization of the heretic, schismatic, infidel, and pagan; the schools.[26] They had an altogether special relationship to Renaissance Humanism.[27]

Perhaps the best indication of how the early Society related to the Council comes from Ignatius himself in the instruction he sent in early 1546 to Laínez, Alfonso Salmerón, and Claude Jay as to how they should deport themselves in Trent.[28] Divided into three parts, the document (once again!) is as important for what it does not say as for what it does. The first part counsels that they should be modest in preseting their opinions, listen with respect to the viewpoint of others, always present and consider both sides of any disputed point. The second instructs them to carry on the usual ministries of the Society – preaching, catechism, the *Exercises*, visiting the sick and poor, "even bringing them a little gift, if possible." Contrary to what we might expect, Ignatius designates these ministries as the principal reason he allowed the Jesuits to be sent to Trent, and, hence, this must be considered the most impor-

26   See my "Priesthood, Ministry, and Religious Life: Some Historical and Historiographical Considerations," *Theological Studies*, 49 (June, 1988), 223–57, especially 237–48.
27   See my "Renaissance Humanism and the Religious Culture of the First Jesuits," *Heythrop Journal*, 31 (October, 1990), 471–87.
28   *Monumenta Ignatiana: Epistolae*, MHSJ, I, 386–9.

tant part of the instruction. The third part concerns their life-style and regimen.

What is missing, of course, is any word concerning the great issues facing the Council. Ignatius obviously assumes that, whatever those issues are, the Jesuits will have something helpful to say when occasion requires. He looks upon them, however, more as mediators than as proponents of specific agenda.

Polanco's account of the Jesuits' contribution to this first period of the Council manifests the same detachment from specific issues under debate. But he adds the significant detail that, since in Ignatius' opinion the Council in 1546 was moving at such a snail's pace, he considered recalling Laínez and assigning him to Florence.[29] In the early summer of 1546 Ignatius had in actual fact written to the three Jesuits asking whether it might not be to God's greater glory for them to withdraw from the Council and engage in the *consueta ministeria* of the Society elsewhere. Salmerón replied that they were of the unanimous opinion they should remain at Trent, and Ignatius acquiesced.[30] Just before the troubled adjournment of the Council in 1547, nonetheless, he assigned Jay to Ferrara, seemingly without second thought that the Council at that critical moment in its history ought to have priority.[31]

The attitude Ignatius here manifests was, as best I can tell, by and large typical of the vast majority of Jesuits at the time. What the Council hoped to accomplish was, of course, important to them, but it was not exactly their business. Convinced of their own orthodoxy, they did not need to take special note of the doctrinal decrees. The disciplinary decrees were pertinent to bishops and pastors of parishes, not directly to them. In fact, like members of the mendicant orders, they feared the consequences for themselves of one of the principal aims of the council, viz., an emphasis on the jurisdiction of bishops that might result in restriction of their ministries and curtailment of their many pastoral "privileges."

From the experience many of us have had of Vatican Council II, we easily imagine Jesuits of the sixteenth century pouring over the documents of Trent and rushing around the world with them in their hands. That is not how it was. Few of them probably ever saw the decrees.

There were, of course, notable and well-known exceptions. Laínez and Salmerón were present for all three periods of Trent over it eighteen-year history, a distinction enjoyed by few other participants in the Council. For them the Council accounts for important years to their

29   *Chronicon Societatis Jesu*, MHSJ, I, 177–83.
30   *Monumenta Salmeron*, MHSJ, I, 16.
31   Polanco, *Chronicon*, MHSJ, I, 225.

lives as Jesuits, and they knew its documents well and contributed to their formulation. Jerónimo Nadal, the person after Ignatius most responsible for the cohesion in the early Society, obviously studied and assimilated the great decrees on Original Sin and Justification. In 1565 Peter Canisius by special request of Pope Pius IV carried the *corpus* of Tridentine legislation with him back to the German bishops after the completion in Rome of the Jesuits' Second General Congregation, and, because of the peculiar situation in which he found himself in the Empire, was subsequently much concerned with that *corpus*. But to judge the rest of the Society by these examples is to engage in unabashed history "from above."

Helpful to the process of osmosis by which Ignatius and the Society began to be designated as focused on the reform of the Church would be a superficial recognition by roles in relationship to Trent played by a few leading Jesuits. If one examines the evidence in its entirety, however, one sees how the Society was in fact riding a trajectory independent of the direct concerns of the Council. In the great bulk of correspondence from Jesuits working in the ministries of the Society, it is amazing how seldom the Council is even mentioned.

In the broadest possible perspective, of course, the Jesuits were in perfect tandem with Trent in so far as it represented opposition to the Reformation. It was in this regard that the early Jesuits themselves made statements that would promote the osmosis. Nadal made his first trip to the Empire in 1555 and was appalled at what he found. Although opposition to the Reformation is only implicit in such foundational Jesuit documents as the *Exercises* and the *Constitutions*, Nadal after 1555 became a strong voice in the Society for assigning a high priority to the German situation. His reflections after that date on Jesuit origins began to see retrospectively a providential relationship to Protestantism.

Once Ignatius died in 1556, Nadal found the temptation to compare and contrast him with Luther too great to resist. The very next year Nadal suggested the comparison in an exhortation to the Jesuits at the Roman College.[32] In his second *Dialogue* some five years later, he portrayed Ignatius as the new David pitted against Luther, the Goliath.[33] In 1567 he reminded the Jesuits at Cologne, with some confusion of dates, that the year Luther was called by the Devil Ignatius heard the call from God.[34]

Sometime later Pedro Ribadeneyra paralleled the two figures in a passage in his biography of Ignatius, the first ever published and prob-

32   *Monumenta Ignatiana: Fontes Narrativi*, MHSJ, II, 5.
33   *Monumenta Nadal*, MHSJ, V, 607.
34   Ibid., p. 780.

ably the most influential. Luther and his followers were destroying the faith; Ignatius and his were raised up by God to confirm and defend it.[35] Other Jesuits took up the theme and its variations, as place and occasion suggested it was appropriate. The facile diptych that has helped create the confusion and further the process of osmosis first derived from the Jesuits themselves. Even as the Jesuits painted it, however, they did not speak of Ignatius as a reformer. Moreover, while the idea was rhetorically effective, it did not for that reason represent the full reality of Jesuit activity everywhere in the world even at that late date.

Was, then, the great saint of the Counter-Reformation a Counter-Reformation saint? Strong in him was his opposition to the Reformation, without doubt, but in his early years his eyes were set on Jerusalem, not Wittenberg. Even in his later years his self-understanding and his understanding of the Society he founded did not primarily define themselves in relationship to that problem, perhaps even less in relationship to "Catholic Reform" as his age understood it. In retrospect some of his disciples eulogized him by comparing and contrasting him with Luther, but these were rare flights into metahistory generally in the course of more factual accounts.

This hasty review of Ignatius and the first Jesuits can serve as a sort of test-case for Jedin's categories. Although it has vindicated their utility, it has also shown how they fail to take account of certain features that are important. They were a great step forward in our analysis of the Catholicism of that troubled period and helped give impetus to almost fifty years of scholarship that have intervened since it was published. This scholarship has, in the meantime, allowed us to see things from a somewhat different perspective. It has, moreover, allowed us to see the limitations under which Jedin worked.

What are some of those limitations? I will mention two. First of all, Jedin's focus was the Council of Trent and, therefore, the abuses in what we have come to call the "institutional church" in the sense of its hierarchy and official leadership. Crucial problems, surely, and often scandalous, but not the whole picture. In that framework, "reform" was the burning issue, and it was easy to latch onto the term and to sweep all changes and religious enthusiasm under its label.

Secondly, even though Jedin was properly critical, he was mightily influenced by Burckhardt, Huizinga, and Pastor in his assessment of the general religious situation and in his understanding of the Renaissance and late Middle Ages. His judgment, like theirs, was largely negative. Social historians in the past several decades have shown how lively reli-

---

35   "Vida del Bienaventura Padre San Ignacio de Loyola," in *Historias de la Contrarreforma*, ed. Eusebio Rey (Madrid, 1945), pp. 140–52.

gious practice was among most of the faithful, carried on in large measure in confraternities and other institutions that fell outside strictly parochial confines. Misguided that practice perhaps may have been in some ways, but not for that reason is it summarily to be dismissed as in every way unhealthy or as crying for reform. Moreover, not all historians would agree that the changes that de facto occurred in the sixteenth and seventeenth centuries as a result of "Catholic Reform" or other causes were in every instance for the better – *in melius*.

Renaissance historians have discovered the religious and moral issues that the Humanists tried to address, and they evaluate them positively. They have dismissed from the scene the category of "pagan Humanists" of whose existence earlier generations were so thoroughly convinced. They do not, of course, fail to see deficiencies in the humanistic enterprise, but they have radically revised many of the assumptions and conclusions of Burckhardt, Huizinga, and Pastor.

From these limitations flow in some measure the limitations of "Catholic Reform and Counter-Reformation" as an adequate category to capture the complexity of the phenomenon under discussion. Just as Jedin objected to "Counter-Reformation" as an adequate category because it took the Reformation as its point of reference, so might we object that "Catholic Reform" in a more subtle way does the same. Wherever Protestantism penetrated, there Reformation was the definition of the game. Not every place where Catholicism extended did "Catholic Reform," "Counter-Reformation," or the combination of the two always define the reality, even where religious enthusiasm was heightened. Catholicism, with its sluggish continuities as well as its new realities, was bigger than "Catholic Reform and Counter-Reformation."

I propose that "Early Modern Catholicism" is a better designation. It suggests both change and continuity and leaves the chronological question open at both ends. It implicitly includes Catholic Reform, Counter-Reformation, and even Catholic Restoration as indispensable categories of analysis, while surrendering the attempt to draw too firm a line of demarcation among them. It does not silently deliver Renaissance Humanism to an early grave. It is open to "confessionalization" when and where that becomes operative. It seems more welcoming to the results of history "from below" than "Catholic Reform" and "Counter-Reformation," which indicate more directly concerns of religious officialdom. Most important, it suggests that important influences on religious institutions and "mentalities" were at work in "early modern society" that had little to do with religion or "reform" as such, and it is thus more sensitive to the theses like those about "modernization" proposed by Reinhard and Prodi. It accounts, in brief, for more of the data.

Our categories of historical analysis do not easily yield their hold on our imaginations, and, even though "Catholic Reform and Counter-Reformation" is a mouthful, its otherwise obvious merits make it deserving of special respect. For reasons I have adduced, I think it might well be replaced by "Early Modern Catholicism," bland and all-too-neutral though such an alternative might sound for that contentious age. I conclude, in any case, not so much with a plea to do so as with the more modest and perhaps more realistic request that we exercise caution in applying Jedin's construct to the sprawling and complex reality he designated by it. That would be a tribute worthy of him.

# Part II Outcomes

# 4

# The Counter-Reformation and the People of Catholic Europe

## John Bossy

Originally appeared as Bossy, John, "The Counter-Reformation and the People of Catholic Europe," *Past and Present* 97 (1970): 51–70.

## Editor's Introduction

Before the 1970s, few historians asked what effects the Counter-Reformation had on the religious and social lives of ordinary Catholics in sixteenth- and seventeenth-century Europe. In this seminal essay, John Bossy argues that from the perspective of the village steeple, the Counter-Reformation amounted to an official campaign to enforce a code of "parochial conformity" involving faithful attendance at Mass, confessing sins and receiving communion at least yearly, at Easter, submitting to the authority of parish priests, and so on. The cumulative effect of this code, Bossy continues, was to disentangle local religious observance from the bonds and feuds of kinship, to superimpose ecclesiastical authority on previously autonomous institutions of village life, and to replace a morality grounded in obligations to extended family with an individualistic, church-regulated Christian ethics. In short, the Counter-Reformation was part of a process by which traditional, village society and culture were "acculturated" into the values and institutions of a dominant religious elite. But the campaign only half-succeeded, mainly because, in Bossy's view, the church failed to cast the nuclear family in the role that kin-groups once played in church life. The implications of Bossy's thesis are weighty: If for most people, the Counter-Reformation spelled only discipline and a loss of pious autonomy, how can it have been the expression of a "religious movement," except among the powerful and the well-educated?

# The Counter-Reformation and the People of Catholic Europe*

## John Bossy

I

An English historian wanting to understand what happened to the popular religion of Catholic Europe in the age of the Counter-Reformation has first to free himself from a latent assumption that the only person whose religious outlook and behavior are worth knowing

*The original sketch for this paper was presented to the *Past and Present* conference on "Popular Religion" in 1966. A slightly shortened version of the present text was read as a paper to the Ninth Irish Conference of Historians in May 1969, and I am grateful to the Irish Committee of Historical Sciences for consenting to its publication here. I have used the following abbreviations in the notes: –

| | |
|---|---|
| Adam | P. Adam, *La vie paroissiale en France au XIVe siècle* (Paris, 1964) |
| Borromeo, *Acta* | *Acta ecclesiae mediolanensis*, ed. F. Borromeo, 2 vols. (Milan, 1599) |
| Borromeo, *Pastorum instructiones* | *S. Caroli Borromaei . . . pastorum instructiones*, ed. E. Westhoff (Münster, 1846) |
| Canons and Decrees | *Canons and Decrees of the Council of Trent*, ed. and trans. H. J. Schroeder (St. Louis/London, 1941, repr. 1960) |
| Delaruelle | E. Delaruelle, E.-R. Labande and P. Ourliac, *L'Eglise au temps du Grand Schisme et de la crise conciliaire*, in *Histoire de l'Eglise depuis les origines jusqu'à nos jours*, eds A. Fliche, V. Martin, et al., xiv, part 2 (1964) |
| Ferté | Jeanne Ferté, *La vie religieuse dans les campagnes parisiennes, 1622–95* (Paris, 1962) |
| Grosso-Mellano | M. Grosso and M.-F. Mellano, *La controriforma nella arcidiocesi di Torino*, 3 vols. (Rome, 1957) |
| Join-Lambert | M. Join-Lambert, "La pratique religieuse dans le diocèse de Rouen sous Louis XIV," *Annales de Normandie*, iii (1953), pp. 247–74. |
| Le Bras, *Études* | Gabriel Le Bras, *Études de sociologie religieuse*, 2 vols. (Paris, 1955–6) |
| Marcilhacy | Christiane Marcilhacy, *Le diocèse d'Orléans sous l'épiscopat de Mgr. Dupanloup: sociologie religieuse et mentalités collectives* (Paris, 1962) |
| Pérouas | Louis Pérouas, *Le diocèse de la Rochelle de 1648 à 1724: sociologie et pastorale* (Paris, 1964) |
| Roncalli, *Atti* | *Atti della visita apostolica di San Carlo Borromeo a Bergamo, 1575*, ii, part 3, ed. A. G. Roncalli [later Pope John XXIII] (Florence, 1957) |

about is, taking the word in a wide sense, the nonconformist. This instinct may help to explain why, at least among historians, little attention has been paid in the British Isles to the work undertaken, chiefly in France, by the school of "religious sociology" inaugurated nearly forty years ago by the canon-law historian Gabriel Le Bras.[1] For this has been above all concerned to investigate the popular reception of a particularly pure example of Christianity conceived as acceptance of an externally enacted code of behavior. Those who have practised in it have, to say the least, presented a body of evidence far too imposing for historians to ignore. I do not know whether they would agree with the conclusions I have drawn from their work, and they might find these somewhat "Anglo-Saxon" in their drift; but I am sure that two schools of inquiry so similar in object and so different in approach must both be enriched by confrontation with one another.

To the ordinary population, and particularly to the rural population, of France and Italy – with whom, I must add, I shall be here almost exclusively concerned – what the Counter-Reformation really meant was the institution among them, by bishops empowered by the council of Trent to enforce it, of a system of parochial conformity similar in character to that which the contemporary Church of England was seeking to impose, though much more comprehensive in its detail. The faithful Catholic was to attend Mass every Sunday and holy-day in his parish church. He was to receive the Church's sacraments, other than confirmation, from the hands of his parish priest, who would baptize him, marry him, give him extreme unction on his deathbed, and bury him. He would receive the eucharist at least once a year, at Eastertide, and with the same regularity the priest would hear and absolve his sins in the sacrament of penance.[2]

Toussaert            Jacques Toussaert, *Le sentiment religieux en Flandre à la fin du Moyen Age* (Paris, 1965)
Vinot-Préfontaine    J. Vinot-Préfontaine, "Sanctions prises dans l'ancien diocèse de Beauvais contre les refractaires au devoir pascal," *Revue d'histoire de l'Eglise de France*, xlv (1959), pp. 76–83.

1   See in particular Le Bras, *Études*, which reprints his original manifesto of 1931, vol. i, pp. 1–24, and partly recapitulates his *Introduction à l'histoire de la pratique religieuse en France*, 2 vols. (Paris, 1942–5). For more recent developments, see his "L'historiographie contemporaine du catholicisme en France," in *Mélanges Pierre Renouvin* (Paris, 1966), pp. 23–32, and the periodical *Archives de sociologie religieuse*, founded by Le Bras and the late E.-G. Léonard. There is a convenient short guide in F. Boulard, *Premiers itinéraires en sociologie religieuse* (Paris, 1955).
2   The most important Tridentine decrees relating to popular religion and behaviour are in *Canons and Decrees*, pp. 305 (catechism), 423–4 (discipline of the Mass), 454–60 (marriage), 465 (catechizing of children), 467 (instruction), 484 (images and saints' days), 516 (duelling): English translations, pp. 26, 150–2, 183–90, 195, 197–8, 216, 251.

It may be thought perverse to describe the Counter-Reformation as having invented this code of religious practice, since most of the enactments which went to make it up had already been in force in the pre-reformation Church and the council of Trent explicitly added to them only in the case of matrimony.[3] Yet, by applying Le Bras's methods of investigation so far as possible to pre-Reformation religious practice – and it is significant that they cannot easily be so applied – Jacques Toussaert has made it highly probable that, whatever the state of legislation, the people of western Europe fulfilled their parochial duties in so spasmodic a manner that it is hard to believe they had any clear sense of parochial obligation at all.[4] The moral of his story is perhaps not, as Toussaert seems inclined to conclude, that the peasants and weavers of fifteenth-century Flanders had no religion, but that the Church of the last medieval centuries was not in actual fact a parochially-grounded institution. The disciplinary significance of the council of Trent and of two centuries of activity on the part of the Catholic hierarchy lay in their determination that it should effectually become so grounded: that the code of parochial observance should be made watertight and universally enforced. This did not require much new legislation, but called for a decidedly new attitude to old legislation: that this attitude existed may, more than from anything else, be gathered from the concern which council, bishops and popes shared with authorities elsewhere in Europe, that parish clergy should keep an accurate record of the acts in question in registers of baptisms, marriages, burials, lists of Easter communicants and *status animarum*.[5] Armed with these weapons, Counter-Reformation bishops were far better equipped to enforce a code of uniform parochial practice, just as historians are to estimate its observance; all soundings confirm that, towards the end of the seventeenth century, after a hundred and fifty years of effort, it was being all but universally observed in all parts of western Europe subject to their unimpeded jurisdiction, and continued to be so observed until the fall of the *ancien régime*.[6]

3   Cf. T. M. Parker, "The Papacy, Catholic Reform and Christian Missions," in R. B. Wernham (ed.), *New Cambridge Modern History*, iii: *The Counter-Reformation and Price Revolution* (Cambridge, 1968), p. 44.
4   Toussaert, esp. pp. 122–204; cf., for England, the preamble to the second Act of Uniformity, 1552, in G. R. Elton, *The Tudor Constitution* (Cambridge, 1960), pp. 396ff.
5   Trent required marriage registers, and made a rather off-hand reference to baptismal registers (*Canons and Decrees*, pp. 455, 456; 184ff, 186); the full series of five registers was imposed by the papacy in 1614: *Enciclopedia cattolica*, vii (Vatican City, 1951), pp. 1312–13. Cf. the English *Injunctions* of 1538, in H. Gee and W. J. Hardy, *Documents illustrative of English Church History* (London, 1921), p. 279; and see P. Laslett, in E. A. Wrigley (ed.), *An Introduction to English Historical Demography* (London, 1966), p. 4, for an interesting comparison between English and French registers.
6   Le Bras, *Études*, i, 275ff.; Pérouas, p. 162. The same emerges from all the similar studies which will be cited below, e.g. Join-Lambert, p. 272. E. Le Roy Ladurie, *Les*

I doubt if historians have measured the importance of this silent revolution in altering the social climate of Catholic Europe from what it had been at the beginning of the sixteenth century, or in distinguishing it from that of adjacent countries where it did not occur. Anglican bishops were, to be sure, trying to do much the same thing at much the same time, but just when their continental counterparts were beginning to see light at the end of the tunnel, they sustained a devastating setback. Those who opposed them would not have thanked historical demography for revealing that they had helped Englishwomen of the late seventeenth century to conceive illegitimate children at three times the rate of the French; but this seems to have been one consequence of their efforts.[7] I can see no way of finding out whether English and French habits had differed in this respect before the Reformation, but it seems unlikely that they had; if they had not, the disparity would testify to the work of the Counter-Reformation episcopate, and help to illustrate their success in the field of parochial observance, the social implications of which I want now to explore.


II


"Medieval society was . . . ," it has been alleged, "largely composed of *nonparticipants*, inactive men."[8] If this had been so, the Counter-Reformation would have had a far less exacting task before it. In proposing to make the parish the sole institution in which the most important acts of popular religion might be practised; in envisaging this as, for such purposes, a passive recipient of hierarchically-conveyed instructions, it innovated on the practice of a Church which had entered the sixteenth century as, in effect, a conglomerate of autonomous communities. These were not necessarily, in a narrow sense, ecclesiastical in character, and before we come to consider the impact of the Counter-Reformation on those which were, a large and obscure territory needs to be looked at where the Church entered into conflict, more openly than it had hitherto done, with the bonds of kinship and the solidarities which presupposed them.

It seems significant that Gian Matteo Giberti, the first bishop to manifest the full range of Counter-Reformation characteristics, had as his diocese the Verona of Montagues and Capulets, from whose mode of

*paysans de Languedoc*, 2 vols. (Paris, 1966), pp. 651ff, 890, shows, here, some falling off after about 1740; cf. below, n. 64.
7  P. Goubert, *Beauvais et le Beauvaisis de 1600 à 1730* (Paris, 1960), p. 31; P. Laslett, *The World We Have Lost* (London, 1965), pp. 128–36.
8  Michael Walzer, *The Revolution of the Saints* (London, 1966), p. 4.

conflict-settling Burckhardt drew illustrations of Italian modernity.[9] This was not simply a matter of duelling, though the council of Trent legislated vigorously against it, and showed a proper sense that it was here dealing with a collective, not individual, disorder.[10] The range of problems involved in this conflict was wide, and the habits which the Counter-Reformation was seeking to eradicate went deep: there is a lot to be said for the view that the great obstacle to Tridentine uniformity was not individual backsliding or Protestant resistance but the internal articulations of a society in which kinship was a most important social bond and feud, in however conventionalized a form, a flourishing social activity.[11] Persuading the whole population of a parish to assemble regularly in its parish church or to communicate together at Easter proved often enough beyond the powers of the clergy. If I may use an example from mid-sixteenth-century Northumberland, Bernard Gilpin, a rare missionary in territory seemingly unevangelized since the days of Saint Cuthbert, found it impossible to get the borderers to hear his sermons, not because they did not wish to listen, but because to enter under the same roof as members of a family with which one's own had a dispute was to violate the rules which alone could maintain some sort of order in so benighted a countryside;[12] illustrations of the same problem could, I am sure, be drawn from any upland region of Europe. Alessandro Sauli, returning as bishop to his native isle of Corsica from the Counter-Reformation heartland of Borromean Milan, found that before he could get on with Tridentine reform he had to set on foot fraternities devoted, with what can have been only a very marginal success, to eliminating feud on the island.[13] In Piedmont, visitations of the late sixteenth century were continually revealing parishes where people had not come to church or made their Easter communion because of social hostilities

9  Cf. A. G. Dickens, *The Counter-Reformation* (London, 1968), p. 54; Jacob Burckhardt, *The Civilisations of the Renaissance in Italy* (London, 1951 edn.), pp. 265–8 – nonetheless an important passage in this context.

10  Loc. cit. above, n. 2.

11  Jacques Heers, *L'Occident aux XIVe et XVe siècles: aspects économiques et sociaux* ("Nouvelle Clio," Paris, 1963), pp. 299ff, is an admirable, and so far as I know unique, discussion of the state of kinship relations in late-medieval Europe. See also ibid., pp. 81ff; and some general remarks in R. Mandrou, *Introduction à la France moderne, 1500–1640* (Paris, 1961), pp. 112ff.

12  M. H. Dodds (ed.), *Northumberland County History*, xv (Newcastle-on-Tyne, 1940), p. 312. Gilpin was not a Catholic.

13  F.-J. Casta, *Evêques et curés corses dans la tradition pastorale du concile de Trente, 1570–1620* (Ajaccio, 1965), p. 110. For Borromeo, see *Pastorum instructiones, cap.* xii, p. 51: nos. 6 and 9 of the sins specially to be preached against. Cf., for England, the second of Cranmer's prefatory instructions to the communion services of 1549 and 1552, in *Liturgies of Edward VI*, ed. J. Ketley (Parker Society, Cambridge, 1844), pp. 76, 265, also 87, 274.

which might or might not be embodied in litigation; parish priests, who were often enough party to such hostilities themselves, responded unwillingly to pressure from above against what seemed to them legitimate social custom.[14] Here, no doubt, manners were a little more civil than in Corsica or Northumberland; but though it may have taken a less dramatic form than there, the situation recurs even in the most settled and prosperous regions of agrarian Europe, and all the way through the seventeenth century. It was in the village of Clichy, then just outside Paris, and in 1671, that Christophe Nicolas failed to go to his parish church for a whole year because "he could not bear to see *(ne pouvait pas voir)* another man of the parish with whom he was at enmity *(contre qui il avait de la haine)*, and last Easter he preferred not to make his Easter duties than to be reconciled to him";[15] inquiry into such village feuds was still high on the agenda of eighteenth-century bishops.[16] By this time the problem had generally assumed a more sophisticated form: various cases from seventeenth-century France indicate that people were prepared to turn up at Mass at the same time as their social enemies, but would not go to confession, since this would signify unilateral disarmament, and so were unable to receive communion at Easter.[17] The Counter-Reformation Church was, of course, doing nothing new in taking up the task of reconciling or suppressing feud; what seems particular to this period is that the motive of imposing Christian ethics on social behavior had lost ground to the motive of imposing conformity in religious observance.

Here the Church had been enjoining a positive obligation where kinship morality might enjoin a negative one; in those acts of religion associated with birth, marriage and death the relation was usually the other way about. The council of Trent, in particular, enacted a matrimonial code which ran counter to the collectivist and contractual traditions of kinship morality by invalidating marriages not performed in public before the parish priest, insisting on individual liberty in the choice of partners, and affirming that marriages contracted by minors without parental consent were valid, though not lawful.[18] It led in consequence to a vigorous attack on the traditional and extra-sacramental espousal or *fiançailles* which had maintained into the sixteenth century

14  Grosso-Mellano, ii, pp. 207ff, 238, 240, 246; iii, p. 202. Likewise, from another part of northern Italy, Roncalli, *Atti*, pp. 128–9. In the *Acta ecclesiae mediolanensis*, pp. 766–7, Borromeo allowed curates to permit postponement of Easter duties "so as to allow time for peace-making."
15  Ferté, p. 318; for other parts of France, Pérouas, p. 161, n. 7; Join-Lambert, p. 272; Vinot-Préfontaine, pp. 78ff.
16  Le Bras, *Études*, i, p. 57.
17  Vinot-Préfontaine, pp. 78ff; Ferté, pp. 318–19.
18  *Canons and Decrees*, pp. 454–60, 183–90: decree *Tametsi*.

the contractual marriage-theory illustrated, for example, in the Anglo-Saxon law-codes.[19] In Normandy, in 1600, *fiançailles* were still a binding contract, cemented by exchange of gifts or passage of money and preceding the church marriage by a considerable time; it was still widely considered, even by canon lawyers, to be entirely proper that the couple should share a bed in the meantime. A century later, with the disappearance of *fiançailles* as a distinct contract, Trent and the principle of parochial conformity had achieved one of its most important victories over kinship solidarity.[20]

It was not possible for the Counter-Reformation to take such decisive action over baptism, since to maintain infant baptism was to maintain godparents and, as the traditional English term "gossip" more precisely expresses, the institution of godparents implies a very strong view of collective solidarity in matters of salvation. There was, perhaps is, a close relation between the rôle of godparents at a baptism and the need of kinsmen to assemble so as to celebrate the advent of a new member and assume their obligations on its behalf. Ecclesiastical and secular authorities, at least since the fourteenth century, had been trying in the interests of public order to restrict the attendance at such occasions;[21] the Church of the Counter-Reformation unified these precedents into a general code. It insisted, not only on parochial baptism, but on a baptism which followed birth with a rapidity which left little or no time for an assembly of kin; from the sixteenth century three days was the maximum delay permitted by diocesan and provincial synods, and in France the secular government of its own accord later reduced this to twenty-four hours. During the eighteenth century practically all children were baptized within the longer period, about half within the shorter.[22] I do not suppose that this prevented people from having their relations in when their babies were born; but it must have done a good

---

19   D. Whitelock (ed.), *English Historical Documents*, vol. i, *c. 500–1042* (London, 1955), pp. 359, 431.

20   Pierre Chaunu, "Une histoire religieuse sérielle," *Revue d'histoire moderne et contemporaine*, xii (1965), pp. 11ff; Ferté, p. 323; see also Laslett, *The World We Have Lost*, p. 144 Cf. the strict instruction of the council of Trent "that spouses shall not cohabit in the same house before they have received the nuptial blessing from the priest in church": *Canons and Decrees*, pp. 455, 184.

21   Delaruelle, p. 739; Adam, pp. 104ff; and especially Toussaert, pp. 94–5, on the baptismal feast and godparenthood as a return for gifts made towards it; the échevins of Ypres tried to restrict attendance to close kinsmen only.

22   F. Charpin, *Pratique religieuse et formation d'une grande ville. Le geste du baptême et sa signification en sociologie religieuse (Marseille, 1806–1958)* (Paris, 1964), pp. 11ff, 19–21 – note the statistics of increasing delay during the nineteenth century, pp. 44–5; Ferté, pp. 299ff; Chaunu, "Une histoire religieuse sérielle," p. 10. The evidence cited by Toussaert, pp. 90–1, for popular pressure for immediate baptism in pre-reformation Flanders, seems mainly to relate to cases where the child was not expected to live, and was therefore baptized at home.

deal to weaken the connection between such collective celebrations and the baptismal ceremony, and to emphasize that one entered the Church as an individual and not as a member of a kin-group. When it reduced the legal complement of godparents to one, or at most to one of each sex, the council of Trent aimed a similar blow at popular instinct;[23] by claiming to submit them to minimum standards of instruction, behavior and religious practice, the Counter-Reformation Church involved itself in a spirited conflict with families, who took it for granted that the choice of godparents was entirely up to them. At Labruyère in the seventeenth-century Beauvaisis, when the parish priest refused to baptize on these grounds, the parents locked him up in the sacristy and christened the child themselves.[24] More trouble arose from attempts to impose qualifications of age, since families commonly demanded the admission as godparents of very young children; the clergy of the archdiocese of Paris had to be content with a minimum age of seven or eight, and were unable to enforce a rule that a godparent should have made his or her first communion.[25] This pressure would seem to have derived from a family instinct to bind together members of the same generation across the boundaries of the single household; and though it had other motives in either case, the Church resisted it, as it resisted multiplication of godparents, precisely for this reason.

One might pursue the same conflict into the arena of the burial and the funeral wake; but since, at least in some parts of the British Isles, this is a fairly familiar problem,[26] I shall venture to take it for granted, and proceed to consider how the Counter-Reformation Church coped with one of the characteristic institutions of medieval popular religion, the fraternity. This was of course an artificial kin-group, and membership might govern behavior in the primary acts of religion, just as natural kinship did. But fraternities were principally active in the secondary field of "devotion": they drew their strength from an unsolicited response of popular feeling to particular features of Christian mythology or the Christian life. Voluntary associations, usually local or professional in recruitment, they possessed officers, funds and a constitution; they maintained a salaried clergy and often had independent chapels. During the later middle ages, they constituted something like an alternative model of the Church, in the sense both that they seem to have

23  *Canons and Decrees*, pp. 456, 185; cf. references above, n. 21.
24  Casta, *Évêques et curés corses*, pp. 107ff; Ferté, p. 302; Pérouas, p. 275; Vinot-Préfontaine, p. 81. Cf. Adam, p. 105: the synod of Soissons of 1403 only refused to allow as godparents people excommunicated, interdicted, not baptized or confirmed.
25  Ferté, pp. 300ff; cf. Adam, p. 105 – the fifteenth-century statutes, quoted here, specifically exclude from restrictions children who were close enough kin to the baptisee for no extra problems about marriage to be created by the "spiritual relationship."
26  Séan ÓSúilleabháin, *Irish Wake Amusements* (Cork, 1967).

recruited a majority of the population, and that, in contrast to the formal hierarchy, they embodied the tradition of kinship and communal solidarity, whose instincts they brought to bear on the problem of salvation.[27] They may very often have expressed these instincts in a crude and materialistic form, and it is probably true that by the sixteenth century they mainly served as societies for mutual secular benefit and regular entertainment. But what exposed them to the thunders of the Counter-Reformation Church was as much the independence of their origins and structure as the flaws in their understanding of Christianity; now, for the first time, they were brought under a rigorous régime of episcopal authorization and supervision.

In this matter as in most others, the activity of Charles Borromeo as archbishop of Milan from 1564 to 1584 was a model for generations of bishops. Like his colleague in Turin, Borromeo believed that dioceses should resemble "well-organized armies, which have their generals, colonels and captains,"[28] and much of his *Acta Ecclesiae Mediolanensis*, the legislative model of the Counter-Reformation episcopate, was concerned with bringing the Milanese fraternities within an all-embracing hierarchical scheme. So, for example, his statutes provided for the incorporation into a single diocesan fraternity of all local fraternities devoted to the eucharist, and remodelled their constitutions in a hierarchical sense.[29] Centralized fraternity-federations of this nature proliferated during the Counter-Reformation; it invented to describe them the term "archconfraternity," which exposes to view the underlying conflict between brotherhood and discipline. There was also room for conflict in this field between clerical and lay *élites*, since the cooperation of the latter was essential if the forms of lay initiative were to be respected: in this spirit, Borromeo ascribed the idea of his superfraternity to the "principal personages, officials and noblemen" of Milan.[30] Where there was genuine lay initiative, as in the best known example of the super-fraternity, the French *Compagnie du très-saint*

27 The fundamental general treatment of the subject is Le Bras, "Les confréries chrétiennes," in *Études*, ii, pp. 418–62; for their rôle in late-medieval church and society, see Delaruelle, pp. 666–93, and Heers, *L'Occident aux XIVe et XVe siècles: aspects économiques et sociaux*, pp. 308–13. See also Adam, pp. 15–79, where a group of fraternity statutes are reproduced; those of the fraternity of St Nicholas of Guérande (ibid., pp. 50ff) are particularly explicit about the character of the fraternity as an artificial kin-group.

28 Archbishop Carlo Broglia, in Grosso-Mellano, iii, p. 216.

29 Borromeo, *Acta*, pp. 896–9; on Federico Borromeo, nephew and successor to Carlo in the see of Milan, see my own "Postscript" to H. O. Evennett, *The Spirit of the Counter-Reformation* (Cambridge, 1968), p. 138, and the article of P. Prodi there cited, n. 3. Cf. Grosso-Mellano, iii, pp. 202, 210, etc.

30 Borromeo, *Acta*, p. 896.

*Sacrement* founded in the reign of Louis XIII, this proved unwelcome: despite the Company's high moral tone and aristocratic background, the bishops smelled competition and had it suppressed.[31] The secular *élite* was always an ambiguous ally for a program of diocesan order and parochial uniformity, and one of the chief objects of the Counter-Reformation hierarchy in dealing with fraternities was to ensure that they should not form centers of religious practice competitive with the parish. "We exhort and warn all fraternity members," wrote Michel Colbert, bishop of Mâcon, in 1668, "that going to Mass in their fraternities . . . in no way exempts them from attendance at their parochial Mass; they must learn . . . that they are parishioners first and *confrères* afterwards."[32] If, as is more than likely, bishops took a less rigorous attitude to forms of spiritual self-determination particular to the nobility, they were entitled to ask the nobility to keep out of a problem which did not concern them.

In the end fraternities ceased to be an obstacle to uniform parochial observance, because they ceased to exist. During the seventeenth century there were still parts to the Catholic west where new ones were spontaneously emerging; but, in a climate so discouraging to their spiritual value and social independence, they could not be expected to thrive, and in the eighteenth century they went into a galloping and universal decline.[33] Whatever its formal continuities, a Church without them was a very different institution from the Church of the fifteenth century.

The purpose of all this negative activity was to divert all streams of popular religion into a single parochial channel; but this would do little good so long as the popular attitude to the parish and its premises remained what it had been up to the sixteenth century. It seems unclear how widely the medieval parish was felt to be, in itself, a collectivity of the kind I have been describing; there was surely a good deal in the view which conservative churchmen in England tried to convey to their Puritan critics, that it served as a mechanism by which tensions accumulated between these communities could be released at special moments of ritual festivity.[34] In either case the indispensable location for these was the parish church. To the Counter-Reformation hierarchy such collective manifestations were suspicious in themselves, improper in buildings reserved for acts of formal religious observance, and as occasions of saturnalian licence incompatible with the regular disci-

31   V.-L. Tapié, *La France de Louis XIII et de Richelieu* (Paris, 1952), pp. 350ff.
32   Le Bras, *Études*, ii, p. 458, n. 5.
33   Pérouas, p. 501; Le Bras, *Études*, ii, p. 637; i, p. 63.
34   Christopher Hill, *Society and Puritanism in Pre-Revolutionary England* (London, 1966 edn.), p. 192; cf. Toussaert, pp. 295–310, 326.

pline of life which these acts were intended to promote. The parish wakes and church-ales of England had their counterparts all over Europe: the wake, vigil or *veille* was a general assembly of the parish, male and female, in or about the church, during the night preceding a notable feast; its most familiar survival is All Souls' Night, the equivalent of Hallowe'en, which reproduced on a more comprehensive scale the licence appropriate to the family funeral wake.[35] Wakes had been attracting clerical criticism well before the sixteenth century: the fourteenth-century preacher Nicholas of Clamanges was as clear about their heathen origins and as convinced of their scandalous character as any Puritan. "On such nights some dance in the very churches with obscene songs, others play at dice, with oaths denying God and cursing of the saints."[36] Medieval bishops had legislated against them, but it is obvious from the visitation reports of the sixteenth and seventeenth centuries that they had not been very successful, and perhaps they had not tried very hard. In this as in other fields the Counter-Reformation succeeded in making its legislation work. The parish wake seems to have been effectively suppressed, in the sense that such occasions ceased to find a home in the parish church, withdrew to alternative accommodation, and lost their integral if ambiguous relation with the ceremonies of the Christian year.[37]

Suppressed likewise was the slightly more decorous church-ale or parochial beanfeast, commonly held in church after the beating of the parish bounds at Rogationtide, or on Maundy Thursday or Good Friday to celebrate the conclusion of Lent.[38] With these feasts, and especially with the latter, it was often hard to distinguish the sacramental liturgy from dinner. Maundy Thursday was after all a commemoration of the Last Supper; and a parish which had reconstituted one part of the gospel story by a washing of feet might reasonably go on to partake of cakes and ale.[39] Good Friday was a popular day for fraternity feats, and it was not unknown for brethren, after communion on Easter Sunday, to sit down in church to a slice of Paschal lamb.[40] At communion itself, the ban on reception in both kinds may or may not have been universally effective, but it was common, perhaps usual, for those communicating

35   Grosso-Mellano, ii, pp. 250, 257; iii, 227; Pérouas, p. 172; Adam, pp. 264ff; Join-Lambert, art. 104 of the visitation questionnaire of 1687, pp. 260ff; Ferté, pp. 332–3.

36   Adam, pp. 266–7.

37   An idea of the process may be got from comparing Grosso-Mellano, ii, p. 277; Join-Lambert, p. 269; and Marcilhacy, pp. 278–9.

38   E.g. Ferté, p. 337; Grosso-Mellano, ii, p. 210. Cf., for the English church-ale, Hill, *Society and Puritanism*, pp. 190ff.

39   Toussaert, p. 333; Grosso-Mellano, iii, p. 225.

40   Roncalli, *Atti*, pp. 13, 15.

at Easter or other feasts to receive wine, in return for a contribution, on the grounds that this was to wash their mouths out.[41] All this may shed some light on the eucharistic experiments of sixteenth-century reformers; it certainly accounts for the rigidity in this matter of the Counter-Reformation Church, obsessed with the problem of distinguishing liturgical from non-liturgical, and convinced that church-feasting was, as Borromeo said, "indecent and contrary to Christian discipline."[42] By the later seventeenth century, eating and drinking, like dancing, gaming and ritual obscenity, had everywhere been expelled from churches, leaving behind them the reverent silence which may already be felt in the visitation enquiry of a bishop of Rouen: "Do people assemble too near the church to chat when there are persons inside trying to say their prayers?"[43]


## III

Sad as it may be, it is no doubt true that the emergence of a modern Catholicism depended on eliminating most of these elements of popular participation, and arguable that real progress was impossible until habits of uniform parochial observance had been instilled. This in itself was, of course, an ambiguous achievement. A code of uniform religious practice might foster interior Christian faith and behavior in millions of Catholics; it might equally well substitute one form of external constraint for another. In trying to find out what actually happened we have, I believe, two essential points to bear in mind: first, that a transition from medieval Christianity to modern Catholicism meant, on the popular front, turning collective Christians into individual ones; and second, that the attempt to achieve this transition was very commonly a failure, as is obvious from the widespread collapse of popular religion in Catholic Europe at the fall of the *ancien régime*.[44] I think we shall be most likely to understand the problems which faced the Counter-Reformation on its more positive side if we start by looking at the article in the code of religious practice which could most naturally serve as a vehicle of interior change.

The history of the sacrament of penance – of "confession" – is for fairly obvious reasons a rather obscure subject, and very little has been

41   Toussaert, pp. 161ff; Grosso-Mellano, ii, p. 206.
42   Borromeo, *Acta*, p. 902.
43   Join-Lambert, p. 260: questionnaire, no. 113.
44   The indispensable introduction to this subject is Le Bras's "Carte religieuse de la France rurale," in *Études*, i, p. 324.

written about it relevant to this period.[45] Nevertheless I think it is clear that the popular practice of confession underwent profound changes at this time, quite apart from the greater regularity with which it was resorted to. For one thing, the Counter-Reformation, apparently in the person of Borromeo, invented the confessional-box. Medieval confession, if spontaneous, took place in a variety of circumstances, but usually in public or semi-public in church; if inspired by illness or impending death, it naturally took place at home. The second case, if Flanders is anything to go by, seems to have been about as common as the first.[46] In practice, it was closer to Cranmer's "ghostly counsel, advice and comfort"[47] than to the anonymous leap in the dark familiar in more modern times; and this change of environment implies a change in what the sacrament was really felt to be for. The ordinary member of the medieval Church seems to have looked to confession mainly as a mediator between an overt offence, particularly one involving violence, and overt acts of "satisfaction." It was, that is to say, more a social than a private act, carried strong undertones of composition-theory which became overtones in the practice of indulgences, and could be felt even by clerical commentators not necessarily to involve interior sorrow for the offence committed. In its own way, the Counter-Reformation Church took to heart Luther's objection that the scriptural phrase, "penitentiam agite," to which it appealed for justification of the traditional practice, did not mean "do penance," but "repent."[48] The Council of Trent defined that, apart from the act of confession itself, both contrition and satisfaction were essential to the validity of the sacrament; but it evidently wished to transfer attention from the second to the first, and remarked on the importance of offences against the last two Commandments, which do not concern overt acts but dispositions of the mind.[49] Since the sixteenth century confession has been primarily concerned with the interior man, and the "satisfactory" element has correspondingly retreated into the background. Here again Borromeo was a sign of the times with his pastoral instructions that absolution should be refused or delayed where there was not felt to the true repentance. Fortified by his example, the clergy began to go in for the novel practice of refusing absolution in these circumstances, and there arose in seventeenth-century France the special pastoral technique of

45 But see Delaruelle, pp. 656–64.
46 *Dictionnaire de droit canonique*, iv, ed. R. Naz (Paris, 1944), p. 63; Delaruelle, p. 660, n. 26; Toussaert, pp. 104–22.
47 *Liturgies of Edward VI*, pp. 82, 274.
48 R. H. Bainton, *Here I Stand* (New York, 1955 edn.), p. 67.
49 *Dictionnaire de théologie catholique*, iii, ed. A. Vacant and E. Mangenot (Paris, 1908), pp. 912, 98ff; cf. Delaruelle, p. 661.

postponing absolution, associated with the Jansenists and underlying the argument about frequent communion.[50] The early Jansenists, at least, were probably quite faithful to the ends of Tridentine reform; but the discipline by which they proposed to achieve them was incompatible with universal and uniform religious practice. You could scarcely combine a Jansenist discipline with a universal obligation of annual Easter confession and communion; and Vincent de Paul was no doubt drawing on his own more intimate experience of the popular mind when he said that, if the clergy applied it, people would simply refuse to come to these sacraments at all.[51] Beyond a certain point, the Counter-Reformation hierarchy had to settle for quantity rather than quality in confession; as a bishop of La Rochelle complained in the 1660s: "The tribunals of confession have never been so thronged with people, and there have never been so few real changes of heart."[52]

Dilemmas of this kind, which were numerous, arose in part from the miserable state of popular religious instruction; without dramatic improvements in this field, habits of church attendance and sacramental practice would never express more than what Le Bras has termed a "sheep-like conformism."[53] The medieval Church had no machinery for catechizing children; if it thought about the matter at all, it may perhaps have assumed that rudimentary instruction was a job for parents; otherwise children received as much or as little enlightenment as everybody else.[54] The Council of Trent gestured rather inconclusively towards making the instruction of children a constitutive element of the code of religious practice;[55] what bishops made of this was a duty upon parish priests to catechize the children of their parish on Sunday and feast day afternoons, and a duty upon parents to send their children to be so catechized.[56] These obligations were, no either side, more easily imposed than accepted; happily, a great deal of private enterprise, much of it

50  Borromeo, *Pastorum instructiones*, pp. 119–22; Pérouas, pp. 282ff; Ferté, p. 319. The argument about "frequent communion" may be approached through the studies of J. Orcibal cited in my "Postscript" to Evennett, *Spirit of the Counter-Reformation*, p. 140, n. 2.

51  J. Laporte, *La doctrine de Port-Royal: la morale*, ii (Paris, 1952), pp. 232ff; P. Coste, *Monsieur Vincent*, 3 vols. (Paris, 1931), iii, pp. 173ff. For later influence see, e.g., Marcilhacy, p. 288.

52  Pérouas, p. 162.

53  See below, n. 64.

54  Pérouas, pp. 272ff; Delaruelle, p. 665; P. Broutin, *La réforme pastorale en France au XVIIe siècle: recherches sur la tradition pastorale après le concile de Trente*, 2 vols. (Paris, 1956), i, p. 49.

55  *Canons and Decrees*, pp. 465, 196.

56  Borromeo, *Acta*, p. 7 – first provincial council of Charles Borromeo, 1565; Grosso-Mellano, ii, pp. 229, 230, 249, 257. Cf., for England, Hill, *Society and Puritanism*, p. 448 – attitude of Archbishop Laud.

eventually embodied in religious orders and the like, had already been put into religious instruction since the early sixteenth century.[57] This was inevitably more effective in towns than in the countryside, and it was, once again, Borromeo who harnessed to the purposes of the rural parish the existing idea of a fraternity devoted to the religious instruction of children. He required such "Schools of Christian Doctrine" – "School" here meaning fraternity, as in Venice – to be erected in every parish subject to his visitation, gave them a hierarchical structure, and set them to work at the organizing and running of what, if his legislation had been universally applied, would have been large and minutely regulated Sunday schools – except that they functioned on feast days as well as on Sundays – under the supervision of the parochial clergy.[58] One may well ask how closely the parish Sunday afternoon in rural Lombardy corresponded to the grand conception of Borromeo's constitutions, but on paper anyway by 1600 these "Schools" formed a uniform network covering much or most of northern Italy. It was another half-century before French bishops had got anything like so far; but after about 1650 all French dioceses seem to have had legislation imposing catechism as a duty on parish priests and parents. Despite the usual resistance, in some it certainly became universal practice. In others it was patchily enforced: a third of the children in the diocese of Rouen were still not getting any religious instruction about 1700, and there may also have been some general falling-back in the eighteenth century.[59] But all in all, and over a period of a century and a half, it seems fairly clear that the vague injunctions of the council of Trent had achieved in this matter a high degree of practical realization.

In Germany from soon after the middle of the sixteenth century, in Italy from somewhat later, in France from a good deal later still, most of the children of Catholic Europe were, in the modern phrase, "learning their catechism": memorizing the contents of, though not of course actually reading, specially designed little books constructed in question-and-answer form. The models for these books were the sixteenth-century Catechisms of the Jesuits Canisius and Bellarmine, much indebted to Luther, and in general use in Germany and Italy respec-

---

57  *Enciclopedia cattolica*, iii, pp. 1110ff; Evennett, *Spirit of the Counter-Reformation*, pp. 84–6.

58  Borromeo, *Acta*, pp. 61, 795, 845–95; cf. T. M. Parker, "The Papacy, Catholic Reform and Christian Missions" (cited above, n. 3), p. 65. For the introduction of the system through Borromeo's visitations, as papal delegate, of other dioceses, see, e.g., Roncalli, *Atti, passim*, pp. 312, 316.

59  Le Bras, "État religieux et moral du diocèse de Châlons au dernier siècle de l'Ancien Régime," in *Études*, i, pp. 63ff; Pérouas, pp. 272ff, 379ff; Join-Lambert, pp. 260, 266ff; Marcilhacy, pp. 239ff.

tively;[60] in accordance with their more independent traditions, many French bishops composed or had composed their own. Exposure to them, even at their least inspired, was bound to mean a real mutation in the popular understanding of religion; yet they were a dubious introduction to a truly individual Christian life. Louis Pérouas, who has investigated the catechisms of the diocese of La Rochelle, shows that, after a more imaginative start, they had come by the beginning of the eighteenth century to consist, on the doctrinal side, of scholastic formulae designed to fill out a logical pattern and, on the practical side, of a set of chilling moral imperatives, presented as "the duties of the Christian religion" and evocative of the enlightened despots, even of Napoleon.[61] It may well be that something like this was inevitable; there is certainly something paradoxical about trying to promote individual Christianity by compulsory legislation, and Counter-Reformation catechism may not, all told, have done much more than superimpose a mental automatism on the behavioral automatisms of the code of external practice. Yet this is perhaps a condition of any educational process, rather than a particular failing of the Counter-Reformation, and I think we need to ask more specifically how it managed to achieve, on so impressive a scale, the contrary of what it intended. One striking attempt to solve this problem has been made.

Whatever ambiguities may have been embedded in the use of the catechism as an initiation into the Christian religion, there is no doubt about the part it played in promoting primary education in backward countrysides. Visual aids might convey some sort of understanding; but what was an illiterate really to comprehend of the formulae he was asked to recite or the sacraments he was required to receive? "The process of diffusing a certain amount of basic understanding" (un certain savoir), to quote Emmanuel Le Roy Ladurie, the historian in question, "is inseparable from the process of teaching the rudiments of Christian doctrine."[62] Besides, since French bishops were unwilling to give even the guarded concession to the fraternal principle which Borromeo had made with his "Schools," it was necessary to help out the

---

60   The examples I have used are *Catechismus Petri Canisii* (in German), and *Dottrina Christiana dell' . . . Rob. Bellarmino* (both edns. Augsburg, 1614). See J. Brodrick, *St. Peter Canisius* (London, 1935), pp. 221–52, and his *The Life and Work of . . . Cardinal Bellarmine*, 2 vols. (London, 1928), i, pp. 389–99. For the Dutch catechism of Louis Makeblijde, also a Jesuit, see Toussaert, p. 69.

61   Pérouas, above, n. 59; cf. *Enciclopedia cattolica*, iii, p. 1112.

62   E. Le Roy Ladurie, *Les paysans de Languedoc*, 2 vols. (Paris, 1966), p. 649, and in general pp. 647–52, 882–6. Cf. M. Venard, "Une histoire religieuse dans une histoire totale," *Revue d'histoire de l'Eglise de France*, liii (1967), p. 46.

hard-worked priest by having in the parish a schoolmaster who, as in a backwoods village of Languedoc, would be found "very useful for teaching religion, how to pray, and for the catechism." So, in the diocese of Montpellier, another episcopal Colbert was busy at the end of the seventeenth century complementing the catechism of Sundays and feast days with a network of parochial schoolmasters giving weekday schooling to at least the male children of the better-off end of rural society; by 1704 there was a schoolmaster in every parish and one child was getting some kind of education for every two or three families in the diocese.[63]

This, in Le Roy Ladurie's view, is enough in itself to explain the misfiring of the popular Counter-Reformation in France: it was obliged to promote education, and in promoting education tended to abolish itself. He brings a certain amount of evidence to show that the spread of education was, in the course of the eighteenth century, so modifying the mentality of the less remote parts of rural France that, while the requirements of religious practice were being most massively fulfilled, the outlook and ambitions of the population were settling more and more firmly on the things of this world.[64] This is a most important suggestion, and there is obviously something in it; but the implication that Catholicism and education are incompatible seems a little a priori, and if they often proved so in eighteenth-century France I should be inclined to blame the sociological weakness of Tridentine Catholicism: its incapacity to provide, within the rigid framework of parochial conformity, the channels and organs of autonomous participation which the medieval Church had fostered in such profusion. The decline of fraternities, the lack of congregational structures, were obviously of great importance; but neither in itself quite reaches the heart of this particular matter, or truly accounts for the common but elusive sense that, all things considered, the medieval Church made for life and the Counter-Reformation Church against it. I have tried to suggest that what made the medieval Church on the popular plane a real, if ignorant and misguided, community, was its admission of the kin-group, natural and artificial, as a constituent element in its life; where the Tridentine Church strikes me as having most damagingly failed was in its

---

63  Le Roy Ladurie, *Les paysans de Languedoc*, pp. 129, n. 7, and 649; also P. Ariès, *Centuries of Childhood*, trans. R. Baldick (London, 1962), pp. 288–94, 305.
64  Le Roy Ladurie, *Les paysans de Languedoc*, pp. 651ff, 890. Le Roy Ladurie associates this change of outlook with evidence of declining religious practice (cf. above, n. 6); I should myself be inclined to associate it with the "conformisme moutonnier" described by Le Bras in the diocese of Châlons (above, n. 59), pp. 64, 68. In both regions religious indifference has been predominant since the nineteenth century: see Le Bras's "Carte religieuse de la France rurale," in *Études*, i, p. 324.

reluctance to admit the nuclear family or household on the same terms.

This may be felt a surprising suggestion to make, considering how prominent a position has been occupied in modern Catholic apologetics by propaganda about the social rights and spiritual importance of the family. But there was little precedent for this in the activity of the Counter-Reformation hierarchy, in whom the notion of the nuclear family as an autonomous entity inspired indifference or distaste. There seems to be no reference to the *familia*, in either of its senses, in the decrees of the council of Trent;[65] the council enacted only two reforms which affected it, about marriage and catechism, and both, if anything, diminished the rights of parents and the independence of the family. Haunted, it may be, by cartoons of the domestic Luther, the Counter-Reformation hierarchy seems to have taken it for granted that household religion was a seed-bed of subversion. It thereby turned its back on a movement which, while it might have anti-sacerdotal implications, was by no means inherently unorthodox or Protestant, and under the influence of the Christian humanists had been making a good deal of progress in early sixteenth-century Europe.[66] Tridentine legislation against the celebration of Mass in private houses may, perhaps, only have inconvenienced the upper classes; but the object this was understood by most of the Counter-Reformation hierarchy as being intended to secure, that all parish members should attend on all days of obligation a single parochial Mass, showed equal disregard for the workings of households large and small, and was for that and other reasons entirely impracticable. In the end, by forcing the hierarchy to duplicate Masses and even to allow for an element of representative attendance, the households of Catholic Europe gained for themselves a minimal status in determining the pattern of religious observance; but in this atmosphere a positive sense of the spiritual value of the household could not grow.[67] Complaint that the Counter-Reformation Church did not encourage domestic bible-reading would no doubt be utopian; it is nonetheless obvious how large a gap was left by its absence, and nothing

65 Not counting the term 'filiis familias," which appears in the decree *Tametsi: Canons and Decrees*, p. 454.

66 See especially richard Whitford, *A werke for housholders* (London, 1533); *Dictionary of National Biography*, lxi (1900), pp. 125–7, should correct the impression which may be given by Hill, *Society and Puritanism*, pp. 150, 446, that Whitford was not an orthodox Catholic. See in general Ariès, *Centuries of Childhood*, pp. 339–415, which does not however deal with the levels of society discussed here.

67 *Canons and Decrees*, pp. 423, 151; Adam, p. 248; Le Bras, *Études*, i, p. 277 and n. 5; Ferté, pp. 269–70, 285–6; Marcilhacy, pp. 320, 333. Cf. the fine passage in Whitford, *A werke for housholders*, sig. D iii-2, providing for domestic convenience "for God is there present where he is duely and devoutly served"; and Hill, *Society and Puritanism*, p. 447.

effective was devised to take its place. Canisius's Catechism does include forms of household prayer, but Bellarmine's does not, nor, so far as I can see, do any of the French Catechisms of the seventeenth century. Borromeo's instructions show, here and there, a desire to encourage family evening prayers and simultaneous examination of conscience,[68] but this was something which appears to have played no part in his pastoral visitations. Nor does it appear in those of his emulators, though they showed interest in other household matters, like where people slept.[69]

In the France of the Second Empire, Bishop Dupanloup took the view that the family had been so corrupted by irreligion that the catechism-class must be made to serve as a substitute.[70] Though it professed to be teaching submission to parental authority, the Counter-Reformation hierarchy acted on similar assumptions. In so acting it divorced the growth of the individual from the environment most likely to foster it, and caused, I believe, its educative program to misfire. It also demonstrated that there was something intrinsically the matter with its idea of the Church: a conviction that all problems could be solved by compulsory legislation was here most evidently false. Domestic participation could not be legislated for. That it was, in effect, legislated against is the one feature of the code of religious practice which I should without hesitation put down to panic about Protestantism. I hope I have communicated my belief that the bishops of the Tridentine Church have more positive achievements to their credit than they are often allowed: from the parish register to the primary school they were laying many of the foundations of the modern state, and perhaps they have as good a claim as English Puritanism to have "eradicate[d] habits which unfitted men for an industrial society."[71] Yet their failure of nerve at this crucial point is enough in itself to justify those who have maintained, against a good deal of objection, that the term Counter-Reformation has a necessary and respectable place in the language of modern European history.

68   *Catechismus Petri Canisii* (cited above, n. 60), pp. 125ff; Borromeo, *Pastorum instructiones*, pp. 143–4 and *Acta*, pp. 899ff.

69   Grosso-Mellano, iii, p. 277; Casta, *Evêques et curés corses*, p. 108; cf. Adam, p. 96. Note Whitford's comment on the difficulties of practising domestic piety when sleeping three in a bed: *A werke for housholders*, sig. b i-2.

70   Marcilhacy, p. 245.

71   Hill, *Society and Puritanism*, p. 188. It will be obvious that Hill's chapter xiii ("The Spiritualisation of the Household") has been much in my mind while writing the two concluding paragraphs of this paper; cf. my own "Character of Elizabethan Catholicism," first published in *Past and Present*, no. 21 (April, 1962), and repr. in Trevor Aston (ed.), *Crisis in Europe, 1560–1660* (London, 1965), pp. 224ff.

# 5

# Reformation, Counter-Reformation, and the Early Modern State: A Reassessment

*Wolfgang Reinhard*

Originally appeared as Reinhard, Wolfgang, "Reformation, Counter-Reformation, and the Early Modern State: A Reassessment," *Catholic Historical Review* 75 (1989): 383–405.

*Editor's Introduction*

Wolfgang Reinhard is one among several scholars who have challenged the idea that there was a fundamentally antithetical relationship between Reformation and "Counter-Reformation" in sixteenth- and seventeenth-century Europe. Reinhard accepts Jedin's positive reassessment of the Counter-Reformation's "grass-roots" origins. But he takes it a step further, arguing that both sixteenth-century Reformations – Protestant *and* Catholic – shared common origins and developed as parallel manifestations of a *single* process of historical change called "confessionalization." Specifically, after a brief "evangelical movement" between 1517 and 1525, the Reformation and Counter-Reformation emerged as competing "conservative operations with authorities in the lead," if not always in full control. In order to compete more effectively, both reform movements established stricter expectations of religious orthodoxy and obedience through education, propaganda, and censorship; and because no church possessed enough resources to achieve these goals on its own, most became dependent, more or less, on the support of princes, magistrates, and kings. Indeed, churches became *part of* the state, in practice if not always in theory. Moreover, by encouraging religious discipline, churches also produced more obedient subjects of princely authority. For these reasons, the Counter-Reformation was profoundly political. Thus "confes-sionalization" contributed, unintentionally, to the modernization of states. Although Reinhard's vantage is that of the princely chancery, he would agree with John Bossy that the Counter-Reformation meant to transform ordinary believers into the mere objects of domination.

# Reformation, Counter-Reformation, and the Early Modern State: A Reassessment

*Wolfgang Reinhard*

Most historians today will agree that there is no history without theory. This is particularly true if the term "theory" is not limited to the elaborate products of refined social science techniques, but rather includes general concepts of history, historical terminology, and, last but not least, the respective system of historical periodization. The less one reflects on such elementary theories the more likely is their uncontrolled influence upon historical thought. This may result in a general bias in research and teaching, blocking the way to necessary corrections of our image of certain periods, until the accumulation of a critical mass of knowledge has made such corrections unavoidable. That this is the case in early modern European history, I shall try to demonstrate, offering at the same time some alternative concepts and an alternative periodization.

Traditionally, German, and to a certain extent European early modern history as well, is divided into three periods: the "Reformation" 1517–1555, the "Counter-Reformation" 1555–1648, and the "Age of Absolutism" 1648–1789. This division has become almost indestructible because of the simple and convincing dialectical pattern it is based upon: a progressive movement, the "Reformation," as thesis, evokes a reaction, the reactionary "Counter-Reformation," as antithesis; their contradiction leads to extremely destructive armed conflicts, until Europe is saved by the strong hand of the absolutist early modern state, which because of its neutrality in the religious conflict is considered the synthesis, a synthesis which opens the way to that culmination point of world history, the modern national power state.[1] This view of history is

---

1   Some examples: Karl Brandi, *Deutsche Geschichte im Zeitalter der Reformation und Gegenreformation* (Munich, 1969; first edition 1930), p. 216; Leo Kofler, *Zur Geschichte der bürgerlichen Gesellschaft. Versuch einer verstehenden Deutung der Neuzeit* (Neuwied-Berlin, 1971; first edition 1948), pp. 7ff, 284, 417 (Marxist analysis); Review of David Parker, *The Making of French Absolutism* (London, 1983) by Ulrich Muhlack, *Zeitschrift für Historische Forschung*, 13 (1986), 239ff; some more in Wolfgang Reinhard, "Gegenreformation als Modernisierung? Prolegomena zu einer Theorie des konfessionellen Zeitalters." *Archiv für Reformationsgeschichte*, 68 (1977), 226–9.

wonderfully convincing, but quite incorrect. If only we were able to free ourselves from its grip, we might easily learn from recent research that "Counter-Reformation," if a reaction, was still not simply reactionary. But we would also recognize that the relation between "Reformation" and "Counter-Reformation" was not just that of action and reaction, but much more that of slightly dislocated parallel processes. Finally, we would see that the early absolutist state was far from neutral in religious matters; it was overtly intolerant and quite correctly considered this intolerance a foundation of its strength. I shall try to prove these points, beginning by an analysis of the character of "Reformation" and "Counter-Reformation," and at the same time give the outline of a new, probably more realistic view of early modern European history.

The labels "progressive Reformation" and "reactionary Counter-Reformation" are no longer viable, either as dialectic contradictions or as successive periods of history, because they are in neither sense mutually exclusive. In particular the so-called "Counter-Reformation period" is at least as much characterized by the "second Reformation," the expansion of Calvinism, as by increasing Catholic activity. And since Calvinism proves much stronger than Lutheranism, the Protestant "Reformation" reached its culmination at the very moment, when traditional historiography placed the "Counter-Reformation" in ascendancy. In addition, the definitive formation of Lutheranism also occurred in those years; the *Konkordienformel* (formula of concord) dates from 1580.

If "Reformation" and "Counter-Reformation" are not mutually exclusive in their temporal aspect, then this is even truer of their material aspect. The discovery that they are closely connected by their origin and background is much older than today's fashionable ecumenism. Catholics had once rejoiced when a Protestant historian, Wilhelm Maurenbrecher, in 1880 published his discovery of a Spanish Catholic reform before "Reformation."[2] In the meantime even Protestant historians[3] have accepted Herbert Jedin's formula "Catholic Reform and Counter-Reformation" of 1946,[4] stressing the fact that the revival of the old Church was more than just a reaction to Protestantism. And if this statement once had a certain apologetic flavor such as: the true Catholic Church has no need of heretics to initiate her own reform, meanwhile this attitude has been neutralized by reducing both Protes-

---

2  Wilhelm Maurenbrecher, *Geschichte der katholischen Reformation*, vol. I (1880).
3  Kurt Dietrich Schmidt, *Die katholische Reform und die Gegenreformation* ("Die Kirche in ihrer Geschichte," vol. 3 L 1 [Göttingen, 1975]).
4  Hubert Jedin, *Katholische Reformation oder Gegenreformation? Ein Versuch zur Klärung der Begriffe nebst einer Jubiläumsbetrachtung über das Trienter Konzil* (Lucerne, 1948).

tant and Catholic reform movements to their common medieval background and origin. Thus the Calvinist Pierre Chaunu came to consider "Reformation" and "Counter-Reformation" just the second and third in a whole series of movements for church reform.[5] Thus the evangelical movement as initiated by Martin Luther in 1517 may be considered the final result of more than 200 years of attempted regeneration of theology and piety.

Of course, the dynamics of those movements had to do with the conditions of society. The list is rather long: population pressure in a "full world" without modern technological escapes, and, later on, in the fourteenth century, economic crisis and plague; next, the increasing importance of cities, and what they stood for, i.e., money economy and educated laity, in other words, increasing division of labor leading to a growing complexity of human existence because of growing numbers of human beings living closely together; then, serious crises of the political and ecclesiastical systems, in particular the Great Schism, and the failure of several councils to reform the Church; finally, new tendencies in intellectual life, intertwined with the beforementioned social developments. All this again and again between the thirteenth and the sixteenth century led to attempts to reform the Church and the world.

Thus "Reformation" and "Counter-Reformation," once considered irreconcilable opposites, today are seen as closely connected by their common origin. But this is not to level them down to one and the same thing, because still the early "evangelical movement" initiated by Luther remains something particular, since it proved an innovative force of modernizing tendency. However, as soon as the princes took over in the 1520s after the Peasants War, the movement became "Reformation," that is, a process of religious change organized by conservative authorities in their legal terms.[6] Therefore the *Confessio Augustana* in 1530 very decisively steers clear of the "Left," of the kind of radicalism the evangelical movement had brought about, and very deliberately approaches the Old Church party again.[7] And whoever, despondent at Lutheran conservatism, hopes to find the principle of progress in more radical

5   Pierre Chaunu, *Les temps réformes. Histoire religieuse et système de civilisation. La crise de la chrétienté. L'éclatement 1250–1550* (Paris, 1975).
6   It has become possible again to distinguish a dynamic "evangelical movement" from a rather conservative "Reformation," cf. Hans-Jürgen Goertz, "Aufstand gegen den Priester. Anti-klerikalismus und reformatorische Bewegungen," in Peter Blickle (ed.), *Bauer, Reich und Reformation. Festschrift für G. Franz* (Stuttgart, 1982), pp. 182–209.
7   Cf. Wolfgang Reinhard, "Das Augsburger Bekenntnis im politischen Zusammenhang," in Horst Jesse (ed.), *Das Augsburger Bekenntnis in drei Jahrhunderten* (Weissenhorn, 1980), pp. 32–50.

Calvinism, is also doomed to disappointment. Since in most cases Calvinism was introduced into the Empire by the authority of princes, its structure consequently assumed a form very similar to that of Lutheranism.[8] On the other hand, the identification of Calvinism with political opposition movements resulted from historic contingency and not from its basic theological character, as has been claimed. John Calvin's doctrine of politics and his political correspondence leave no doubt about that.

The study of the history of political ideas, such as the sovereignty of the people and right to resist authority, demonstrates beyond doubt that their development depended much more on the contemporary political constellation than on the supposed properties of any theology. Political resistance was first legitimized by conservative Lutherans, when their stronghold Magdeburg was in danger after the "Interim" of 1548. From there the doctrine migrated to Geneva, where it was adapted to the necessities of West European Calvinism at the very moment when German Lutherans dropped the notion altogether. Unlike the Calvinists, the German Lutherans enjoyed the political protection of the Peace of Religion of Augsburg and had no need to resist the emperor any more. But resistance theory reached its first culmination point with the Calvinist *Monarchomachs*, who wrote in the aftermath of the massacre of St. Bartholomew's Night, when the French monarchy threatened the very existence of their community. However, as soon as a new king became their protector and provided them with a guaranteed minimum of toleration, Calvinists were converted to absolutism. Instead, it was the Catholics who now became *Monarchomachs*, for the growing power of monarchy seemed to threaten their religion and the traditional authority of the pope. Defending their faith and their pope, they developed theories of resistance and sovereignty of the people which, particularly in the case of some Spanish Jesuits, went further than anything Calvinists have ever written. But as soon as an alliance between throne and altar had been established, Catholic writers became advocates of absolutism, too.[9] Thus sixteenth-century Jesuit authors could be denigrated as fathers of revolution by conservative historiography,[10] or elevated as

8   The outstanding case is that of the Palatinate, cf. Paul Münch, *Zucht und Ordnung. Reformierte Kirchenverfassungen im 16. und 17. Jahrhundert* (Stuttgart, 1978).

9   Cf. Hans Fenske, Dieter Mertens, Wolfgang Reinhard, Klaus Rosen, *Geschichte der politischen Ideen von Homer bis zur Gegenwart* (Koenigstein, 1981), pp. 225–47; W. Reinhard, "Gegenreformation" (as in note 1), pp. 245ff.

10   Leopold von Ranke, *Die Idee der Volkssouveränität in den Schriften der Jesuiten* (1835), in "Sämmtliche Werke," vol. 24 (Leipzig, 1877), pp. 223–36.

forefathers of democracy by historians of liberal observance,[11] whereas other members of the same order may serve as proof of a sinister alliance between reactionary forces of oppression.[12] The positions of modern historiography depend as much on the respective political constellation as sixteenth-century theoreticians did.

The Jesuit order, still considered one of the leading institutions of Catholic regeneration, provides us with particularly good examples of modern tendencies inside the supposedly reactionary "Counter-Reformation." Compared with traditional monastic and mendicant orders, the Society of Jesus leaves an almost revolutionary impression; for sound reasons conservative forces of the Old Church, such as the later Pope Paul IV, had become its opponents.[13] And it was not by mere chance that attempts to found a corresponding female order had to fail. The innovations of the Jesuits, combined with a kind of "Women's Liberation" in ecclesiastical terms, were completely intolerable for Roman hierarchs.[14] In the case of the Jesuits, the very fact of a *new* foundation could be considered scandalous, because for centuries nobody had gone beyond reforming existing orders. The elite-conscious way of recruiting members and the carefully planned training they had to undergo were also without precedent. The "Spiritual Exercises," which played a central role in that training, today may look all but modern, as far as their contents are concerned. Nevertheless, they are still of fascinating modernity in a threefold respect. The book organizes the internalization of fundamental values of a group with remarkable psychological rationality. In doing so, it aims at the education of the particular individual in a comprehensive manner without precedent in western history. Finally, this particularly intensive internalization of group values by the individual allows religious life without the traditional instruments of monastic communitarian discipline, such as chancel office and enclosure, and therefore becomes the precondition for an unrestricted

11   Gunther Lewy, *Constitutionalism and Statecraft during the Golden Age of Spain: A Study of the Political Philosophy of Juan de Mariana, S.J.* ("Travaux d'humanisme et renaissance," vol. 36 [Geneva, 1960]).
12   Cf. René Fülöp-Miller, *Macht und Geheimnis der Jesuiten. Eine Kultur- und Geistesgeschichte* (Berlin, 1932), pp. 426–53.
13   Peter A. Quinn, "Ignatius of Loyola and Gian Pietro Carafa: Catholic Reformers at Odds," *Catholic Historical Review*, 67 (July, 1981), 386–400.
14   Joseph Grisar, "'Jesuitinnen.' Ein Beitrag zur Geschichte des weiblichen Ordenswesens von 1550 bis 1650," *Reformata Reformanda. Festschrift H. Jedin* (Münster, 1965), II, 70–113; *idem, Die ersten Anklagen in Rom gegen das Institut Maria Wards (1622)* ("Miscellanea Historiae Pontificiae," vol. 22 [Rome, 1959]); *idem, Maria Wards Institut vor römischen Kongregationen (1616–1630)* ("Miscellanea Historiae Pontificiae," vol. 27 [Rome, 1966]).

activity of the Jesuits in the world. It is not at all surprising, therefore, that the order proved particularly efficient in education; probably the Jesuit schoolmaster was the most successful agent of "Counter-Reformation."[15]

The Jesuits also ran the economy of their colleges in a strikingly modern fashion[16] that challenges the notion of Catholic economic inferiority, as "proved" once and for ever by Max Weber's famous essay on the *Protestant Ethic and the Spirit of Capitalism*.[17] Certainly, the Protestant open admission of a moderate rate of interest was more honest than covert Catholic casuistic solutions of that problem, but it proved also less elastic from the economic point of view. In fact, the tortuous acceptance of certain forms of credit and interest by Catholic theologians was more favorable to modern economic practice than Calvinist rigorism.[18] Thus the financial system of the papacy remained superior to that of most European monarchies for quite a time. Indeed, it was not the "Spirit of Counter-Reformation" that produced the eventual economic lapse of Catholic southern Europe, as Herbert Lüthy has claimed, by inverting Weber's thesis.[19] It was rather the unfavorable development of the economy itself compared with that of northern Europe: the south

15   Cf. Mabel Lundberg, *Jesuitische Anthropologie und Erziehungslebre in der Frühzeit des Ordens (ca. 1540–ca. 1650)* (Uppsala, 1966); John W. Donohue, *Jesuit Education. An Essay on the Foundation of Its Idea* (New York, 1963); Gian Paolo Brizzi, "Studia humanitatis' und Organisation des Unterrichts in den ersten italienischen Kollegien der Gesellschaft Jesu," in Wolfgang Reinhard (ed.), *Humanismus im Bildungswesen des 15. und 16. Jahrhunderts* (Weinheim, 1984), pp. 155–70; Heinrich Boehmer, *Die Jesuiten* (1904), ed. K. D. Schmidt (Stuttgart, 1957), p. 57.

16   See, e.g., Friedrich Zoepfl, "Geschichte des ehemaligen Mindelheimer Jesuitenkollegs," *Archiv für die Geschichte des Hochstifts Augsburg*, 6 (1929), 1–96.

17   First published in 1904/5, when capitalism was fashionable in Europe. When during the Great Depression this was no longer the case, the origins of capitalism were sometimes not claimed for Calvinism, but Jesuits were made responsible for it; cf. James Brodrick, *The Economic Morals of the Jesuits. An Answer to Dr. H. M. Robinson* (Oxford, 1934).

18   Marjorie Grice-Hutchinson, *The School of Salamanca: Readings in Spanish Monetary Theory, 1544–1605* (Oxford, 1952); John T. Noonan, *The Scholastic Analysis of Usury* (Cambridge, Massachusetts, 1957), pp. 202–29, 249–93; Wilhelm Weber, *Wirtschaftsethik am Vorabend des Liberalismus. Höhepunkt und Abschluß der scholastischen Wirtschaftsbetrachtung durch Ludwig Molina S. J. (1535–1600)* (Münster, 1959), pp. 175–186; Marc Venard, "Catholicisme et usure au XVIe siècle," *Revue d'Histoire de l'Église de France*, 52 (1966), 59–74; Jelle C. Riemersma, *Religious Factors in Early Dutch Capitalism, 1550–1650* (The Hague-Paris, 1967); Clemens Bauer, "Rigoristische Tendenzen in der katholischen Wirtschaftsethik unter dem Einfluß der Gegenreformation," *Adel und Kirche. Festschrift Gerhard Tellenbach* (Freiburg, 1968), pp. 552–79.

19   Herbert Lüthy, "Variationen über ein Thema von Max Weber: die protestantische Ethik und der Geist des Kapitalismus," in *Gegenwart der Geschichte. Historische Essays* (Cologne-Berlin, 1967), pp. 67ff, 92ff.

was unable to keep up with changing patterns of demand and suffered from higher costs of production.[20] This kind of explanation represents a methodological reaction, but historical research indeed once again prefers to explain economic development by economic causes first, and not by immediate resort to the forces of intellectual history.

The same is true of social history. Once it seemed obvious that modern poor relief was an achievement of the "Reformation."[21] Did not suppression of begging and takeover of relief by secular authorities correspond exactly to Protestant theology, where pious works of charity had ceased to be a way to heaven, and laboring according to your personal calling had become a part of everybody's human dignity? Without doubt Protestant theology was perfectly adapted to legitimize the new policy. But the Middle Ages were far from considering poverty nothing but a praiseworthy state of Christian existence; since the thirteenth century it had also become a curse and a threat for society.[22] When after the "Black Death" the widening price gap between city and countryside had forced the rural poor into the cities, and the later increase of population made the situation even more critical, authorities had to react, and did that in ways remarkably similar, whatever their religious affiliation.[23]

Thus, empirical research leads us to the inevitable conclusion that the labels "Reformation" and "Counter-Reformation" simply do not correspond, either chronologically or materially, to the images of "progressive action" and "reactionary reaction" that once seemed so self-evident. Obviously, it would be more appropriate to separate a comparatively

20   Carlo M. Cipolla, "The Italian 'Failure'," in Frederick Krantz and Paul M. Hohenberg (eds), *Failed Transitions to Modern Industrial Society: Renaissance Italy and Seventeenth Century Holland* (Montreal, 1975), p. 9; Richard Tilden Rapp, "The Unmaking of the Mediterranean Trade Hegemony. International Trade Rivalry and the Commercial Revolution," *Journal of Economic History*; 35 (1975), 499–525; *id., Industry and Economic Decline in Seventeenth-Century Venice* (Cambridge, Massachusetts, 1976); Domenico Sella, *Crisis and Continuity in the Economy of Spanish Lombardy during the 17th Century* (Cambridge, Massachusetts, 1979).
21   E.g., Otto Winckelmann, *Das Fürsorgewesen der Stadt Straßburg vor und nach der Reformation* (2 vols; Leipzig, 1922).
22   Jean-Pierre Gutton, *La société et les pauvres. L'exemple de la généralité de Lyon, 1534–1789* (Paris, 1971), pp. 215–18.
23   Cf. Natalie Z. Davis, "Assistance, humanisme et hérésie: le cas de Lyon," in Michel Mollat (ed.), *Etudes sur l'histoire de la pauvreté* (Paris, 1974), II, 761–822 (first in English *Studies in Medieval and Renaissance History*, 5 [1968], 217–75); Bronislaw Geremek, "Criminalité, vagabondage, paupérisme: la marginalité à l'aube des temps modernes," *Revue d'Histoire Moderne et Contemporaine*, 21 (1974), 337–75; Ingomar Bog, "Über Arme und Armenfürsorge in Oberdeutschland und in der Eidgenossenschaft im 15. und 16. Jahrhundert," *Jahrbuch für Fränkische Landesforschung*, 34/35 (1975), 983–1001.

short-lived spontaneous "Evangelical Movement" from 1517 to 1525 from these two almost parallel organized processes of "Reformation" and "Counter-Reformation," which both began in the early 1520's and lasted two centuries. According to our sources, both could be defined as rather conservative operations with authorities in the lead and legal devices predominating. In this regard, Calvinists, Catholics, Lutherans, and to a certain extent even Anglicans, all acted in remarkably similar ways. No wonder: each faced the same problem. Under the pressure of mutual competition the religious groups had no choice but to establish themselves as "churches," i.e., stable organizations with well defined membership. These new "churches" had to be more rigid than the old pre-Reformation Church, where membership was self-evident and required no careful preservation. Particular confessions of faith served to distinguish these separate religious communities from each other. And since the German word *Konfessionen* covers both the confessions of faith and the respective communities, I have decided to call the formation of the new churches *Konfessionalisierung* (confessionalization). In my opinion it began with the first Lutheran visitations and some tentative measures on the Old Church side in the 1520s and ended after the later seventeenth century, when France re-established religious unity by force (1685), when England secured the Protestant character of its monarchy (1688–1707), and when the Prince-Archbishop of Salzburg expelled the Protestants from his country (1731). Obviously "Church" and "State" collaborated everywhere to cut autonomous parts out of the body of one single Christian community (*Kristenheit*) by establishing a particular group conformity of religious doctrine and practice among their members. However, the instruments used, and the institutions and personnel to handle them, deserve a closer look, just to demonstrate once again how closely they corresponded to each other in all communities, in spite of theological differences.[24]

As already mentioned, the basic procedure consisted in the establishment of the respective pure doctrine and its handy formulation in a confession of faith, which could be used to measure everybody's orthodoxy. The Lutherans took the first step in this direction with their "Augs-

---

24  This concept is based on ideas of Ernst Walter Zeeden, *Die Entstebung der Konfessionent. Grundlagen und Formen der Konfessionsbildung im Zeitalter der Glaubenskämpfe* (Munich, 1965; the original version was published in 1958 in the *Historische Zeitschrift* and has been reprinted recently in his *Konfessionsbildung. Studien zur Reformation, Gegenreformation und katholischen Reform* [Stuttgart, 1985], pp. 67–112). I tried to "improve" it with the help of sociological theory; see Wolfgang Reinhard, "Konfession und Konfessionalisierung in Europa," in Reinhard (ed.), *Bekenntnis und Geschichte* (Munich, 1981), pp. 165ff, 174–9.

burg Confession" of 1530. But the decisive years were the late 1550's and early 1560's, when various Calvinist confessions were followed by the Catholic *Professio Fidei Tridentina* (the confession of the Council of Trent). Then, in 1580, the majority of German Lutherans agreed to the *Formula Concordiae* (formula of concord).

A complementary measure to this establishment of pure doctrine was the extinction of possible sources of confusion which might lead the faithful astray. It should no longer be possible that a priest out of naiveté or necessity served two masters, said Mass in the morning and preached to the Protestants in the afternoon, as sometimes had happened in Germany.[25] And the lay chalice, a few years before still considered a way to reunify the churches by concessions to the Protestants, now came under suspicion of crypto-Protestantism, and was abolished as soon as possible.[26]

Then the new rules had to be spread and, if necessary, enforced. Propaganda might be the first instrument to that purpose. The invention of printing had made Luther's initial success possible; the calculated use of the printing press now became essential for indoctrination as for fighting the enemy.[27] Theology under those conditions deteriorated from lofty speculations to continuous battles and almost by definition became controversial.[28] Colloquies between theologians of different observance were no longer serious attempts at reunification, but tended to become ritualized exchanges of arguments to demonstrate the strength of irreconcilably antagonistic positions.[29] On a lower level, indoctrination of simple believers developed into an elaborate technique, employing a broad range of instruments. Catechisms, sermons (printed collections included), and church music were in use everywhere. Catholics had

25  Zeeden, *Die Entstehung der Konfessionen*, p. 74.

26  Gustave Constant, *Concession à l'Allemagne de la communion sous les deux espèces. Etude sur les débuts de la réforme catholique en Allemagne (1548–1621)* (2 vols.; Paris, 1923); August Franzen, *Die Kelchbewegung am Niederrhein im 16. Jahrhundert* (Münster, 1955); Heinrich Lutz, "Bayern und der Laienkelch," *Quellen und Forschungen aus italienischen Archiven und Bibliotheken*, 34 (1954), 203–34.

27  Cf. Karl Eder, *Die Kirche im Zeitalter des konfessionellen Absolutismus (1555–1648)* (Freiburg, 1949), pp. 205–10; Paul Chaix, Alain Dufour, Gustave Moeckli, *Les livres imprimés à Genève de 1550 à 1600* ("Travaux d'humanisme et Renaissance," vol. 86 [Geneva, 1966]); Hans Joachim Bremme, *Buchdrucker und Buchhändler zur Zeit der Glaubenskämpfe. Studien zur Genfer Druckgeschichte* ("Travaux d'humanisme et Renaissance," vol. 104 [Geneva, 1969]).

28  Cf. Wilbirgis Klaiber (ed.), *Katholische Kontroverstheologen und Reformer des 16. Jahrhunderts. Ein Werkverzeichnis* (Münster, 1978); Erwin Iserloh (ed.), *Katholische Theologen der Reformationszeit* (4 vols.; Münster, 1984–7).

29  Cf. Janusz Tazbir, "Die Religionsgespräche der Reformationszeit," in G. Müller (ed.), *Die Religionsgespräche der Reformationszeit* (Gütersloh, 1980), pp. 127–43.

something of an advantage in that their liturgy appealed to the senses and incorporated popular spectacles such as religious processions, pilgrimages, and the veneration of saints and their relics.

Censorship was the negative complement of propaganda, keeping away competitors. the Roman and the Spanish Indexes of prohibited books have become famous, but censorship was common practice in Calvinist and Lutheran churches as well, because very church considered it its duty to protect its members against dangerous contamination.[30]

Therefore, it was particularly important to secure the orthodoxy of persons in strategic positions, such as people responsible for teaching or preaching or able to intervene at decisive hours of human life. Theologians, priests, ministers, teachers, doctors, midwives, and sometimes even secular officials in general were examined on their orthodoxy and made to swear to the respective confession of faith.[31] Then they could train the younger generation in internalizing the new doctrine and rules of behavior.

Each church tried to win the future by expanding and streamlining its educational system so as to safeguard the "right" alignment of its children. New school ordinances mushroomed, stressing religious education and exercises together with the control of religious and moral behavior.[32] If necessary, new orthodox educational institutions had to be created to prevent future elites from studying abroad, where they might be exposed to dangerous influences. In Spain, this was formally prohibited in 1559.[33] But even if there was no formal prohibition, it was still advisable to graduate at the prince's own academy, if one desired to be employed by him.

The new groups should become as homogeneous as possible. Minorities which could not be amalgamated either emigrated or were expelled, as happened to the Salzburg Protestants as late as the early eighteenth

30   Franz Heinrich Reusch, *Der Index der verbotenen Bücher* (2 vols.; Bonn, 1883–5); cf. Bernhard Lohse, "Glaube und Bekenntnis bei Luther und in der Konkordienformel," in Wenzel Lohff and Lewis W. Spitz (eds), *Widerspruch, Dialog und Einigung* (Stuttgart, 1977), p. 29; Münch, *zucht und ordung*, p. 135.

31   Cf. Klaus Schreiner, "Iuramentum Religionis. Entstehung, Geschichte und Funktion des Konfessionseides der Staats- und Kirchendiener im Territorialstaat der frühen Neuzeit," *Der Staat*, 24 (1985), 211–46.

32   With more success than Gerald Strauss, *Luther's House of Learning. Indoctrination of the Young in the German Reformation* (Baltimore, 1978), is willing to admit; cf. James Kittelson, "Successes and Failures in the German Reformation: The Report from Strasbourg," *Archiv für Reformationsgeschichte*, 73 (1982), 153–75; cf. also the Jesuits.

33   Henry Kamen, *The Spanish Inquisition* (London, 1965), p. 97ff of the German translation of 1967.

century.[34] The remaining orthodox majority was allowed al most no contact with neighbors of different religion to prevent possible contamination, or even temporary escape from the strict discipline of their own group. Catholics should have no chance to eat meat on Fridays in Protestant restaurants, nor should Puritans be able to drink in Catholic inns.[35] Finally, discipline was applied to group members in an active way by the instrument of visitation, when ecclesiastical superiors or, more often than not, mixed commissions of clerical and secular officials arrived to investigate in minute detail the religious and moral life of the parish.[36] In Calvinist congregations, which did not recognize a superior institution, the local presbytery or consistory served as the functional equivalent;[37] it had been created for that very purpose. Social control by senior members of your own community probably is more effective than that of an outside authority, even when that authority possessed its own police force or, as in the case of the Catholic Church, such a formidable organization as the Spanish or the Roman Inquisition.

However, group coherence cannot be produced by repression alone, regular participation in a distinctive group ritual is even more important. Therefore the churches established control of that participation by careful record-keeping on baptisms, marriages, communions, and burials. Moreover, they stressed, and sometimes even overstressed, those rites which were particularly useful at distinguishing them from their competitors, even if their theology did not demand such practices. Thus, adoration of the sacrament of the altar and veneration of saints and relics became exclusively characteristic features of Catholicism, whereas practising the lay chalice from now on automatically implied Protestant inclinations.[38] And if a Protestant community indulged in iconoclasm, eliminated the remaining elements of the Catholic mass, and dropped

34 Cf. Franz Ortner, *Reformation, katholische Reform und Gegenreformation im Erzstift Salzburg* (Salzburg-Munich, 1981).

35 Felix Stieve, *Das kirchliche Polizeiregiment in Baiern unter Maximilian I. 1595–1651* (Munich, 1876).

36 Important: E. W. Zeeden and Peter Thaddäus Lang (eds), *Kirche und Visitation, Beiträge zur Erforschung des frühneuzeitlichen Visitationswesens in Europa* (Stuttgart, 1984).

37 Cf. Jean Estèbe and Bernard Vogler, "La genèse d'une société protestante: étude comparée de quelques registres consistoriaux languedociens et palatins vers 1600," *Annales*, 31 (1976), 362–88; Heinz Schilling, "Reformierte Kirchenzucht als Sozialdisziplinierung? Die Tätigkeit des Emder Presbyteriums in den Jahren 1557–1562," in Wilfried Ehbrecht and Heinz Schilling (eds), *Niederlande und Nordwestdeutschland* (Cologne and Vienna, 1983), pp. 261–327.

38 In 1610 a papal dispensation was granted to a candidate "non obstante quod eius mater sub utraque specie communicet" (Archivio Segreto Vaticano, Sec. Brev. 460, fol. 43).

exorcism in baptism, everybody was to realize that they were moving on from Lutheranism to Calvinism.[39]

Even performances with almost no religious significance were considered confessional property, and therefore became unacceptable to others in spite of obvious advantages. When Pope Gregory XIII achieved the overdue reform of the calendar in 1582, most Protestants refused to accept that new reckoning. The Lutheran estates of the Empire did not adopt it until 1699; and in a mixed city like Augsburg the new calendar led to a major conflict just short of civil war.[40]

No wonder that in such a situation even language did not escape confessional regulation. Of course, churches tried to secure an adequate name for themselves. The Old Church somehow managed to reserve for herself the venerable designation "Catholic," whereas the new churches were called after their leading reformers. The Lutherans reluctantly accepted this labelling; Calvinists, however, dislike it right down to the present day. (Though, for the purposes of this essay I had no other choice, for "Calvinist" *is* the most unequivocal term.) But the churches went further than that; even the first names given in baptism became "confessionalized." True, there remained a common mass of names of New Testament origin, but in Calvinist Geneva certain names of saints and others typical of Old Church piety were banned and replaced by that inflation of Old Testament names which soon became a characteristic feature of Calvinism. On the other hand, Catholics from 1566 on were legally obliged to choose a saint's name.[41] But there is still much research to be done in that field; we in fact do not know very much about how "confessionalization" changed patterns of everyday life such as language.

Certainly, all this socio-religious change could not be realized within a short time. But the notorious inertia of all established social structure is not the only reason for the slowness of "confessionalization." The churches simply lacked adequate institutions staffed with personnel qualified for that task. The Old Church on the one hand, the new

39  Cf. Thomas Klein, *Der Kampf um die zweite Reformation in Kursachsen 1586–1591* (Cologne and Graz, 1962); Heinz Schilling (ed.), *Die reformierte Konfessionalisierung in Deutschland–Das Problem der "Zweiten Reformation"* ("Schriften des Vereins für Reformationsgeschichte," vol. 195 [Gütersloh, 1986]).

40  Ferdinand Kaltenbrunner, *Beiträge zur Geschichte der Gregorianischen Kalenderreform* (Vienna, 1880); id., "Der Augsburger Kalenderstreit," *Mitteilungen des österreichischen Instituts für Geschichtsforschung*, 1 (1880), 497–540; F. Stieve, *Der Kalenderstreit des 16. Jahrhunderts in Deutschland* ("Bayerische Akademie der Wissenschaften," Abhandlungen, vol. 15, 3 [Munich, 1880]).

41  Cf. in particular Willi Richard, *Untersuchungen zur Genesis der reformierten Kirchenterminologie der Westschweiz und Frankreichs mit besonderer Berücksichtigung der Namengebung* (Bern, 1959).

churches on the other, had complementary advantages and disadvantages in this respect. In the beginning, when it had to react to the "evangelical movement," the Old Church suffered a kind of deadlock because of a completely inadequate personnel in most of its positions, the papacy included. Though not necessarily irreligious, those members of the clergy were much more preoccupied with their social status and political success than with orthodox faith and an immaculate life. But once this deadlock had been broken, in particular when the papacy was "conquered" by the reform movement,[42] the Old Church had the advantage of an elaborate institutional structure. In spite of its traditional ponderosity, this institutional apparatus was still capable of reorganization, once the Council of Trent and a series of reform-minded popes started to create new institutions or to revitalize ancient ones. Thus, an elaborate network of papal nuncios was not only employed to enforce "Counter-Reformation" policy, but also to initiate "Catholic Reform" in local churches. Bishops now had to visit the pope and to report on their churches every three to five years. They were required to hold provincial councils and diocesan synods to publish the new reform legislation, and to coordinate and guide reforming activities in their dioceses. In addition, religious orders were still the strongest force the Old Church had at her disposition. New ones were created and took over new tasks, mainly in the fields of propaganda and education. Capuchins, Ursulines, and the institute of Mary Ward deserve to be mentioned besides the Jesuits. Apart from their ordinary work, Capuchins and Jesuits developed a new tool of religious propaganda, strategically planned missionary campaigns in regions of doubtful observance.

The new churches, on the other hand, had to start without any institutional infrastructure, except in those countries like England where they took over the old church institutions. Often secular authorities of cities and states stepped in instead, a kind of substitution favored by Luther's notorious indifference toward institutions. However, the new churches made up for that inherent weakness of their position by their personnel, which, even if not sufficiently trained, still consisted of convinced and enthusiastic innovators. And the necessary training was soon provided by new or reformed institutions of higher education such as the University of Wittenberg and the academies at Strasbourg and Geneva.[43]

42   Cf. Wolfgang Reinhard, "Reformpapsttum zwischen Renaissance und Barock," in Remigius Bäumer (ed.), *Reformatio Ecclesiae. Festgabe für Erwin Iserloh* (Paderborn, 1980), pp. 779–96.
43   Cf. Robert Kingdon, *Geneva and the Coming of the Wars of Religion in France 1555–1563* (Geneva, 1959).

Thus indeed higher education became of crucial importance for the new churches – a fact soon noticed and answered by the Old Church. The foundation of seminaries as ordered by the Council of Trent was meant to provide the Old Church with adequately qualified priests able to stand comparison with Protestant ministers. And the rapidly spreading Jesuit colleges soon became the training ground of a new Catholic elite, who might then continue their studies at one of the new Catholic universities.[44] In the Holy Roman Empire alone the sixteenth and seventeenth centuries saw the foundation of twelve Catholic, twelve Lutheran, and eight Calvinist universities or institutions of similar status; we might add five more academies to the number of the Calvinist ones, if we take Switzerland into account.[45]

However, neither church was content with creating institutions of higher education; they were all in need of institutions of control and repression, too. Thus, they revived the old medieval visitation and adapted it to their new needs, with the exception of autonomous Calvinist churches, where a new institution, the presbytery or consistory, was created to fulfill the same function. In addition, the Catholic Church founded the Inquisition, whose functional equivalent in Protestant countries – and some Catholic ones, too – was provided by spies and police officers in the service of the respective state.[46]

Because of the shortage of institutions and personnel, *all* churches had to rely to a lesser or greater extent on the support of secular powers, a fact of far-reaching consequences, even if solutions greatly differ from case to case according to local conditions. In fact, each of the local churches which served as a model of "Confessionalization" to the three major groups – i.e., Saxony to the Lutherans, Geneva to the Calvinists, Milan to the Catholics[47] – practised a different kind of church-state relationship. Therefore, we have to keep the crucial role of the State in mind, when we examine the results of "Confessionalization."

Without doubt, in the long run the churches succeeded in "confessionalizing" their members to a remarkable extent. However, in reaching the goal they had in mind, they produced several unintended results. First, society after "Confessionalization" was certainly more "modern"

44    Cf. Karl Hengst, *Jesuiten an Universitäten und Jesuitenuniversitäten* (Munich, 1981); Peter Schmidt, *Das Collegium Germanicum in Rom und die Germaniker. Zur Funktion eines römischen Ausländerseminars (1552–1914)* (Tübingen, 1984).
45    *Atlas zur Kirchengeschichte* (Freiburg, 1970), p. 80; Ulrich Im Hof, "Sozialdiszi-plinierung in der reformierten Schweiz vom 16. bis zum 18. Jahrhundert," *Annali dell'istituto storico italo-germanico in Trento*, VIII (1982), 127ff.
46    One example: Stieve, *Der Kalenderstreit des 16. Jahrhunderts in Deutschland.*
47    Saxony and Geneva are well known; for Milan see *Acta Ecclesiae Mediolanensis* (Milan, 1599ff) and Wolfgang Reinhard, *Die Reform in der Diözese Carpentras* (Münster, 1966), p. 134.

than before: education was improved and more widespread, and the first media revolution in history had taken place, the victory of printing. By these means, and by their demand for a much higher degree of religious consciousness, churches had contributed to the further development of rationality. At the same time, they had trained their members in discipline and made them accustomed to being objects of bureaucratic administration – both essential preconditions of modern industrial societies.[48]

On the other hand, the constant pressure they and their secular allies exercised on the people must have created stress and a potential of latent aggressiveness. I think that the notorious witch-craze of the late sixteenth and early seventeenth centuries is nothing else but an unconscious collective expurgation of these aggressions at the expense of victims provided by traditional superstition. It cannot be mere coincidence that the witch-craze reached its climax in time and space precisely where "Confessionalization" was practised with particular intensity, but nevertheless very rarely identified witches directly with the "confessional" enemy.[49]

Last but not least, "Confessionalization" made an important contribution to the growth of the modern state in Europe. Not that the churches intended to do so; more often than not it was quite the opposite. However, they all needed the help of secular authorities, a help which was granted willingly, but not free of charge. The churches had to pay for it in some cases in the literal sense of the word. Early modern state-builders, on the other hand, knew very well that joining the process of "Confessionalization" would provide them with three decisive competitive advantages: enforcement of political identity, extension of a monopoly of power, and disciplining of their subjects. Therefore, it was obvious that a policy of religious toleration would not pay at that stage of state-building. Indeed, tolerant states were powerless states during the first centuries of modern history!

But what was the concrete relationship between religion and political identity? When medieval "Christianity" broke down into different churches, national and territorial states, these new entities still maintained the traditional claim of total commitment. Society was still not split up into more or less autonomous subsystems as is the case today, such as "politics," "religion," "economy," "family life," etc., where members may be different, but membership is compatible. Quite the

48   John Bossy, "The Counter-Reformation and the People of Catholic Europe," *Past and Present*, No. 47 (1970), 51–70.
49   This suggestion appeared obvious after studying a large number of regional studies on witch-hunting in the sixteenth and seventeenth centuries, which cannot be quoted here.

opposite: society remained unitarian; "religion" included "politics" as "politics" included "religion," and it was not possible to pursue economic purposes or to lead a family life outside of both. Under such conditions, the development of the early modern state could not take place without regard to "Confession," but only based upon "fundamental consent on religion, church, and culture, shared by authorities and subjects" (Heinz Schilling).[50] That is why Catholicism came to constitute the national political identity of Portugal, Spain, and after some time even of France, exactly as Protestantism did for England. The Swedish case is even more symptomatic: the Swedes overcame confessional ambiguity only when their national identity was threatened by the impending succession to the throne of the Catholic king of Poland. At that point Sweden finally accepted the Augsburg Confession in 1593, closed down the convent of Vadstena, the Catholic national sanctuary, in 1595, and outlawed Catholics.[51]

In the case of German territorial states, the appeal to religious differences is even more essential, because these principalities lacked a "national" culture to legitimize their political independence. Sometimes there were not even different dynasties to draw clear lines of demarcation between territories, but just rival branches of the same noble house. It cannot be mere coincidence that in such cases the individual lines preferred different "confessions": Wittenberg Lutheranism – Leipzig Catholicism; Kassel Calvinism – Darmstadt Lutheranism; Munich Catholicism – Heidelberg Lutheranism, later on Calvinism. Even princes of the same religion carefully separated their respective territorial churches from each other,[52] and if they were Catholic, they tried at least to establish an exclusively territorial bishopric in their country. The different Swiss republics had drawn their definite "confessional" borderlines as early as 1531[53] – obviously advanced state-building favored effective "Confessionalization" just as "Confessionalization" favored state-building.

50   H. Schilling, *Konfessionskonflikt und Staatsbildung. Eine Fallstudie über das Verhältnis von religiösem und sozialem Wandel in der Frühneuzeit am Beispiel der Grafschaft Lippe* (Gütersloh, 1981), p. 34.
51   Paul Georg Lindhardt, *Skandinavische Kirchengeschichte seit dem 16. Jahrhundert* ("Die Kirche in ihrer Geschichte," vol. 3, M 3. [Göttingen, 1982]), pp. 281ff; Georg Schwaiger, *Die Reformation in den nordischen Ländern* (Munich, 1962), pp. 142ff; Oskar Garstein, *Rome and the Counter-Reformation in Scandinavia*, vol. 2 (Oslo, 1980).
52   Cf. Schilling, *Konfessionskonflikt und Staatsbildung*, p. 367.
53   Peter Stadler, "Eidgenossenschaft und Reformation," in Heinz Angermeier (ed.), *Säkulare Aspekte der Reformationszeit* (Munich, 1983), pp. 91–9; very important Ernst Walder, "Reformation und moderner Staat," *Archiv des Historischen Vereins des Kantons Bern*, 64/65 (1980), 441–583.

Closed borders, limited mobility, and intermarriage to prevent religious contamination also served to enforce political group identity. Religious obedience to authorities outside the state was considered treacherous. The enlightened John Locke still refused toleration to Catholics, because their loyalty to a foreign prince, the pope, might become a danger for the British state.[54] The elector of Brandenburg made every effort to keep his neighbor, the prince-archbishop of Cologne, away from the Duchy of Cleves, although that duchy's Catholics belonged to the Archdiocese of Cologne.[55]

However, political identity is enforced not only by isolation of the population, but also by a thorough "Confessionalization" of the subjects. This is not to be confused with abusing faith for political purposes. The "civic religion" of Machiavelli and of Rousseau was still far away from the cynical strategies of today's election managers, because in those days those who used religion for political purposes nevertheless still believed in it. From 1615 to 1628 Duke Maximilian of Bavaria had a "Bavaria Sancta" published. In his preface the Jesuit Matthew Rader explained what the book wanted to demonstrate: "Cities, castles, market-towns, counties, villages, fields, forests, mountains and valleys all breathe and demonstrate Bavaria's Catholic religion . . . , because the whole region is nothing but religion and one common church of its people."[56] *Tota regio nil nisi religio* is much more than just playing with the words of the famous formula *Cuius regio eius religio*. This was the program of Maximilian's reign, and he proved so successful in its implementation that still today *Bavarian* and *Catholic* remain almost synonyms![57]

This kind of close affinity between religion and politics made it much easier to overcome the traditional Christian dualism of the spiritual and

54   Epistola de Tolerantia 1689, cf. John Locke, *Ein Brief über Toleranz*, ed. Julius Ebbinghaus ("Philosophische Bibliothek," vol. 289 [Hamburg, 1975]), pp. 92–5 (English and German).
55   Dorothea Coenen, *Die katholische Kirche am Niederrhein* (Münster, 1965); Martin Lackner, *Die Kirchenpolitik des Großen Kurfürsten* (Witten, 1973); Klaus Deppermann, "Die Kirchenpolitik des Großen Kurfürsten," *Pietismus und Neuzeit*, 6 (1981), 99–114. Brandenburg-Prussia accepted certain minorities for practical reasons, but it did *not* become a tolerant state before the eighteenth century!
56   Cf. Peter Bernhard Steiner, "Der gottselige Fürst und die Konfessionalisierung Altbayerns," *Um Glauben und Reich. Kurfürst Maximilian I.* ("Wittelsbach und Bayern," vol. 2, 1 [Munich, 1980]), pp. 252ff.
57   Cf. Stieve, *Der Kalenderstreit des 16. Jahrhunderts in Deutschland; Landrecht/Policey: Gerichts- Malefitz und andere Ordnungen Der Fürstenthumben Obern und Nidern Bayern* (Munich, 1616), pp. 583–5; Hans Rössler, "Warum Bayern katholisch blieb. Eine Strukturanalyse der evangelischen Bewegung im Bistum Freising 1520–1570," *Beiträge zur altbayerischen Kirchengeschichte*, 33 (1981), 91–108.

the secular spheres, just re-established by Luther in the most radical way, in favor of a unitarian regime, this time, however, with the secular authority in the lead, and not the ecclesiastical, as once in the Middle Ages. "Your Grace shall be our pope and emperor," some peasants wrote to their lord, Philip of Hesse, as early as 1523.[58] "Confessionalization" meant gains of power for the State, because the Church became a part of the State in theory as well as in practice. And if not in theory, as in the Catholic case, then at least in practice! The duke of Bavaria did not decide on the orthodoxy of doctrine as the elector of Saxony did, but his "Spiritual Council" at Munich resembled the "High Consistory" at Dresden and the "Church Council" at Heidelberg very closely. No wonder, as all those bodies served the same purpose; they had to govern the territorial church in the name of the prince.[59] Thomas Hobbes's claim that church government was nothing but a part of political sovereignty, and that consequently the spiritual power of the pope did not extend beyond the territory where he was also temporal sovereign, the Papal States, this claim is not to be considered an aggressive anticipation of a future state of things, but a simple description of seventeenth-century reality![60] Had not the electors of Saxony very carefully obstructed the establishment of Protestant bishops as required by the Augsburg Confession of 1530?[61] Of course, the Catholic Church maintained a certain autonomy of its institutions and elites. That is why the expansion of state power is accompanied by a continuous series of conflicts between "Church" and "State." It is amazing that this is true even of the Papal States, where the political hierarchy is recruited from the same clergy as the ecclesiastical one. Nevertheless, here too the "State" dominates the "Church," sometimes at the expense of the very same principle of episcopal autonomy proclaimed by the Council of Trent and enforced by the papacy wherever possible – outside the Papal States![62] But also Ferdinand of Bavaria in his capacity of prince-bishop

58   Walter Heinemeyer, "Die Territorien zwischen Reichstradition, Staatlichkeit und politischen Interessen," in Angermeier, *Säkulare Aspekte*, p. 77.
59   Cf. *Handbuch der Bayerischen Geschichte*, vol. 2 (Munich, 1969), pp. 51, 583; Irmgard Höss, "Humanismus und Reformation," *Geschichte Thüringens*, vol. 3 (Cologne and Graz, 1967); Volker Press, *Calvinismus und Territorialstaat. Regierung und Zentralbehörden der Kurpfalz 1559–1619* (Stuttgart, 1970); imitations of the Bavarian model: Helmut Steigelmann (ed.), *Der Geistliche Rat zu Baden-Baden und seine Protokolle 1577–1584* (Stuttgart, 1962); Herbert Immenkötter, *Die Protokolle des Geistlichen Rats in Münster* (Münster, 1972).
60   Thomas Hobbes, *Leviathan*, ch. 42.
61   I. Höss, "Episcopus Evangelicus. Versuche mit dem Bischofsamt im deutschen Luthertum des 16. Jahrhunderts," in Erwin Iserloh (ed.), *Confessio Augustana und Confutatio* (Münster, 1980), pp. 499–516.
62   Paolo Prodi, *Il sovrano pontefice. Un corpo e due anime: la monarchia papale nella prima età moderna* (Bologna, 1982), pp. 249–93.

of Münster in Westphalia was able to separate a part of the bishopric of Osnabrück and add it to his own diocese just because that part belonged to the principality of Münster politically. He simply claimed the *cura religionis* over it, as it was exercised by temporal princes in other cases.[63] Nevertheless, almost no German Catholic prince ever gained control of his territorial church by establishing a new territorial bishopric, not even in Bavaria. The system of the German imperial church with its politically independent prince-bishops proved an obstacle to further growth of State power, as becomes obvious by a comparison with western and southern Europe. The kings of France and Spain as well as most of the Italian princes and republics held complete control of their respective churches and in some cases were even able to have them reorganized according to their wishes, as in the case of the Spanish Netherlands.[64]

It would be a mistake to consider church government by the secular sovereign grossly dysfunctional from the ecclesiastical point of view, as it turned out in France because of dubious royal appointments to bishoprics and abbeys. The "Catholic Kings" in Spain enforced church reform as did the dukes of Bavaria.[65] One should not forget that "Reformation" by Protestant princes basically was the same thing, in particular when it claimed not to found a new church, but just to purify the old one. On the other hand, purely religious actions might also serve political purposes. The electors of Saxony used "Reformation" and church visitation to enlarge their political power at the expense of neighboring bishops and local nobility.[66] And in Bavaria the restructuring of popular piety proved helpful in undermining the political autonomy of that country's powerful old monasteries. The expansion of the cult of the Virgin as favored by the duke and realized by Jesuits and mendicants went forward at the expense of the traditional patron saints of those monasteries. Thus the "Patrona Bavariae" replaced the patron saint of the local lord exactly as the latter himself was replaced by the duke.[67]

To be saved from competition, churches had to pay a high price to their princes. They not only lost autonomy, but estates and revenues, too. This expropriation of church property was by no means a Protestant peculiarity. In some cases, it had already taken place before the

63  Cf. Immenkötter, *Die Protokolle des geistlichen Rats in Münster*, p. 19.
64  Michael Leopold Dierickx, *De oprichting der nieuwe bisdommen in de Nederlande onder Filips II 1559–1570* (Antwerp, 1950); idem (ed.), *Documents inédits sur l'érection des nouveaux diocèses aux Pays-Bas 1521–1570* (3 vols.; Brussels, 1960–2).
65  Cf. *Historia de la Iglesia en Espana*, vol. 3, 1 (Madrid, 1980), pp. 115–210; *Handbuch der Bayerischen Geschichte*, vol. 2 (Munich, 1969), pp. 626–56.
66  Cf. Höss, "Episcopus Evangelicus," p. 87.
67  Cf. Hermann Hörger, *Kirche, Dorfreligion und bäuerliche Gesellschaft*, vol. 1 (Munich, 1978), pp. 124–36.

"Reformation."[68] And the Protestant secularizations have their less-known counterpart in extensive expropriations by Catholic princes. The French crown, for example, financed the religious wars to a large extent by selling church property.[69] And the clergy was exempt from taxation, in canon law only, since in reality they were taxed by the pope in the Papal States and by the duke of Bavaria as well as by the kings of Spain and France.

Finally, church government by the State and abolition of clerical privilege as practised by both Protestant and Catholic rulers was a decisive step in the direction of a general levelling of their subjects, toward a modern equality not so much of rights as of their loss. In this respect, the Protestant "Reformation" proved a particularly strong promoter of state power. Protestant theology abolished the clergy as a separate estate of society. However, Catholics had their own ways to catch up. A certain prince-abbot of Fulda, for example, used the paternal authority ascribed to the abbot by the monastic observance to overcome the resistance of his estates and to establish his princely absolutism.[70]

Both the "Reformation" and the Council of Trent modernized church administration on bureaucratic lines. The Protestant *Superintendents* or *Superattendants* took their titles from the *Episcopoi*, literally the *overseers*,[71] of the ancient church, but in reality they were, like the later French *Intendant*, modern bureaucratic officials of the *Commissioner*-type, and no longer holders of a benefice as their predecessors had been. According to G. R. Elton, the beginnings of the English "Reformation" are nothing else than one aspect of a major administrative reform of the kingdom.[72] And the Catholic Church overcame the premodern society of privilege-holders by concentrating control of the faithful in the hands of the parish priest and the bishop, and by closing gaps in this control by the new matrimonial legislation combined with the establishment of church records.[73] Administration by writing and an overflow of detailed

---

68 For example, Wilfried Schöntag, "Die Aufhebung der Stifte und Häuser der Brüder vom gemeinsamen Leben in Württemberg," *Zeitschrift für Württembergische Landesgeschichte*, 38 (1979), 82–96.

69 Following earlier studies by Ivan Cloulas now: Claude Michaud, "Les aliénations du temporel ecclésiastique dans la seconde moitié du XVIe siècle. Quelques problemes de méthode," *Revue d'Histoire de l'Église de France*, 67 (1981), 61–82.

70 Klaus Wittstadt, *Placidus von Droste, Fürstabt von Fulda 1678–1700* (Fulda, 1963).

71 Cf. Höss, "Episcopus Evangelicus," p. 86.

72 Cf. G. R. Elton, *The Tudor Revolution in Government* (Cambridge, 1953); idem, *Policy and Police. The Enforcement of the Reformation in the Age of Thomas Cromwell* (Cambridge, 1972).

73 Council of Trent, Sessio XXIV, Decretum de reformatione matrimonii, H. J. Schroeder, O. P. (ed.), *Canons and Decrees of the Council of Trent* (St. Louis, 1941), pp. 183–90 (English translation), pp. 454–60 (Latin).

regulations heralded the age of bureaucracy. By joint efforts of Church and State subjects became accustomed to a stricter discipline of life. And where the State still lacked a well organized bureaucracy able to reach every single subject in the countryside, the Church stepped in with its parish ministers.

This alliance of Church and State during the process of "Confessionalization" reached its culmination in the field of ideas and emotions, where it secured the consent of the subjects to their own subjugation. This had been noticed as early as 1589 by Giovanni Botero:

> No law is more favorable to princes than the Christian one, because it submits to them not only the bodies and means of the subjects, but their souls and consciences, too, and it binds not only the hands, but also the feelings and thoughts.[74]

Of course, in 1653 the Lutheran Dietrich Reinkingk would still agree with him:

> Religion and Reason of State both begin with an R, for they both together contain the greatest secret of statecraft, in particular, if a new empire or government has to be stabilized. . . . One religion in one country and state connects the minds of the subjects among themselves and with their superiors more than anything else, and is the true basis of mutual confidence.[75]

It paid for an early modern authority to regularize the very intimacy of the religious and moral lives of its subjects, and to supervise them by officials and spies; it paid not only through political stability, but also by the gain of new political territory. Whereas a purely political expansion of state power had to reckon with a stubborn resistance of subjects and traditional intermediate authorities, it was obviously easier to risk a move in the field of religion in accord with the subjects. This strategy proved successful in Sweden, England, and certain German territorial states, when "Reformation' was introduced with the help of the estates. However, in a more subtle way, it was also the essential precondition of success for "Confessionalization" as described above. Resistance against measures which are legitimized by their consequence for the eternal salvation of subjects was not only condemned by authorities and by public opinion, but by the very consciences of the subjects themselves. Who

---

74   Translated from Giovanni Botero, *Della ragione di Stato*, ed. Luigi Firpo (Turin, 1948), p. 137.
75   Translated from Dietrich Reinkingk, *Biblische Policey* (Frankfurt, 1681 [first edition 1653]), pp. 14, 35.

dares to doubt, after all, that early modern monarchies could do no better than participate in the process of "Confessionalization"? In 1835, Alexis de Tocqueville still knew only two consensus-producing forces in history: religion and patriotism, which by itself is also a kind of religion:

> In the present age they [the Turks] are in rapid decay because their religion is departing, and despotism only remains. Montesquieu, who attributed to absolute power an authority peculiar to itself, did it, as I conceive, an undeserved honor; for despotism, taken by itself, can maintain nothing durable. On close inspection we shall find that religion, and not fear, has ever been the cause of the long-lived prosperity of an absolute government. Do what you may, there is no true power among men except in the free union of their will; and patriotism and religion are the only two motives in the world that can long urge all the people towards the same end.[76]

---

76  Alexis de Tocqueville, *De la démocratie en Amérique*, I 5, in the American translation by Henry Reeve, ed. Phillips Bradley (New York, 1945), vol. 1, p. 97.

# 6

# How to Become a Counter-Reformation Saint

## *Peter Burke*

Originally appeared as Burke, Peter, "How to Become a Counter-Reformation Saint," in Kaspar von Greyerz, ed., *Religion and Society in Early Modern Europe, 1500–1800* (London: German Historical Institute, 1984), 45–55.

### Editor's Introduction

Proponents of the "acculturation" thesis often adopt the perspective of everyday religious life in the parishes of Catholic Europe; but what did the process look like from the vantage of Rome? Peter Burke uses patterns of canonization in Counter-Reformation Europe to weigh the balance of forces in the centuries-long transaction between learned and popular religious cultures. He demonstrates that in the sixteenth century, this balance shifted decisively toward the centers of power: By 1625 or so, Rome had successfully imposed a papal monopoly over canonization. As in matters of "parochial discipline," moreover, the period was one in which the rules became stricter, and the standards of orthodoxy more exacting. Finally, the group characteristics of saints canonized during the Counter-Reformation have much to say about the dominant religious mentalities of the age. In contrast to earlier periods, this cohort included few martyrs and no theologians; nor can "heroic virtue" explain why some were canonized and others not. Instead, the Counter-Reformation church was most likely to honor the founders of new religious orders, missionaries, model bishops, and saints notable for their charitable works. Together, these roles described the church's main priorities; and although Burke does not pursue the point, his examples also suggest the important role that gender played in the construction of new religious identities. Finally, Burke's analysis also describes the church's loss and recovery of "nerve": Canonizations ceased abruptly in 1523; then no saints were canonized until 1588; from then on, canonizations resumed, but at a slow, highly regulated pace.

# How to Become a Counter-Reformation Saint

*Peter Burke*

I

A volume concerned with the ideas of the sacred and the profane would hardly be complete without some consideration of those holy people, the saints. In any case, saints are well worth the attention of historians because they are cultural indicators. Like other heroes, they reflect the values of the culture which sees them in a heroic light. As western culture has changed over time, so have the kinds of people reverenced as saints: martyrs, ascetics, bishops, and so on. To complicate the story, the way in which saints are created has itself changed over the long term. It has always been the outcome of some sort of interaction between clergy and laity, center and periphery, learned culture and popular culture, but at various times the balance of forces has shifted towards the center. One of the periods in which this happened was the Counter-Reformation.

In the early church, sanctity was essentially an unofficial phenomenon, as it still is in Islam.[1] Some people became the object of cults after their deaths, and some of these cults spread outside their original locations. However, the process of saint-making gradually became more formal and more centralized. At the end of the eleventh century Pope Urban II emphasized the need for witnesses to the virtues and miracles of candidates for sanctity. In the thirteenth century Gregory IX formalized the rules of procedure in cases of canonization. It was the same Gregory IX who set up the tribunal of the Inquisition. This was no coincidence: Like a good lawyer, Gregory was concerned to define both saints and heretics, the opposite ends of the Christian scale. He used similar legal methods in both instances: trials. The trial for sanctity required witnesses; it required judges; and it required the notorious devil's advocate, the equivalent of counsel for the prosecution.[2]

---

1 P. Brown, *The Cult of the Saints* (London, 1981); E. Gellner, *Saints of the Atlas* (London, 1969).
2 M. R. Toynbee, *St. Louis of Toulouse and the Process of Canonisation* (London, 1929); E. W. Kemp, *Canonisation and Authority in the Western Church* (Oxford, 1948); A. Vauchez, *La Sainteté en occident aux derniers siècles du moyen âge* (Rome, 1981).

However, side by side with the formally canonized saints, defined by the center of religious authority, Rome, there survived informally chosen holy people, whose cult was local not universal and permitted not obligatory. It was a two-tier system, not unlike the dual structure of local and international trade. Holy people are not unique to Christianity. What does appear to be uniquely Christian, though, is the idea that saints are not only extremely virtuous people, but also efficacious mediators with God on behalf of the living; more powerful, more valuable dead than alive. This was, of course, an idea which came under fire at the Reformation. Erasmus, for example, pointed out that the veneration of the saints was "not a great deal different from the superstitions of the ancients," such as sacrificing to Hercules or Neptune.[3] Specific saints were identified with characters from classical myth: St George with Perseus, for example (since the cult of St George went back to "time immemorial," he was exempt from the new strict verification procedures).

These criticisms worried the authorities, as can be seen from the discussion of the question of the saints at one of the last sessions at the Council of Trent. The fathers admitted that there had been abuses. However, the decree which emerged from the discussion reaffirmed the desirability of venerating the images and relics of the saints and of going on pilgrimage to their shrines. St George survived the criticisms of humanists and reformers and was not removed from the calendar till our own day. Changes were made, but they were limited ones.

In the first place, an attempt was made to emend the accepted accounts of the lives of the saints and to replace these accounts with something more reliable, judged by the criteria of humanist historical criticism. The most elaborate and systematic attempt at criticism and emendation was of course the work of the Bollandists in the seventeenth century, but the way had been shown by Erasmus himself in the life of St Jerome prefixed to his edition of Jerome's works.[4]

In the second place, the procedure for admitting new saints was tightened up. The last canonizations under the old regime were those of St Bruno (1514), St Francis de Paul (1519), St Benno and St Antonino of Florence (both 1523). There followed a hiatus of sixty-five years during which no more saints were canonized. It does not seem unreasonable to explain this hiatus in terms of a failure of nerve and to speak of a "crisis of canonization" at a time when, as we have seen, the very idea of a saint was under fire. In Lutheran Saxony, the canonization of St Benno

3  Erasmus, *Enchiridion Militis Christiani*, in J. P. Dolan (ed.), *The Essential Erasmus* (New York, 1964), p. 60.
4  H. Delehaye, *L'Oeuvre des Bollandistes*, 2nd edn (Brussels, 1959); Erasmus's life of Jerome reprinted in his *Opuscula*, ed. W. K. Ferguson (The Hague, 1933).

(a local worthy) was mockingly celebrated with a procession in which horses' bones figured as relics.[5] On the other hand, the Protestants developed the cult of their own holy people, notably the martyrs to Catholic persecution.[6] Thus the church authorities were placed in a dilemma. To create saints was to invite mockery, but to refrain from creating them was to yield the initiative in propaganda to the other side. The immediate response of the authorities was to do nothing. It was not until 1588, twenty-five years after the close of the Council of Trent, that saints began to be made again, starting with St Didacus, otherwise known as Diego of Alcala. There were only six formal canonizations in the sixteenth century, but there were twenty-four in the seventeenth century and twenty-nine in the eighteenth.[7]

The revival of saint-making was accompanied by an increase in the central control of the sacred, or of the right to define the sacred. 1588 was not only the year of the elevation of St Didacus but also that of the setting up of the Congregation of Sacred Rites and Ceremonies, a standing committee of cardinals whose responsibilities included canonizations. A treatise of 1610 affirmed that "the authority to canonize saints belongs to the Roman pontiff alone."[8] Saint-making procedures were made increasingly strict and formal by Pope Urban VIII in 1625 and 1634. The distinction between saints and the second-class *beati* was made sharper than it had been, and formal beatification was instituted. A fifty-year rule was introduced: in other words, proceedings for canonization could not begin until fifty years after the death of the candidate for sanctity. This was a break with tradition. Carlo Borromeo, for example, had been canonized only twenty-six years after his death, and Filippo Neri twenty-seven years after (in Filippo's case, the canonization process began within months of his death). The fifty-year rule was followed by another hiatus: there were no canonizations between 1629 and 1658. The final touches to the new system were added in 1734 by the canon lawyer Prospero Lambertini, later Benedict XIV.[9]

5   K. H. Blaschke, *Sachsen im Zeitalter der Reformation* (Gütersloh, 1970), p. 116.
6   D. Kelley, *The Beginning of Ideology* (Cambridge, 1981), p. 121n., emphasizes Protestant consciousness of this process. S. Bertelli, *Ribelli, libertini e ortodossi* (Florence, 1973), p. 59, emphasizes Catholic consciousness of the need to respond.
7   I follow the list compiled by G. Löw from the archives of the Congregation of Rites, given in his article "Canonizazzione" in *Enciclopedia Cattolica*, 12 vols (Rome, 1948–54). Slightly higher figures are given elsewhere, possibly by adding non-formal canonizations.
8   A. Rocca, *De canonizatione sanctorum* (Rome, 1610), p. 5.
9   P. Lambertini, *De canonisatione* (Rome, 1766). On Urban VIII, as on other popes of the period, the standard work is, of course, L. von Pastor's *Geschichte der Päpste*. The relevant volumes are XXI–XXXVII. I have used the English translation: *History of the Popes* (London, 1932–50). On Sixtus V, vol. XXI, p. 138; on Clement VIII, vol.

According to this system, sanctity was explicitly defined in terms of the Aristotelian-Thomist concept of a "heroic" degree of virtue.[10] As for the procedures by which the possessors of this heroic virtue were recognized, they had become more "bureaucratic," in Max Weber's sense of the term. The distinction between sacred and profane was made sharper than it had been, while recruitment procedures for the saints were made uniform and formal. In the trials for sanctity, the supernatural was defined, graded, and labelled with increasing care. There was also an increase in the central control of the sacred, at the expense of local, unofficial, or "wildcat" devotions. A papal monopoly of saint-making had effectively been declared. At a time of centralizing monarchies, the next world was remade in the image of this one.[11]

These changes still did not mean that unofficial saints disappeared altogether, for the new rules were not made retroactive and the status of some individuals remained ambiguous – that of the plague-saint Roche, for example. His cult had spread widely in the later fifteenth century and popes had authorized confraternities and masses in his name. The Venetians made his cult official at the time of the great plague of 1576, during the hiatus in canonizations already discussed. However, this cult was hardly from time immemorial, since Roche had lived in the fourteenth century. He was an awkward case, as the popes recognized. According to the Venetian ambassador, Sixtus V meant "either to canonise him or to obliterate him" (*o di canonizzarlo o di cancellarlo*), but in fact the pope died without having made his choice. Urban VIII authorized a special mass of St Roche, but even he, who defined so much, did not clear up the ambiguity of this saint's status.[12]

Local cults not only continued but also sprang up. Some were simply premature honours paid to those whose canonization might reasonably be expected. In Milan, Carlo Borromeo was venerated before his canonization in 1610, and scenes from his life were displayed in the cathedral.

XXIV, pp. 234ff; on Paul V, vol. XXV, pp. 257ff; on Gregory XV, vol. XXVII, pp. 119ff; on Urban VIII, vol. XXIX, pp. 8ff; on Alexander VII, Clement IX and Clement X, vol. XXXI, pp. 128ff, 338ff, 468ff; on Alexander VIII, vol. XXXII, p. 540; on Clement XI, vol. XXXIII, pp. 343ff; on Benedict XIII and Clement XII, vol. XXXIV, pp. 165ff, 410ff; on Benedict XIV, vol. XXXV, pp. 312ff; on Clement XIII, vol. XXXVII, pp. 401ff.

10   R. Hofmann, *Die heroische Tugend* (Munich, 1933); cf. R. De Maio, "L'ideale eroico nei processi di canonizzazione della Contro-Riforma," *Ricerche di Storia Sociale e Religiosa*, vol. II (1972), pp. 139–60.

11   For a development of Weber's ideas on religious power and legitimacy which emphasizes the interaction between clergy and laity, see P. Bourdieu, "Une interpretation de la théorie de la religion selon Max Weber," *Archives Européennes de Sociologie*, vol. XII (1971). pp. 3–21.

12   *Bibliotheca Sanctorum*, 12 vols (Rome, 1961–70), s.v. "Rocco." Perhaps the most useful modern work of reference o the lives of saints.

In similar fashion, at Antwerp, Rubens painted scenes of the miracles of Ignatius Loyola and Francis Xavier about 1617, although the two men did not become saints officially until 1622.[13] In 1631 the Venetians instituted an official cult of their former patriarch, Lorenzo Giustinian, who was not canonized until 1690.[14]

Other unofficial saints were less conventional. In Castille, Luisa de Carrión, who died in 1636, was treated as a saint and as a miracle worker at court as well as in popular circles, although the Inquisition accused her of imposture and even witchcraft.[15] In Naples, the fisherman turned rebel Masaniello was treated as a saint after his murder in summer 1647. The hair of the corpse was torn out for relics; his name was added to the litany (*Sancte Masanalle, ora pro nobis*); there were stories of his miracles and it was believed that he would rise again.[16] Even in Rome itself, unofficial cults could still grow up. In 1648, for example, "in the monastery of the Quattro Coronati, a nun called Sister Anna Maria died with the reputation of a saint, and her body was exposed to public view for three days." The Franciscan Carlo da Sezze, who died in 1670, had lived in Rome with the reputation of a saint and was consulted on occasion by Pope Clement IX.[17]

However, people like this who died in the odor of sanctity could not be tried for fifty years, and if they failed, the cult would be suppressed. Many were examined, but few passed. There have been very few studies of the unsuccessful, despite the potential interest and importance of a historical sociology of failure.[18] The remainder of this paper will, therefore, be concerned with the successful, the happy few, the fifty-five individuals canonized between 1588, when the practice was revived, and 1767, which was followed by another hiatus, this time of forty years.[19]

---

13   R. Wittkower, *Art and Architecture in Italy 1600–1750* (Harmondsworth, 1958), p. 61; J. R. Martin, *The Ceiling Paintings for the Jesuit Church in Antwerp* (London and New York, 1968), pp. 29ff. I should like to thank David Freedberg for bringing the point about Rubens to my attention.

14   A. Niero, "I santi padroni," in S. Tramontin et al., *Culto dei santi a Venezia* (Venice, 1965), pp. 77–95.

15   B. Bennassar et al., *L'Inquisition espagnole* (Paris, 1979), p. 200, cf. pp. 208–9 and also W. Christian, *Local Religion in Sixteenth-Century Spain* (Princeton, NJ, 1981), p. 133.

16   Details and references in Peter Burke, "The Virgin of the Carmine and the Revolt of Masaniello," *Past and Present* 99 (1983); 3–21.

17   G. Gigli, *Diario romano* (1608–70), ed. G. Ricciotti (Rome, 1958) p. 311.

18   An exception: L. Ciamitti, "Una santa di meno," *Quaderni Storici*, vol. XLI (1979). In the same issue J. M. Sallmann, "Il santo e le rappresentazioni di santita," notes the existence of about a hundred unsuccessful candidates in the Kingdom of Naples between 1550 and 1800.

19   For a full list from 1594 on, see Löw, "Canonizazzione," cited n. 7 above.

II

That the prosopography of the saints might be of value for an understanding of Catholic society is no new idea. A number of historians and sociologists have studied the changing social origins and career patterns of the saints as indicators – or even indices – of social and cultural trends.[20] They have pointed out the rise of martyrs in the sixteenth century and the rise of the middle class into sanctity in the eighteenth and nineteenth centuries.[21]

However, these historians and sociologists have not always been sufficiently conscious of a central problem of method, of the need to decide whether to treat the saints as witnesses to the values of the age in which they lived or the age in which they were canonized. In some cases, like those already mentioned of Carlo Borromeo and Filippo Neri, the problem is not acute, because they were canonized so quickly. On the other hand, several Counter-Reformation figures, now venerated as saints, received this title long after their deaths. John Berchmans, for example, died in 1621 and was canonized in 1888, while Peter Canisius died in 1597 but was not canonized until 1925. It is true that biographies of Canisius were published in 1614 and 1616 and that his beatification process lasted over 250 years, but if he is to be included as a Counter-Reformation saint, so should all those whose processes began in the period. They may, after all, be canonized one day. Conversely, among the saints canonized 1588–1767 were eight who died in the fifteenth century, six who died in the fourteenth century, four who died in the thirteenth century and one who died in the twelfth century.

Most students of the saints have assumed that they are witnesses to the age in which they lived. For a historian of mentalities, however, they have to be treated as witnesses to the age in which they were canonized; there is no other justification for confining oneself to this particular for-

20    G. G. Coulton, *The Medieval Village* (Cambridge, 1925), appendix 32; P. A. Sorokin, *Altruistic Love* (Boston, Mass., 1950), pt 2; K. George and C. H. George, "Roman Catholic Sainthood and Social Status," *Journal of Religion*, vol. V (1953–4), reprinted in R. Bendix and S. M. Lipset (eds), *Class Status and Power*, 2nd edn (Glencoe, Ill., 1967), pp. 394–401; P. Delooz, *Sociologie et canonisations* (Liège and The Hague, 1969); D. Weinstein and R. M. Bell, "Saints and Society," *Memorie Domenicane* (1973); M. Goodich, "A Profile of Thirteenth-Century Sainthood," *Comparative Studies in Society and History*, vol. XVIII (1976), pp. 429–37; Vauchez, *La Sainteté en occident*; W. O. Chadwick, *The Popes and European Revolution* (Oxford, 1981), pp. 81ff. This essay was in proof before I was able to consult D. Weinstein and R. M. Bell, *Saints and Society* (Chicago and London, 1982) and S. Wilson (ed.), *Saints and their Cult* (Cambridge, 1983).

21    These points are made by Sorokin and George.

mally defined group.[22] It might also be worth looking at saints who were, one might say, "reactivated" in the period, but since the criteria for reactivation are not likely to be precise, it may be more useful , in this brief sketch, to concentrate on the newly canonized alone, with the fifty-five saints formally canonized between 1588 and 1767. It might have been worth adding the formally beatified, of which there were forty-three between 1662 and 1767 (twenty-four individuals and the collective beatification of the nineteen martyrs of Gorkum).[23] However, sixteen of the individual *beati* were canonized later in our period, so the addition of this group would not affect the conclusions very much.

Since the total "population" of the saints is so much less than one hundred, precise statistics will be of little use, let alone percentages. In any case, too much emphasis has been placed on "objective" factors such as social origins and career patterns. As the Belgian sociologist Pierre Delooz has remarked, the saints have to be studied as part of the social history of perception. The objective factors will, therefore, be discussed only briefly here.

What kind of person had the best chance, during the Counter-Reformation, of achieving this particular form of upward mobility? Men had better chances than women: there were forty-three males to twelve females in the group. Italians (twenty-six saints) and Spaniards (seventeen) had better chances than anyone else (twelve altogether, comprising four French, three Poles, two Portuguese, one German, one Czech and one Peruvian). Nobles had better chances of becoming saints than commoners. At least twenty-six of the fifty-five saints were of noble origin, including some from leading families like the Borjas and the Gonzagas, while Elizabeth of Portugal was of royal blood. There is little or no precise information about the social origins of a number of the saints, but at least five were of peasant stock, while two more worked for a time as shepherds (Pascual Baylón and John of God) and one as a ploughman (Isidore). As for the "middle classes," we know at least that John of the Cross was the son of a silk-weaver, Jean-François Régis the son of a merchant and Filippo Neri the son of a lawyer.

To have a good chance of becoming a saint it was better to be clerical than lay, and much better to be a member of a religious order than one of the secular clergy. Of our fifty-five individuals, only six were members of the laity (Isidore the ploughman, John of God, Francesca Ponziani, Elizabeth (Isabel) of Portugal, Caterina of Genoa and Margherita of Cortona), and of these, Margherita of Cortona was a

---

22  See Delooz (or his contribution in Wilson, ch. 6) and Weinstein and Bell, *Saints and Society*, pt 2.
23  *Enciclopedia Cattolica*, s.v. "Beatificazione."

member of the "third order" of Franciscans, while John of God is asso-ciated with the Brothers Hospitallers and Francesca Ponziani with the Benedictines. Three of the fifty-five were lay brothers, on the margin between the lay and clerical worlds: Pascual Baylón, Felice of Cantalice and Serafino of Montegranaro. The secular clergy account for another eight of the fifty-five, making seventeen altogether who were not full members of religious orders.

Of the thirty-eight remaining saints, the Franciscans have the largest share, with one nun (Caterina of Bologna) and seven friars (Diego of Alcalá, Pedro of Alcántara, Giovanni Capistrano, Giacomo della Marca, Francisco Solano, Pedro Regalado and Giuseppe of Copertino). Close behind came the Dominicans and the Jesuits. The Dominicans had three nuns (Rose of Lima, Agnese Segni and Caterina de'Ricci), and four friars (Hyacinth [Jacek], Raimondo Peñaforte, Luis Bertrán and Michele Ghislieri, better known as Pope Pius V). There were six Jesuits canonized in the period: Ignatius Loyola, Francis Xavier, Francisco Borja, Aloysius (Luigi) Gonzaga, Stanislas Kostka and Jean-François Régis. Then came the Carmelites, with two nuns (Teresa of Avila and Maria Maddalena de'Pazzi) and two friars (Andrea Corsini and John of the Cross). The Servites had three saints: a nun, Giuliana Falconieri, and two friars, Filippo Benizzi and Pellegrino Laziosi. The capuchins had two saints, Fidelis of Sigmaringen and Giuseppe of Leonessa, not counting their two lay brothers, Felice and Serafino. The Theatines had two saints, Gaetano of Thiene and Andrea Avellino. There was one Benedictine (Juan of Sahagún), one Augustinian (Tomaso of Villanueva) and four saints who founded their own orders (Camillo de Lelis, Jeanne de Chantal, José de Calasanz and Girolamo Miani).

It is obvious enough that these fifty-five men and women were not a random sample of the Catholic population at large. However, the ques-tion remains, why these particular individuals achieved recognition rather than the many people of similar social background. It is not sufficient to say that they possessed "heroic virtue": it is also necessary to discover who saw them as virtuous. There are two places to look for the answer to this question: at the grass roots, where a particular cult grew up, and at the center, where it was made official.

To begin with the periphery. Delooz was surely right to view the problem of the saints as essentially one of collective representations, or the social history of perception. Some societies are, as he put it, "pro-grammed" to perceive sanctity, while others are not.[24] Italy and Spain were clearly programmed in this way. Saints were also perceived in stereotyped ways: there is a relatively small number of saintly roles, or

24  Delooz, *Sociologie et canonisations*, p. 179.

routes to sanctity. It may be useful to draw up a typology and distinguish five main routes or roles.

The first is that of the founder of a religious order. No fewer than twelve out of our fifty-five fall into this class. Francesca Ponziani founded the Benedictine Oblates; Teresa of Avila the strict ("discalced") Carmelite; Ignatius Loyola founded the Jesuits. François de Sales and Jeanne de Chantal between them founded the Visitation nuns. Gaetano of Thiene was one of the founders of the Theatines. Vincent de Paul founded both the Congregation of the Mission and the Daughters of Charity. Camillo de Lelis founded the Camilliani, Girolamo Miani the Somaschi and José de Calasanz the Piarists. Filippo Neri is now regarded as the founder of the Oratorians, although he did not have a formal institution in mind, and, in a similar way, John of God may be described as the "posthumous founder" of the Brothers Hospitallers.

A second important road to sanctity was that of the missionary. Nine of our fifty-five fall into this class, if we include an organizer of missions, Tomaso of Villanueva. Diego of Alcalá was a missionary in the Canaries; Raimondo Peñaforte in North Africa; Francis Xavier in the Far East. Luis Bertrán and Francisco Solano both worked in Spanish America, in modern Colombia and in Peru respectively. Jean-François Régis tried to convert the Huguenots of the Cévennes, while Fidelis of Sigmaringen met his death on a mission to the Swiss. Giuseppe of Leonessa worked in Italy as well as outside Europe.

A third route to sanctity was that of charitable activity. There are seven obvious cases in the fifty-five, three women (Elizabeth of Portugal, Margherita of Cortona, Caterina of Genoa) and four men. Vincent de Paul's work among the galley-slaves is famous, and there was also John of God who worked among the sick in Granada; Camillo de Lelis; and José de Calasanz who set up schools for the poor.

A fourth route was that of the pastor, the good shepherd, with seven cases, of which the most famous is surely that of the model bishop of the Counter-Reformation, Carlo Borromeo, with François de Sales, Bishop of "Geneva" (actually based at Annecy), close behind. The others are Pope Pius V; Turibio, Archbishop of Lima; Patriarch Lorenzo Giustinian; Jan Nepomuk, said to have been murdered for refusing to divulge the secrets of confession; and Tomaso of Villanueva, Archbishop of Valencia, who overlaps with the missionary group.

The fifty and last main route was that of the mystic or ecstatic, subject to trances, levitation, and so on. Again there are seven obvious cases, four women and three men. The women were Teresa of Avila (another overlap), Rose of Lima, Maria Maddalena de'Pazzi and Caterina de'Ricci, while the men were John of the Cross, Pedro Regalado and Giuseppe of Copertino. There were, of course, saints who did not fit any of these categories very well. Aloysius Gonzaga and Stanislas Kostka, for example, who were both Jesuit novices who lived ascetic lives and died young. Jan Kanty was a professor at Cracow. However, the five roles which have just been described seem the most important by far, although some omissions may seem surprising. These Counter-Reformation saints include no theologians, no equivalent of Thomas Aquinas (although Nicholas of Cusa was proposed for canonization). Equally surprising is the relative lack of martyr-saints, in a period in which many people (some of whom have been canonized subsequently) did die for the Catholic faith, a period which did also reactivate the cult of the martyrs of the early church (encouraged by the discovery of the Roman catacombs at the end of the sixteenth century). Jan Nepomuk and Fidelis of Sigmaringen fall into the martyr category, while the nineteen martyrs of Gorkum, executed by the Calvinists, were beatified in 1675. That other martyrs were unofficially regarded as saints seems likely. A historian of the mission to Japan remarked that "pour obéir au decret du Pape Urbain VIII, je déclare que s'il m'arrive de qualifier de Saints et de Martyrs ceux qui ont souffert la mort dans le Japon, je ne prétends point prévenir le jugement du Saint Siège: mais j'entends par le nom de Saints, des personnes signalées en vertu . . ."[25] Was this a case of reluctant obedience?

The clustering of our fifty-five saints around five roles suggests that a key factor in the imputation of sanctity to an individual is the "fit" between his or her career and the best-known stereotypes of sanctity. The process is, of course, circular or self-confirming. There are few lay saints, for example, because the stereotypes are biased in favour of the clergy and the stereotypes are biased partly because the clergy form the majority of saints. Individuals are matched with roles. They are perceived as similar to individuals who have already been recognized as saints. In some cases, the later saint consciously modelled himself or herself on an earlier figure. Maria Maddalena de'Pazzi and Rose of Lima are both said to have imitated Catherine of Siena, who was canonized in the fifteenth century. Carlo Borromeo is said to have modelled himself on St Ambrose, his great predecessor as Archbishop of Milan.[26] One may suspect that Filippo Neri, renowned for his gaiety and humility, was perceived as another St Francis; Francisco Borja, general of the Jesuits, as another St Ignatius; Ignatius himself as another St Dominic (another Spaniard who founded an order); and Aloysius Gonzaga, famed for his heroic degree of chastity, as another St Alexis. There were, of course,

25  P. Crasset, *Histoire de l'église du Japon* (Paris, 1715), preface.
26  V. Puccini, *Vita di M. M. Pazzi* (Florence, 1611), p. 1; G. B. Possevino, *Discorsi della vita di Carlo Borromeo* (Rome, 1591), p. 121; A. Valier, *Vita del beato Carlo Borromeo* (Milan, 1602), p. 53.

many lesser imitators of the saints. One of the main reasons for having saints, as the church officially saw it, was to provide models with which the faithful could identify.

In the imputation of sanctity, contiguity was important as well as similarity (or as Roman Jakobson would say, metonymy as well as metaphor).[27] The sacred seems to be contagious. At any rate, we find that Francis Xavier, Filippo Neri, Pius V and Felice of Cantalice were all associated with Ignatius Loyola; Felice of Cantalice, Camillo de Lelis, Maria Maddalena de'Pazzi and Caterina de'Ricci with Filippo Neri; Francisco Borja, Pedro of Alcantara and John of the Cross with Teresa of Avila; Andrea Avellino and Aloysius Gonzaga with Carlo Borromeo.[28]

So much for the growth of cults at the periphery. It remains to try to explain how and why certain cults were adopted by the center and made official. The "heroic virtue" of the candidates had to satisfy the examiners. To understand what happened it is not sufficient to study the trials themselves. One needs to remember, for example, that particular popes took a special interest in saint-making – Sixtus V, for example, whose recovery of nerve put the whole process back into motion in 1588; Paul V, who only canonized two saints himself but left five more cases pending, to be completed by Gregory XV; Clement X and Alexander VIII, who canonized five saints apiece; Benedict XIII, who canonized eight in one year; and Benedict XIV, who had written a treatise on the subject.[29] Papal interests also help to explain particular choices. Only one pope, Clement XI, canonized another, Pius V; but regional loyalties were extremely strong. The Roman Paul V canonized the Roman Francesca Ponziani. The Florentine Urban VIII canonized one Florentine, Andrea Corsini, and beatified another, Maria Maddalena de'Pazzi. The Venetian Alexander VIII canonized the Venetian Lorenzo Giustinian. Another Venetian, Clement XIII, canonized one Venetian, Girolamo Miani, and beatified another, Gregorio Barbarigo (who, like the pope, had been Bishop of Padua). In one case a process like the "old school tie" loyalty seems to have been at work: Benedict XIV, an old pupil of the Somaschi, beatified the order's founder, Girolamo Miani. And Alexander VII, in spite of the fifty-year rule, canonized his old friend François de Sales.

The center did not simply select from candidates presented by the periphery, but sometimes yielded to pressure. The religious orders were powerful pressure-groups and the high proportion of saints from their

27  R. Jakobson, "Two aspects of language," reprinted in his *Selected Writings*, vol. II (The Hague and Paris, 1971), pp. 239–59.
28  Some of these associations are pointed out by De Maio, " 'L' ideale eroico," cited n. 10 above.
29  See Pastor, *Geschichte der Päpste*.

ranks has surely to be explained in these terms, among others.[30] Robert Bellarmine, for example, who was strategically placed at Rome, is said to have been responsible for the beatification of his fellow Jesuit, Ignatius. There were also pressures from rulers. If there was a "Spanish preponderance" in the field of sanctity as in that of international relations, the two phenomena may not be unconnected. The first Counter-Reformation saint, Diego of Alcalà, was canonized following pressure from Philip II. Philip III pressed for Raimondo Peñaforte, Isidore and Carlo Borromeo. The bull canonizing Ignatius refers to requests from both Philip II and Philip III.[31] Sigismund of Poland pressed successfully for the canonization of Hyacinth and Louis XIII for Caterina of Genoa. Henri IV, Ferdinand II and Maximilian of Bavaria were other rulers who tried to exert pressure on behalf of particular candidates. As for Andrea Corsini, his case was urged by an alliance of his order, the Carmelites, the ruler of the region he came from, Tuscany, and his family.[32] For family pressure must not be forgotten: It was to the advantage of Carlo Borromeo that he had his nephew and successor, Federigo, to plead for him. Foreign visitors to Italy, including Burnet and Montesquieu, picked up gossip about Italian noble families paying large sums to have relatives canonized. 100,000 crowns was a figure quoted for Carlo Borromeo and 180,000 crowns for Andrea Corsini.[33]

Such stories do not have to be taken too literally. Suffice it to say, pending further research, that it is impossible to explain the achievement of sanctity entirely in terms of the qualities of the individual, or even by the qualities which the witnesses saw in each individual. The imputation of sainthood, like its converse, the imputation of heresy or witchcraft, should be seen as a process of interaction or "negotiation" between center and periphery, each with its own definition of the situation.[34] This process involved the official management of unofficial cults, which were, like religious visions, sometimes confirmed and sometimes suppressed.[35] It also involved the implantation of official cults in parts of the periphery other than the region where they first sprang up. The cults of Ignatius Loyola and Francis Xavier, for example, seem to have become part of German Catholic popular culture in the course of the seventeenth and eighteenth centuries, a process which involved their

30   Bertelli, *Ribelli*, p. 118. On orders as pressure groups in the late Middle Ages, Vauchez, *La Sainteté en occident*, pp. 131ff.
31   F. Contelorus, *De canonizatione sanctorum* (Lyons, 1634), pp. 789ff.
32   S. di S. Silverio, *Vita di S. Andrea Corsini* (Florence, 1683), pp. 54ff.
33   G. Burnet, *Some Letters* (Amsterdam, 1686), p. 106.
34   On "negotiation," F. Parkin, *Class Inequality and Political Order* (London, 1971), p. 92; R. Q. Gray, *The Labour Aristocracy of Victorian Edinburgh* (Oxford, 1976), ch. 7.
35   W. Christian, *Apparitions in Late Medieval Spain* (Princeton, NJ, 1981).

"folklorization" or assimilation to earlier local cults. Thus curative properties were now assigned to "Ignatius water."[36]

This process of negotiation deserves further study. Enough has been said here, perhaps, to suggest that saints are indeed cultural indicators, a sort of historical litmus paper sensitive to connections between religion and society.

## Acknowledgment

I would like to thank the audiences to whom drafts of this paper were read in Cambridge, Warwick and Wolfenbüttel for a number of helpful comments.

36   On "Ignatius water," *Handwörterbuch des deutschen Aberglaubens*, Vol. IV (Berlin and Leipzig, 1931–2), p. 671. I should like to thank Bob Scribner for drawing my attention to this phenomenon. I have not been able to consult A. Schüller, "Sankt Franciscus Xavier im Volksglauben," *Zeitschrift des Vereins für Rheinische Volkskunde* (1931), or H. Schauerte, *Die Volkstümliche Heiligenverehrung* (Münster, 1948).

# 7

# Little Women: Counter-Reformation Misogyny

*Alison Weber*

Originally appeared as Weber, Alison, "Little Women: Counter-Reformation Misogyny," in her *Teresa of Avila and the Rhetoric of Femininity* (Princeton: Princeton University Press, 1990), 17–41.

## Editor's Introduction

In this selection, Alison Weber analyzes the changing attitudes of church authorities toward Saint Teresa of Ávila (1515–84), the Spanish ecstatic visionary and reformer of her Carmelite religious order. Weber reveals a profound shift in sensibilities concerning the relationship between gender and spirituality after the late fifteenth century. At that time, Catholic reformers such as the powerful grand inquisitor, Cardinal Francisco Ximénez de Cisneros, rejected the old doctrine that women were intellectually inferior and therefore unqualified to speak or teach on matters of faith. After Cisneros' death in 1517 – well before the Council of Trent – misogynistic anxieties about female piety revived. Weber traces the change in intellectual climate through the language church officials used to describe Teresa, first as a "little woman" (*mujercilla*), later as a kind of de-sexualized she-man. The consolidation of Counter-Reformation misogyny put Teresa on the defensive: Only by embracing stereotypes of the weak and imbecilic "little woman" was she able to defend herself against charges of heresy. Teresa's "rhetoric of femininity," as Weber calls it, was therefore double-edged. On the one hand, it reinforced dominant, male ideologies of female inferiority; but Teresa was also able to use the language of feminine inferiority to defend her own spiritual authority and her reformist activism – the very things that gender stereotypes did not allow. True, the Counter-Reformation made official Catholicism more masculine; but Teresa's rhetoric also exposed the vulnerability of Counter-Reformation misogyny to creative manipulation, even in the increasingly intolerant culture of sixteenth-century Spain.

# Little Women: Counter-Reformation Misogyny

*Alison Weber*

"A virile woman," "a manly soul," "She endured all conflicts with manly courage."[1] These are some of the most reiterated encomiastic expressions to appear in the documents related to Teresa's beatification and canonization. Teresa as a "virile woman" was the central conceit in many of the poems produced for contests in her honor: "You well deserve this name, because your deeds are not those of woman but of glorious man. . . . A Sage said (since it seemed impossible) that to find a strong woman, one must search to the ends of the world. Therefore it is appropriate that you were found among us, oh rare and divine miracle, since Spain was always thought to be at the end of the world."[2] When Teresa was proclaimed co-patron saint of Spain, a Carmelite friar declared in a celebratory sermon that she had succeeded in transcending the congenital inferiority of her sex altogether: "This woman ceased to be a woman, restoring herself to the virile state to her greater glory than if she had been a man from the beginning, for she rectified nature's error with her virtue, transforming herself through virtue into the bone [i.e., Adam's rib] from which she sprang."[3] A 1614 text describes

---

1  *Procesos de beatificación y canonización de Santa Teresa de Jesús*, ed. Silverio de Santa Teresa, vols 18–20 of Biblioteca mística carmelitana (Burgos: Tipografía de "El Monte Carmelo," 1934–5), 20: xiii, xxii, xlii. Many other examples could be cited.

2  Diego de San José, *Compendio de las solenes fiestas que en toda España se hicieron en la Beatificación de N. B. M. Teresa de Jesús Fundadora de la Reformación de Descalzos y Descalzos de N. S. de Carmen* (Madrid: Viuda de Alonso Martín, 1615), 11v–12v. With almost identical phrases a Dominican preacher wrote: "If Solomon sought a strong, courageous and virtuous woman in his age, and could not find a single one, blessed is our age which has seen one of the most courageous and virile women that the Church has ever had" (cited in Félix G. Olmedo, "Santa Teresa de Jesús y los predicadores del siglo de oro," *Boletín de la Real Academia de la Historia* 84 [1924]: 165–75 and 280–95; quotation p. 170).

3  Fray Francisco de Jesús, in *Relación sencilla y fiel de las Fiestas que el rey D. Felipe IIII nuestro Señor hizo . . .* (Facticio volume: Vatican Library, 1627), cited in Francis Cerdan, "Santa Teresa en *Los sermones del patronato*" (1627), in *Santa Teresa y la literatura mística hispánica*, ed. Manuel Criado de Val (Madrid: EDI–6, 1984), pp. 601–8; quotation p. 606. Also see Francisco López Estrada, "Cohetes para Teresa: La relación de 1627 sobre las Fiestas de Madrid par el Patronato de España de Santa Teresa de Jesús y la polémica sobre el mismo," in *Congreso internacional Teresiano 4–7 octubre, 1982*, ed. Teófanes Egido Martínez et al. (Salamanca: Universidad de Salamanca, 1983), 2: 637–81, esp. 654–5.

a hieroglyph depicting Teresa with walls in the middle of her body and towers growing out of her breasts. The accompanying Latin inscription reads: "Ego murus et ubera mea sicut turris" "I am a wall and my breasts are like towers." Saints Elijah and Elisha float above her on a cloud, proclaiming "Soror nostra parvula, ubera non habet" "Our little sister does not have breasts."[4]

It is understandable that a misogynist society would need to engage in this kind of linguistic (and pictorial) gender reassignment in order to designate a woman as virtuous. (The etymological correlation between virtue and masculinity needs no elaboration.) But it is remarkable that Teresa should have been the object of this transformation, since she had so often during her lifetime endured and embraced the derogatory epithet of *mujercilla* or "little woman."

## Women and Pauline Silence

Teresa was considered a *mujercilla* because, among other things, she "taught others, against the commands of St. Paul."[5] That is, she engaged in theological discourse at a time when this was a proscribed activity for women. Paul's justification for the exclusion of women from an apostolic role bears repeating: "Let your women keep silence in the churches: for it is not permitted unto them to speak; but they are commanded to be under obedience, as also saith the law. And if they will learn any thing, let them ask their husbands at home: for it is a shame for women to speak in the church" (1 Cor. 14:34–37). The position against women is even more restricted in the pastoral Epistles, written near the end of the first century AD: "Let the woman learn in silence with all subjection. But I suffer not a woman to teach, nor to usurp authority over the man, but to be in silence. For Adam was first formed, then Eve. And Adam was not deceived, but the woman being deceived was in the transgression" (1 Tim. 2:11–14).

The early Church fathers believed that women's intellectual inferiority and sensuality make them especially susceptible to deception by false prophets: "For [false prophets] are they which creep into houses, and lead captive silly women laden with sins, led away with divers lusts, ever learning, and never able to come to the knowledge of the truth" (2 Tim. 3:6–7).[6] John Gerson's (d. 1429) words are representative of a particularly rigid interpretation of these biblical passages:

4   Diego de San José, *Compendio*, 73r.
5   This was the pronouncement of Papal Nuncio Felipe Sega.
6   For the historical background on women in early Church history see Constance F. Parvey, "The Theology and Leadership of Women in the New Testament," in *Reli-*

The female sex is forbidden on apostolic authority to teach in public, that is either by word or by writing. . . . All women's teaching, particularly formal teaching by word and writing, is to be held suspect unless it has been diligently examined, and much more fully than men's. The reason is clear: common law – and not any kind of common law, but that which comes from on high – forbids them. And why? Because they are easily seduced and determined seducers; and because it is not proved that they are witnesses to divine grace.[7]

The belief in feminine spiritual inadequacy is perhaps best summarized in Kramer and Sprenger's 1486 handbook on witchcraft, *Malleus Malleficarum*. According to the fantastic etymology proposed by these authors, *femina* is derived from *fe minus* – lacking in faith.

Nevertheless, at various times in Church history women have been permitted to express their religious experience in writing. Thomistic theology, while essentially androcentric, did concede the possibility of a prophetic role for women.[8] The explosion of female piety in the late medieval Church is recorded in the visions of women mystics such as Julian of Norwich, Mechtild of Magdeburg, and Catherine of Siena. Such literature was not only a socially sanctioned activity for women;[9] as Caroline Bynum has argued, women's visionary writings propagated new forms of late medieval Christian piety and created a religious language inspired by uniquely female experiences.[10]

## Mulierculae and the Pre-Reformation

At the beginning of the sixteenth century Christian humanists began to reject explicitly the idea of the spiritual inferiority of women and to advocate expanded religious education for them. In the *Paraclesis* or *Exhorta-*

gion and Sexism, ed. Rosemary Ruether (New York: Simon and Schuster, 1974), pp. 117–49. Parvey notes that the later pastoral Epistles reflect a heightened concern over the influence of Gnostic teachers and ecstatic sects among women (p. 136).

7   *De examinatione doctrinam*, pt. 1, cited in Edmund Colledge and James Walsh, eds, *Book of Showings* by Julian of Norwich, 2 vols. (Toronto: Pontifical Institute of Mediaeval Studies, 1978), 1: 151.

8   Eleanor Commo McLaughlin, "Equality of Souls, Inequality of Sexes: Women in Medieval Theology," in *Religion and Sexism*, ed. Rosemary Ruether (New York: Simon and Schuster, 1974), pp. 213–66; quotation p. 236.

9   "Visions were a socially sanctioned activity that freed a woman from conventional female roles by identifying her as a genuine religious figure. They brought her to the attention of others, giving her a public language she could use to teach and learn" (Elizabeth Petroff, *Medieval Women's Visionary Literature* [New York: Oxford, 1986], p. 6).

10   Bynum, *Jesus as Mother: Studies in the Spirituality of the High Middle Ages* (Berkeley: University of California Press, 1982).

*tion to Diligent Study of Scripture* (1516). Erasmus exhorted all Christians – including women – to study the "philosophy of Christ," declaring that specialized learning was not necessary to approach the Scriptures: "But this delectable doctrine doth apply herself equally to all men submitting herself unto us while we are children tempering her tune after our capacity, feeding us with milk. She refuseth no age, no kind, [whether man or woman] no fortune no state and consideration."[11] Jesus did not want his teachings to remain secret but to be widespread, Erasmus argued. Accordingly, the Scriptures should be translated into the vernacular to make them accessible to all: "I would desire all women [*mulierculae*] should read the gospels and Paul's Espistles, and I would to God they were translated into the tongues of all men." Erasmus' defense of the rights of women to study the Scriptures is reflected in his vindication of the diminutive *mulierculae*: in the *Exhortation mulierculae* are not Pauline "silly women" but simple, unlettered women.

This movement of evangelical democratization, transcending gender and class barriers, flourished in early sixteenth-century Spain during the ascendancy of Cardinal Ximénez Cisneros. Under his tutelage portions of the Scriptures and numerous devotional and mystical works were translated into Spanish and distributed to convents and monasteries. The accessibility of works of St. Catherine of Siena, Saint Claire, Saint Juana de Orvieto, Gerson, and St. John Climaco in the vernacular meant that many more women were inspired to participate in the wave of renewed evangelism. Furthermore, the cardinal, a former confessor to Queen Isabel, was an enthusiastic supporter of female piety. Many of his monastic reforms were directed specifically toward improving the religious life of nuns and women tertiaries. During the years of his ascendancy women were granted a greater role in the educational and administrative life of convents. He was, to the dismay of some of his biographers, a devotee and defender of women visionaries who flourished as a result of his reforms.

### The Alumbradas and the Beginnings of Reaction

Although Cisneros had opened up the Church to women and laity, the later years of his reformation witnessed another religious phenomenon

---

11    For Erasmus' Latin text I have used the edition by Werner Welzig in vol. 3 of *Ausgewahlte Schriften* (Darmstadt: Wissenschaftliche Buchgesellschaft, 1968). I have modernized the spelling of the anonymous English translation of 1529 (facsimile reprint, Amsterdam: Theatrum Orbis Terrarum, 1973). Dámaso Alonso has edited and reprinted the 1555 Spanish translation of *La Paráclesis o exhortación al estudio de las letras divinas* along with the *Enchiridion* (Madrid: Centro Superior de Investigaciones Científicas, 1971).

that was to have a profoundly negative impact on women's relationship to the Church in general and on the life of Teresa de Jesús in particular. Groups of men and women, laity and religious, began to meet in private homes to read and comment on the Scriptures. Although the groups did not share a unified doctrine, they held the common belief that the individual was capable of understanding the Scripture when inspired or "illumined" by the Holy Spirit. This is the assumed origin of the derogatory appellation *alumbrados* or Illuminists. There are two distinguishing sociological features of Spanish Illuminism. First of all, many of its adherents were *conversos*. The direct influence from Jewish theology is not at issue; rather, as neophyte Christians, subjected to ever increasing racial discrimination, they may have been especially attracted to a nonceremonial form of Christianity centered on a loving and forgiving God.[12] A second sociological anomaly is that women held major leadership roles in these circles. Isabel de la Cruz was recognized as the "true mother and teacher" of the Toledo *alumbrados*; María de Cazalla preached the Gospel to women in her home in Guadalajara; and Francisca Hernández exercised enormous influence over Franciscan preachers in Valladolid. It is difficult to determine why women should have played such dominant roles in Spanish Illuminism. We can only speculate that the translation of the Scriptures into the vernacular, together with the general receptivity of the Cisneros period to an anti-scholastic Christianity, afforded women domestic evangelical roles for which they could find precedent in the history of the primitive Church.

As Marcel Bataillon has shown, this movement of interior Christianity initially arose independently from Protestantism, although it sprang from common European roots of spiritual unrest. Later it easily incorporated analogous Erasmian ideas, which began to penetrate Spain with Erasmus' vernacular translations in the early 1520s. But a confluence of events – the death of Cisneros in 1517 and the beginnings of Luther's rebellion in the same year, the growing suspicion of Erasmian anticlericalism, and the intensification of anti-*converso* racism – moved the Inquisition to repress what it could only define as a native protestantism in the making.[13]

12   See Angela Selke, "El iluminismo de los conversos y la Inquisición. Cristianismo interior de los alumbrados: Resentimiento y sublimación," in *La Inquisición española: Nueva visión, nuevos horizontes* ed. Joaquín Pérez Villanueva (Madrid: Siglo veintiuno, 1980), pp. 617–36. For speculation on why *conversos* were attracted to heterodox movements also see Antonio Domínguez Ortiz, *Los Judeoconversos en España y América* (Madrid: Istmo, 1971), pp. 159–60.
13   The best introduction to the spiritual history of sixteenth-century Spain is Marcel Bataillon's authoritative *Erasmo y España*, trans. Antonio Alatorre, 2nd rev. edn. (1966; reprint ed., Mexico: Fondo de cultura económica, 1982). His thesis that Spanish Illuminism reveals common roots with but little direct influence from

In 1525 the Inquisition published an edict against the *alumbrados*, an attempt at codification of their doctrine based on the trials of its main teachers. As far as can be determined from the edict, the *alumbrados'* heresy was one of protestantism *sensu latu*: they denied the necessity of any sacramental intermediary between God and man and thus rejected the efficacy of external works as well as the authority of the Church to interpret Scripture.[14] What the doctrine of *dejamiento* meant to the *alumbrados* is still not entirely clear. The term appears to refer to a direct experience of God, achieved through a form of mental prayer that emptied the mind of thoughts. In the state of *dejamiento* the advanced adepts could surrender themselves to God's will, with the assurance that they would not be led into sin. The Inquisition considered two equally heretical implications: justification by faith alone and impeccability or the belief that once united with God a person could not sin. The 1525 Edict did not identify Illuminism as an orgiastic sect, but their supposed doc…ne of impeccability, together with the free association between men and women in small groups, were seen as dangers to public morality.[15] In short, the fear of Protestantism nourished by anti-Semitism transformed a tiny sect of evangelicals, in the Inquisition's eyes, into a threatening band of heretics. The prominence of women in such dangerous sects provided the justification for reaffirming traditional ecclesiastical misogyny.

The Counter-Reformation's increased skepticism toward female spirituality and its eagerness to reinforce male hierarchical authority is broadly reflected in the decline in the percentage of female saints from 27.7 percent in the fifteenth century to 18.1 percent in the six-

Lutheranism has not been seriously challenged since first formulated in 1937. Antonio Márquez, *Los alumbrados: Orígenes y filosofía, 1525–1559*, 2nd rev. edn. (Madrid: Taurus, 1980), gives the best overview of the early *alumbrado* movement and reproduces the 1525 Edict and summaries of the trial of Alcaraz.

14   Unlike Bataillon, who considered Illuminism to be a "movement" of interior Christianity akin to Erasmism, Antonio Márquez insists that the Toledo *alumbrados* constituted a native, heretical protestant sect, with justification *sola fe* and *sola scriptura* as basic doctrine (*Los alumbrados*, pp. 219–21).

15   Isabel de la Cruz and Alcaraz were never accused of sexual impropriety. However, Francisca Hernández' relationships with her male cohorts were condemned as licentious. Charges of illicit erotic relationships between beatas and their confessors did figure prominently in Inquisitorial trials in Extremadura in the 1570s. The Inquisition considered this movement Illuminist, although there is no evidence of direct link between the Toledo Illuminists of the 1520s and this later manifestation, which was essentially thaumaturgical rather than evangelical. On the Extremadura Illuminists see Bernardino Llorca, *La Inquisición española y los alumbrados (1509–1667)* (Salamanca: Universidad Pontificia, 1980), and Alvaro Huerga, *Historia de los alumbrados (1570–1630)*, vol. 1, *Los alumbrados de Extremadura* (Madrid: Fundación universitaria española, 1978).

teenth.[16] However, the rapidity in the change of climate can also be appreciated by comparing the fates of women religious figures during the Cisneros period and its immediate aftermath. The enthusiastic sanction of a female ecstatic in the first decade of the century contrasts sharply with the persecution of the *alumbradas* only fourteen years later.

The life of María de Santo Domingo, the Beata or Holy Woman of Piedrahíta, in many ways exemplifies the favored role of women ecstatics during the Cisneros period. Born of peasant stock in 1486, María never learned to read or write. Around 1507 she began to acquire a reputation for saintliness because of her mortifications, trances, and gift of prophecy. Although she was a tertiary or lay sister, she became so influential in the Dominican order that she was entrusted with reforming the convents and monasteries in the area around Toledo. Her raptures at court won her the support of the Duke of Alba, who endowed a convent for her. Cisneros was one of her devoted admirers – he even gave her a rope belt of St. Francis and solicited her prayers.

In 1508, at the height of her fame, the Pope sent his own envoys to investigate the authenticity of her reported visions and ecstasies. Fortunately she could count on the active support of Cardinal Cisneros, who considered her the embodiment of "living Christian doctrine."[17] After two years of investigation the papal envoys not only declared her innocent of wrongdoing but also issued an edict proclaiming the miraculous nature of her raptures, visions, extended fasts, stigmata, and prophecies.[18] One of the marvels adduced in the 1510 Edict was María's ability to answer profound questions on theology and the Scriptures while she was in a trance: "Those who have seen and heard her agree that it is indeed marvelous that a poor ignorant woman [*mujercilla ignorante*] like Sor María, born and raised in a village should be able to answer such questions as well as and sometimes even better than any master of Theology or man of science."[19] One witness quoted the opinion of a professor of theology at the University of Valladolid: "He could not help but weep greatly upon hearing the marvelous answers

16 Donald Weinstein and Rudolph Bell, *Saints and Society: The Two Worlds of Western Christendom, 1000–1700* (Chicago: University of Chicago Press, 1982), pp. 220–1,225.

17 Cited by Vicente Beltrán de Heredia, *Historia de la reforma de la provincia de España (1450–1550)* (Rome: Institutum Historicum FF. Praedicatorum, 1939), p. 82.

18 For the history of Sor María, see ibid. and Llorca, *Inquisición*, pp. 37–64. He reproduces the edict in her defense in appendix I, pp. 259–71.

19 Llorca, *Inquisición*, p. 260.

that Sor María gave to his questions; and he told me, because we were very close, that he did not know why men bothered to learn anything other than to serve God, since that little woman [*mujercilla*], who had been instructed by the Holy Spirit, knew more than all the learned men of the Realm."[20] Here the diminutive *mujercilla* has the same positive connotation we saw in Erasmus' *Exhortation*: in the eyes of Cisneros and his followers a woman's humble ignorance was no obstacle to spiritual knowledge – ignorance could even give a woman the moral advantage.[21]

This willingness to concede interpretive and even vatic powers to an unlettered woman would be inconceivable just fourteen years later. In the 1524 trials against the Toledo *alumbrados* the Inquisition pronounced such apostolic activity by women "*atrevimieto*" – an act of effrontery. The woman leader of this group, Isabel de la Cruz, was accused of numerous breaches of magisterial authority: she read and taught the Scriptures "according to her own opinion" and encouraged others to do likewise with "simplicity of spirit"; she was said to believe that learned men were incapable of surrendering their will to the love of God.[22] According to several witnesses, "She wanted to teach and not be taught, and she contradicted what learned men said."[23] Her disciple, Alcaraz, gave her more authority to interpret the Bible "than Saint Peter and all the other saints."[24] Her role as principal teacher of the sect earned her the epithet of "mujercilla ignorante y soberbia" "ignorant, proud, little woman."[25] After five years of imprisonment she was induced to confess "that she lacked humility since she was certain that she could not be deceived and hence came all her effrontery in speaking of the Holy Scripture and teaching it to others, . . . and she confesses that she was in error in committing this act of effrontery, since she was an unlearned

20  Beltrán de Heredia, *Historia de la reforma*, p. 107.
21  After Cisneros' death María's activities were severely restricted. Although other political factors were undoubtedly involved in the controversy surrounding this woman, her "vindication" in the 1510 Proceedings indicates the extent to which Cisneros was willing to expand and defend the apostolic role granted to women. For further evidence of Cisneros' support of women visionaries see Ronald E. Surtz, "La madre Juana de la Cruz (1481–1534) y la cuestión de la autoridad religiosa femenina," *Nueva revista de filología hispánica* 33 (1984): 483–91. William A. Christian, Jr., notes that after Cisneros' death in 1517 the Inquisition and the papacy began to examine cases of lay visionaries much more rigorously (*Apparitions in Late Medieval and Renaissance Spain* [Princeton, N.J.: Princeton University Press, 1981], pp. 150–1).
22  Márquez, *Los alumbrados*, pp. 164, 261, 262.
23  Ibid., pp. 280–1.
24  Ibid., p. 101.
25  Ibid.

woman."[26] In a 1529 *auto da fe* Isabel and Alcaraz, their property confiscated, were sentenced to public penance, lashes, and life imprisonment.

The language used to describe feminine theological presumption is even stronger in the trial records of María de Cazalla, a *conversa* and follower of Erasmus, who was denounced to the Inquisition in 1532. One anonymous witness after another testified that she had gone to María's house and heard her read the Epistles in Spanish and that María, while "in the kitchen," had tried to teach things about God "in a way which was not good for women to talk."[27] In the opinion of one prosecutor, "This prisoner holds many arrogant, fatuous, scandalous and suspect propositions, assuming the office of preacher and teacher of doctrine which is conceded only to wise men who have taken Holy orders."[28] The proceedings include such accusations as

> Said María de Cazalla, teacher and dogmatizer of said *alumbrados*, preached to them in public and indoctrinated them, quoting for this purpose sacred authorities and psalms from the Holy Scriptures and declaring this to them in the vernacular, twisting the meaning of the Holy Scriptures and its doctors to her own evil and harmful end, and many persons went to hear her and they listened to her as a preacher, which was scandalous for the people, since she cannot and should not preach, being a woman, and even if she were a man, it would be contrary to apostolic right and precept.

Although she acknowledged she was guilty of presumption for speaking about doctrine, she denied that she intended to teach or held heretical doctrine.[29] After two years of imprisonment she was tortured but made no further confessions. Her sentence was moderate for one accused of heresy – a fine of one hundred gold ducats and public penance in the parish church.[30]

26    J. E. Longhurst, "La Beata Isabel de la Cruz ante la Inquisición, 1524–1529," *Cuadernos de historia de España* 25–26 (1957): 279–303, quotation p. 285. Also see J. C. Nieto, "The Heretical Alumbrados Dexados: Isabel de la Cruz and Pedro Ruiz de Alcaraz," *Revue de littérature comparée* 52 (1978): 293–313.

27    Milagros Ortega-Costa, ed., *Proceso de la Inquisición contra María de Cazalla* (Madrid: Fundación universitaria española, 1978), pp. 259–60.

28    Ibid., p. 32.

29    Ibid., pp. 100, 132.

30    As Bataillon makes clear, María was persecuted for her admitted Erasmian beliefs, redefined by the Inquisition as Lutheranism, at a time when Erasmus' thought had not yet been officially condemned by the Church (*Erasmo*, pp. 209–11, 470–5). The reaction against women's charismatic leadership is reflected in Francisco de Osuna's 1527 work, *Third Spiritual Alphabet*, in which he warns his Franciscan brothers to consult the superiors for spiritual advice rather than "*mujercillas devotas*" who may be deceived (*Tercer abecedario espiritual*, ed. Melquíades Andrés [Madrid: Católica, 1972], p. 567).

## The Consolidation of Counter-Reformation Misogyny

In opposition to the charismatic evangelical freedom championed by Cisneros, and enthusiastically embraced by the *alumbrados*, the Inquisition was moving, in essence, to consolidate the power of a hierarchical mystery religion hermetically controlled by priests. In order to do so it was necessary to ensure that sacred texts were inaccessible to the laity in general but to women in particular, who were deemed to be mentally incapable of understanding the texts and inherently susceptible to diabolical influence. The struggle to regain control over the Scriptures and Christian doctrine, and the effort to exclude women from all but ceremonial forms of Christianity, is most dramatically illustrated by the trial of Carranza, Bishop of Toledo, and the censure of his *Commentaries on the Christian Catechism.*

Bartolomé Carranza de Mendoza at first would appear to have impeccable orthodox credentials. He was twice the Spanish representative at the Council of Trent in 1545 and 1551 and was a prelate favored by Philip II, having distinguished himself in his service during the Catholic Reformation in England. In 1558 Carranza published a Christian catechism in Antwerp that, in many respects, is a prototypical Counter-Reformation treatise. From his preface, "To the pious reader," we can see that his motivation was to produce a book of Christian doctrine that would correct the errors being disseminated by the Lutheran heresy. On the issue of scriptural translation, which had been left unresolved at Trent, his position is cautious: he acknowledges that before Luther the Scriptures were not prohibited in the vernacular. In fact, in Spain Bibles were translated at the order of the Catholic kings. But, he argues, this practice has become dangerous now that Lutherans have taught simple unlettered people to understand the Bible according to individual whim. In Spain the situation has become such that women are declaring the meaning of the Scriptures to men, against the commandment of Saint Paul. The Scriptures are like wine: they are not for the young and inexperienced, but they can be imbibed profitably if they are "watered down" with glosses and commentaries.

The compromise Carranza proposes is that parts of the Scriptures, those that contain advice, precepts, and examples of good behavior, can be read by everyone, men and women. Other parts of the New Testament that are relatively clear can be read provided the translations are not literal and are accompanied by marginal comments. The most obscure passages, like strong wine, must be kept from the laity. But there are some good and devout people, he adds, who are capable of reading even the most difficult portions of the Bible as well and better than those who know Latin and other languages. I don't say this because the sciences that God has communicated to men do not have their place in the Scriptures, but because the Holy Spirit has His disciples and illumines them [*los alumbra*] and gives them help. . . . I have experience of this and can certify that with my advice some people have read the Holy Scriptures and this has helped them live a better life. These included some women, for neither Paula nor Julia Eustoquium, noble Roman women at whose request Saint Jerome translated the Scriptures . . . were more worthy of reading them.

In future, more serene days, Carranza concludes hopefully, the Church will once again be able to distribute freely the "spiritual nourishment" of the Scripture.[31]

Carranza's moderate position of partial, guided access to the Scriptures for men as well as women was roundly attacked by a group of theologians who denounced the *Catechism* to the Inquisition immediately after its publication in 1558. In the following year Inquisitor General Fernando de Valdés not only placed it on the Index but also arrested Carranza, submitting him to imprisonment and a trial that would last nearly seventeen years. When a sentence was finally handed down in 1576, the *Catechism* was condemned, although Carranza himself was not judged a heretic.

The most conservative of the prosecuting theologians, Melchor Cano, found dozens of Illuminist and Lutheran heresies in the *Catechism*. What concerns us here in particular is Cano's articulation of the extreme position of Counter-Reformation misogyny. Cano was adamantly opposed to vernacular translations of the Bible, which he saw as the common denominator of the *alumbrados*, Erasmists, and Lutherans.[32] He repeatedly attacked Carranza for entrusting the Scriptures to women: the divine word is a man's issue, "like arms and money";[33] even if some women should read the Scriptures in Latin, they would inevitably misinterpret them;[34] encouraging women to read the Scriptures with their confessors "in corners" would only result in more Illuminist scandals. He also condemned Carranza's belief that laymen and women could aspire to interior spirituality, arguing that the *Catechism* only urged

31  Carranza, "Al pío letor [*sic*] de este libro," in *Comentarios sobre el Catechismo christiano*, ed. José I. Tellechea Idígoras (Madrid: Católica, 1972), pp. 109–15; quotation p. 115.
32  *Censura de Carranza*, ed. José I. Tellechea Idígoras, vol. 33 of Archivo documental español (Madrid: Real Academia de la Historia, 1981). Annie Fremaux-Crouzet offers a perceptive analysis of Cano's misogyny in relation to his overall philosophy of political repression; see "L'antifeminisme comme theologie du pouvoir chez Melchor Cano," in *Hommage à Louise Bertrand (1921–1979): Etudes ibériques et latino-américaines* (Paris: Les Belles lettres, 1983), pp. 139–86.
33  *Censura de Carranza*, p. 234.
34  Ibid., p. 235.

"ignorant and lazy little men and women" ('mugercillas y hombrecillos ignorantes e ociosos') to disdain oral prayer and the exterior ceremonies of the church,[35] distracted them from their labors, and promoted laziness.[36] Cano's elitist position, so antithetical to Carranza's image of the Scriptures as "spiritual nourishment," resounds ominously in the following categorical statement: "No matter how much women demand this fruit [the Scriptures] with insatiable appetite, it is necessary to forbid it to them, and apply a knife of fire so that the common people cannot get at it."[37] As one Jesuit remarked in a 1559 letter, "These are times when there are those who preach that women should stick to their distaff and rosary, and not worry about other forms of devotion."[38]

Teresa's lifetime spans this period of misogynist retrenchment, which is reflected in the semantic shift of the term *mujercilla*. In the Erasmian context the diminutive is not pejorative but descriptive: *mulierculae* are unlettered women – those who can read in the vernacular but not in Latin, and according to the *Exhortation*, any Christian, with or without Latin, can be a "theologian." In the first decades of sixteenth-century Spanish *mujercilla* was also used to connote unlettered women, as it does in the investigations of the Beata de Piedrahita and in the Spanish translation of the *Exhortation*. However, as the religious climate became more hostile toward women, it took on the decidedly pejorative connotation: "The literal, let alone the spiritual meaning of the Eistles, is difficult for wise men to understand. How much more so for the silly woman [*mujercilla*] who neglects her spinning and has the presumption to read Saint Paul. Holy angels, what a tempest! What business has a silly woman, however pious she may be, reading the Epistles of Saint Paul?"[39] Teresa was born when *mujercilla* could imply spiritual humility, "holy ignorance," evangelical poverty in spirit,[40] but during her adulthood the term came to connote any woman whose spiritual goals were too

35  Ibid., p. 310.
36  Ibid., pp. 353–4.
37  Ibid., p. 238.
38  *Monumenta historica Societatis Iesu* 8 (Madrid, 1896), cited in Francisco Trinidad, "Lectura 'heterodoxa' de Santa Teresa," *Cuadernos del norte* 2 (1982), 2–8; quotation p. 4.
39  Luis de Maluenda, *Excelencias de la fe* (Burgos, 1937), fol. 50, 1, cited in Melquíades Andrés, *La teología española en el siglo XVI*, 2 vols (Madrid: Católica, 1977), 2: 558, n. 161.
40  Although the disdain for human knowledge dates from the early years of the Church, Renaissance humanists had endowed such expressions as "holy ignorance" and "discrete ignorance" with new significance, reaffirming the universality of Christ's message. Without rejecting erudition, the humanist tradition stressed the need for knowledge to be accompanied by charity and love of God. See Aurora Egido, "Los prólogos Teresianos y la 'santa ignorancia,'" in *Congreso internacional Teresiano 4–7 octubre, 1982*, ed. Teófanes Egido Martínez et al. (Salamanca: Universidad de Salamancai, 1983), 2: 581–607.

great, in short, presumptuous female spirituality that bordered on the heretical.[41]

## Teresa in the Shadow of the "Alumbradas"

Teresa de Jesús was not an *alumbrada*, if we define Illuminism in terms that the Toledo group themselves would have accepted: she did not share their disdain for sacraments and exterior works, the veneration of saints, and the mortification of the flesh. She could never be said to have espoused their belief in justification by faith alone. But as a *conversa*, a woman, a reader of Scripture, and a practitioner of mental prayer, she was suspect on multiple grounds and associated inevitably with the Inquisition's ever-expanding definition of Illuminism. By the 1550s the Inquisition was beginning to perceive any form of interior Christianity as a screen for Protestant pietism or other forms of heterodoxy. Moderate theologians were willing to accept mental prayer, provided its practitioners did not reject the legitimacy of vocal prayer. But the opinions of theologians like Cano were in ascendancy: contemplative prayer should be limited to "learned men" with specialized theological training; it was not for women, be they religious or lay, and any opinion to the contrary had "the savor of Illuminist heresy." With the Index of 1559 all vernacular translations of the Scriptures and all vernacular guides to prayer and devotion were banned, including works by Luis de Granada, Saint Juan de Avila, and Saint Pedro de Alcántara.[42]

---

41   The first appearance of the diminutive that I have been able to find in Spanish is from a ca. 1260 translation of the New Testament. The text is precisely the second epistle to Timothy which treats women's susceptibility to deception by false prophets: "ca daquestos son los que traspassan las casas e aduzen catiuas a las mugerciellas cargadas de pecados que son aduchas por muchos deseos." See Thomas Montgomery and Spurgeon Baldwin, eds, *El nuevo testamento según el manuscrito escurialense I–I–6* (Madrid: Anejos del Boletín de la Real Academia Española, 1970). The diminutive does not appear in Covarrubias' 1611 *Tesoro de la lengua castellana o Española* (Madrid: Turner, 1997). In the 1732 *Diccionario de autoridades* (Madrid: Gredos, 1963), *mugercilla* is defined as "a woman of little esteem; foolish. Regularly applied to one who has thrown herself into the world." In modern usage the connotation of sexual license has become more prominent: "A woman of little esteem, especially a prostitute" (Julio Casares y Sánchez, *Diccionario ideológico de la lengua española*, 2nd edn. [Barcelona: Gustavo Gili, 1959]). Fremaux-Crouzet also observes that, among sixteenth-century theologians like Cano and Vergara, the diminutive *"mugercillas"* was a common expression of "irritated derision" applied to women with high spiritual aspirations ("L'antifeminisme," p. 150).
42   For the debate on mental prayer see Daniel de Pablo Maroto, *Dinámica de la oración: Acercamiento del orante moderno a Santa Teresa de Jesús* (Madrid: Editorial de espiritualidad, 1973), and Joseph Pérez, "Cultura y sociedad en tiempos de Santa

Teresa thus lived under the shadow of Illuminism and the ecclesiastical misogyny with which it was inextricably associated. Her writing must be understood as an attempt to differentiate her form of religious experience from charges of Illuminism, salvaging what she could of its affective mental prayer. Thus, she accepted the veneration of images but preferred to use them as an inspiration to mental prayer.[43] She repeatedly acknowledged her dependence on the guidance or correction of the educated clergy or *letrados*, while maintaining that those who had not practiced mental prayer were incapable of judging its orthodoxy. She accepted that contemplation was neither a necessary nor sufficient path to salvation yet urged her friends to pursue it in spite of all dangers. She did not deny the efficacy of vocal prayer, provided it was accompanied by the mental effort of sincere devotion. She avowed her obedience to hierarchical authority but placed the authority of her inner revelations above that of the Church. She acknowledged the necessary mediation of the Church and the merit of works yet professed that the divine union was ultimately gratuitous.

Stripped of their concessions and qualifications, any number of her beliefs could have been formulated by the Inquisition as heretical propositions. Teresa did in fact believe that true prayer is not words but meaning, that spiritual experience is superior to learning, and that God can be apprehended intimately. Historically the alliance between mysticism and Church has often been an uneasy one, for the mystic's ineffable, antiintellectual experience of the divine is, ultimately, nonhierarchical and antiinstitutional. Nonetheless, Teresa moved between orthodoxy and heterodoxy, holding the explosive theological issues of her day in oxymoronic tension, and came perilously close to losing all. *The Book of Her Life* was in Inquisitorial hands for thirteen years. In 1580 her confessor ordered her to burn her meditations on *The Song of Songs*, and in 1589, seven years after her death, theologians for the Inquisition urged that all her books be burned.

## Teresa as "Mujercilla"

That Teresa was, of course, eventually successful in claiming her right to doctrinal discourse is manifested in the hundreds of editions and translations of her works, her canonization in 1622, and perhaps most

Teresa," in *Congreso internacional Teresiano 4–7 octubre, 1982,* ed. Teófanes Egido Martínez et al. (Salamanca: Universidad de Salamanca), 1: 31–40.
43   Juventino Caminero makes a number of interesting observations on Teresa's strategic antiheretical statements in "Contexto sociocultural en el sistema místico de Santa Teresa," *Letras de Deusto* 14, no. 30 (1984): 27–48.

significantly and most ironically in her election as Doctor of the Church in 1969.[44] But this success would have been impossible had Teresa not made some accommodations to the gender ideology of her audience. She has given us one of the earliest and best definitions of pragmatic stylistics: "Estamos en un mundo que es menester pensar lo que pueden pensar de nosotros, para que hayan efecto nuestras palabras"[45] 'We are living in a world in which we have to think of people's opinions of us if our words are to have any effect.'[46] And Teresa knew that this "opinion" – her identification as *mujercilla* – constrained the conditions of her discourse. After all, the famous theologian Bartolomé de Medina had denounced her as a "*mujercilla*," declaring that she and her nuns would be better off "in their convents praying and spinning."[47]

Teresa's defensive strategy was to embrace stereotypes of female ignorance, timidity, or physical weakness but disassociate herself from the double-edged myth of woman as seducible/seductive. In the following passage, for example, the diminutive *mujercitas*[48] is subtly ironic, as she argues that "little" women may receive more spiritual favors from

44    Teresa was the first woman to be accorded this honor, which was proposed by Pope Paul VI in 1967 in the aftermath of reforms of Vatican II. The Promoter General of the Faith wrote in the 1969 Decree: "The difficulties in conceding the title of Doctor to holy women which have customarily been adduced, based on Pauline texts and historical reasons arising from former heresies, have disappeared in our times. . . . Certainly, since the circumstances of our times have changed, not only in civil life, but in the very life of the Church, it seems opportune to concede the title of Doctor also to certain saintly women who have excelled in the eminence of their divine wisdom" (*Santa Teresa de Jesús, Doctora de la iglesia: Documentos oficiales del Proceso Canónico* [Madrid: Editorial de espiritualidad, 1970], p. 254).

45    *Libro de las fundaciones*, in *Obras completas*, edición manual, ed. Efrén de la Madre de Dios and Otger Steggink (Madrid: Católica, 1962), ch. 8, p. 520. All other Spanish citations to Teresa's works in this chapter follow this edition, hereafter abbreviated as *Obras*, 1962.

46    *The Book of Foundations*, in *The Complete Works of Saint Teresa of Jesus*, trans. E. Allison Peers, 3 vols (London: Sheed and Ward, 1944–6); 3: 43; hereafter abbreviated as Peers, *CW*.

47    *Procesos*, 19: 349.

48    In Teresa's idiolect the ending -*illo* is more strongly derogatory than -*ito*, which can simultaneously convey positive and negative affect. Note the combination of affectionate and depreciatory connotations in the following stateent: "Pues comenzando a poblarse estos palomarcitos de la Virgen Nuestra Señora, comenzó la Divina Majestad a mostrar sus grandezas en estas mujercitas flacas, aunque fuertes en los deseos" (*Fundaciones*, ch. 4, p. 507) 'Now when these little dovecotes of the Virgin Our Lady [i.e., the reformed convents] began to be filled, His Divine Majesty began to show forth His greatness in these poor weak women, who none the less were strong in desire' (Peers, *CW*, 3: 17). For other examples of *mujercilla* see *Fundaciones*, ch. 2, p. 501, and ch. 15, p. 538; *Cartas*, p. 1061. *Mujercita* also occurs in *Vida*, ch. 36, p. 153, and *Fundaciones*, ch. 12, p. 530. (All examples can be found in *Obras*, 1962.)

God precisely because they are weak, whereas learned men have less need of these divine consolations: "Para mujercitas como yo, flacas y con poca fortaleza, me parece a mí conviene, como Dios ahora lo hace, llevarme con regalos, porque pueda sufrir algunos travajos que ha querido Su Majestad tenga; mas para siervos de Dios, hombres de tomo, de letras, de entendimiento . . . cuando no la tuvieren [devoción], que no se fatiguen" (*Libro de la vida*, ch. 11, p. 49) 'In the case of a poor little woman like myself, weak and with hardly any fortitude, it seems to me fitting that God lead me with gifts, as He now does, so that I might be able to suffer some trials He has desired me to bear. But servants of God, men of prominence, learning, and high intelligence . . . when they don't have devotion, they shouldn't weary themselves.'[49] She concedes to feminine timidity to show that she respects and suffers from the male admonishments that she nonetheless disregards: "Contradición de buenos a una mujercilla ruin y flaca como yo y temerosa, . . . con haver yo pasado en la vida grandísimos travajos, es éste do los mayores" (*Vida*, ch. 28, p. 115) 'For the opposition of good men to a little woman, wretched, weak, and fearful like myself, . . . among the very severe trials I suffered in my life, this was one of the most severe' (K, 1: 188). She disavows her leadership role in the Carmelite reform by acknowledging her incompetence, which necessitated God's intervention: "Si bien lo advertís, veréis que estas casas en parte no las han fundado hombres las más de ellas, sino la mano poderosa de Dios. . . . ¿De dónde pensáis que tuviera poder una mujercilla como yo para tan grandes obras, sujeta, sin solo un maravedí ni quien con nada me favoreciese?" (*Libro de las Fundaciones*, ch. 27, p. 576) 'If you examine the matter carefully, you will see that the majority of these houses [convents] have been founded not so much by men as by the mighty hand of God. . . . Where do you think a poor woman like myself, subject to others and without a farthing of her own or anyone to help her, found the means to perform such great works?' (Peers, *CW*, 3: 143).

With disarming modesty she concedes to women's intellectual inferiority in a way that frees her to explore a new theological vocabulary:

Havré de aprovecharme de alguna comparación, aunque yo las quisiera escusar por ser mujer, y escrivir simplemente lo que me mandan; mas este lenguaje de espíritu es tan malo de declarar a los que no saben letras, como yo, que havré de buscar algún modo, y podrá ser las menos veces acierte a que venga bien la comparación; servirá de dar recreación a vuestra merced de ver tanta torpeza.               (*Vida*, ch. 11, p. 47)

49   *The Book of Her Life*, in *The Collected Works of St. Teresa of Avila*, trans. Kieran Kavanaugh and Otilio Rodríguez (Washington, D. C.: Institute of Carmelite Studies, 1976), 1: 84; hereafter abbreviated as K.

> I shall have to make use of some comparison, for which I should like to apologize, since I am a woman and write simply what I am ordered to write. But this spiritual language is so difficult to use for anyone who like myself has not gone through studies, that I shall have to find some way of explaining myself, and it may be that most of the time I won't get the comparison right. Seeing so much stupidity will provide some amusement for your Reverence.                                                (my translation)

Writing on the *Song of Songs*, she argues that because of women's intellectual inferiority they are more receptive to an effortless, though fragmentary, understanding of the Scriptures: "Mujeres no han menester más que para su entendimiento bastare; con esto las hará Dios merced. Cuando Su Majestad quisiere dárnoslo sin cuidado ni travajo nuestro, lo hallaremos sabido" (*Meditaciones sobre los cantares*, ch. 1, p. 323) 'Women need no more than what their intelligence is capable of. If they have that, God will grant them His grace; and, when His Majesty is pleased to teach us anything, we shall find that we have learned it without any trouble or labour of our own' (Peers, *CW*, 2: 360). In *The Way of Perfection* she champions women's right to engage in contemplative prayer as a vital Counter-Reformation "work": "Pues todas hemos de procurar de ser predicadoras de obras, pues el Apóstol y nuestra inhabilidad nos quita que lo seamos en las palabras" (*Camino de perfección* [Valladolid Codex], ch. 15, p. 228) 'We women must all try to be preachers in our works, since the Apostle [Paul] and our own mability prevent us from being such with words' (my translation). When, objecting to her active participation in the Carmelite reform, her enemies cited Pauline Scripture against her, she answers: "[D]íjome [Dios]: 'Diles que no se sigan por sola una parte de la Escritura, que miren otras, y que si podrán por ventura atarme las manos'" (*Cuentas de conciencia*, no. 16, p. 444) 'The Lord said to me: "Tell them they shouldn't follow just one part of Scripture but that they should look at other parts, and ask them if they can by chance tie my hands"' (K, 1: 328).[50]

In these passages (and in many others) Teresa concedes to women's weakness, timidity, powerlessness, and intellectual inferiority but uses the concessions ironically to defend, respectively, the legitimacy of her own spiritual favors, her disobedience of *letrados*, her administrative initiative, her right to "teach" in the Pauline sense, and her unmediated

---

50   As part of the reforms of the Council of Trent, nuns were required to observe strict enclosure. Teresa's extensive travels in her efforts to found sixteen new convents were seen by her opponents as a clear contravention of this imperative. Her detractors had apparently used Pauline admonitions that women's activities be confined to the home (Titus 2:5 and 1 Cor. 14:34).

access to the Scriptures. In sum, Teresa's pejorative references to her sex – with or without the depreciatory diminutive – concede to Paul but allude to Matthew.

Not all of Teresa's pejorative references to her sex constitute pragmatic concessions. She also took pains to differentiate herself from *alumbradas*, continually consulting her confessors and other *letrados* over her visions precisely to reassure them that she was not involved in *"cosas de mujercillas"* – a clear allusion to Illuminist raptures (*Cuentas* no. 53, p. 455).[51] Though her faith in the divine nature of her own raptures remained firm, events later in life shook her confidence in women's stability. The life of asceticism, enclosure, and prolonged periods of mental prayer in the reformed Carmelite convents, a life that she had hoped would open the mystical path for more women, had led several nuns along another path, which Teresa was forced to recognize as illness. She began to acknowledge the difficulty of judging ecstasy from without and of distinguishing divine communication from the effects of poor diet, self-inflicted pain, and sensory deprivation. Whereas Teresa consistently resisted the opinion that such women were victims of diabolical possession, she reluctantly came to accept the notion that women's physical weakness (*flaqueza*) had unfortunate mental consequences.

Teresa did make one unequivocal apology for women in the introduction to *The Way of Perfection*: "[No] aborrecistes, Señor de mi alma, cuando andávades por el mundo, las mujeres antes las favorecistes siempre con mucha piedad y hallastes en ellas tanto amor y más fe que en los hombres"[52] 'Lord of my soul, you did not hate women when You walked in the world; rather you favored them always with much pity and found in them as much love and more faith than in men' (my translation). This is Teresa's most radical and perhaps most unorthodox statement, for here she claims not simply women's spiritual equality with men but their *superior* capacity for faith and their *favored* status in God's

51  Writing of herself in the third person, Teresa records that she felt more shame in confessing her divine favors than her sins because "le parecía que se reirían de ella y que eran cosas de mujercillas, que siempre las havía aborrecido oír" (*Cuentas* no. 53, p. 455) 'it seemed to her that her confessors would laugh at her and attribute these favors to the foolish things of women [and she had always hated hearing about such things]'(K, 1: 350), Alfred Rodríguez and Darcy Donahue note that out of fifteen references to women in Teresa's autobiography, thirteen are pejorative. They propose that many of Teresa's prejudicial remarks about woment are motivated by the desire to differentiate herself from *alumbradas*. See "Un ensayo de explicación razonada de las referencias de Santa Teresa a su propio sexo en *Vida*," in *Santa Teresa y la literatura mística hispánica*, ed. Manuel Criado de Val (Madrid: EDI–6, 1984), pp. 309–13.

52  *Camino de perfección*, transcripción del autógrafo de Valladolid, ed. Tomás de la Cruz, 2 vols. (Rome: Tipografia poliglotta vaticana, 1965), 2: 68.

compassionate eyes. Her spiritual life was dedicated to finding and knowing this God who did not hate but rather pitied women. It is not surprising that these words never reached their intended audience but lay obliterated beneath heavy cross-hatches, twice censored by her confessor and by her own hand, until deciphered by modern editors. For a *mujercilla* the alternative to concession was silence.

# 8

# The Thirty Years' War and the Failure of Catholicization

## Marc R. Forster

Originally appeared as Forster, Marc R., "The Thirty Years' War and the Failure of Catholicization," in his *The Counter-Reformation in the Villages: Religion and Reform in the Bishopric of Speyer, 1560–1720* (Ithaca: Cornell University Press, 1992), 144–77.

### Editor's Introduction

Like conversion in the Americas, reclaiming territories lost to Protestantism in Europe was an integral component of Counter-Reformation. And like conversion, "Catholicization" proved to be a difficult challenge. In this chapter from his book on the Counter-Reformation in the German prince-bishopric of Speyer, Marc R. Forster reveals the many local pitfalls and unintended consequences of attempts to "Catholicize" Protestant villages during the seventeenth century. In contrast to Bavaria and Bohemia, Catholicization failed in the region around Speyer, in part because of fierce resistance from villagers, for whom Protestantism had become the "traditional" religion, but also because the Thirty Years' War had dampened missionary zeal and enthusiasm for reform among many Catholics, great and small. With his description of confessional struggles in the mostly Protestant village of Oberöwisheim, Forster shows that Catholicization efforts were implemented unevenly and often succumbed to the cumulative force of peasant insubordination. By the 1650s, villagers were resolving religious differences on their own, creating a bi-confessional religious landscape. Similarly, leading clerics supported catholicization to the extent that it reinforced traditional authorities, but hesitated to use force. While the experience of Speyer was not typical of catholicization everywhere, Forster's discoveries contradict the stereotype of a triumphal and repressive Counter-Reformation. Without the determined application of force, no amount of decree-making could impose the new Catholicism on unwilling hearts, and even in success, Catholicization sometimes exacerbated tensions among Catholic leaders. Thus Forster's essay should warn against interpretations that would portray the Counter-Reformation simply as a binary conflict between elite and popular religious cultures.

# The Thirty Years' War and the Failure of Catholicization

*Marc R. Forster*

In many parts of Catholic Germany, indeed throughout Catholic Europe, the Counter-Reformation began with an effort to convert Protestant populations to Catholicism. In Würzburg in the 1570s, officials of the prince-bishop forced Protestants to convert or emigrate.[1] Elsewhere in the empire Catholic princes followed similar policies in the decades before the outbreak of the Thirty Years' War, exacerbating political and religious tensions.[2] These policies were an integral aspect of Tridentine reform as well as part of the attempt to strengthen state power.

In Germany, the Thirty Years' War gave further impetus to this aspect of the Counter-Reformation. Catholic military victories in the early 1620s allowed the Church to reintroduce Catholicism in many areas and seemed to threaten the survival of Protestantism in a Habsburg-dominated empire. The thorough and often brutal Catholicization of Bohemia after the Battle of White Mountain (1620) became the symbol of the Counter-Reformation at its most violent and oppressive.[3]

Catholic victories even brought Catholicization to the Bishopric of Speyer. This was a new focus, for the Catholic establishment in Speyer had never considered the conversion of Protestants a part of Church reform. Catholic armies, however, dominated the Rhine valley for most of the war, and the defeat of the Protestant Electoral Palatinate removed one of the political restraints on the policies of the Catholic reformers in this region. In the 1620s the Catholics attempted to reintroduce Catholicism in Protestant villages and, even before the Edict of Restitution in 1629, sought to restore the monasteries to Church control.

This effort to convert Protestant areas failed for three fundamental reasons. The first was the determined resistance of rural communes to

---

1  Hans-Christoph Rublack, *Gescheiteste Reformation: Frühreformatorische und prefestantische Bewegungen in süd-und westdentschen geistlichen Residenzen* (Stuttgart: Klett-Cotta, 1978).
2  See especially Martin Heckel, *Deutschland in konfessionellen Zeitatter* (Göttingen: Vandenhoeck und Ruprecht, 1983), part 4.
3  I prefer to call the process of converting Protestant regions "Catholicization" rather than "Recatholicization." First, this term is less awkward. Second, the process of establishing Catholic practice in areas that had been Protestant for three or more generations meant building from the ground up. "Recatholicization" implies the (simple, easy) restoration of a previously existing conditions, which was not the case.

religious change, which they understood as a threat to both their political and religious autonomy. By the 1620s, Protestant religious practices had become traditional in Palatine villages and the introduction of Catholic services an innovation. It is never easy to impose new practices on an unwilling population.

The second reason for the failure of Catholicization in the Bishopric of Speyer was that it was never carried out forcefully. A thorough Catholicization, as practiced in some places in Germany during the war, was a three-stage process. First, Catholic priests were installed in the parishes. Second, there was an effort to persuade or convert the population to the benefits of the new religion. The third step was to devise and enforce legal restrictions on dissenters (and even waverers), such as punishments for failing to attend services and restrictions on the civil rights of those who resisted religious change. Eventually, these punishments could include imprisonment, banishment, or death for the most stubborn non-Catholics. In Speyer the local Catholics, led by the Cathedral Chapter, considered such an ambitious course too risky. Instead, they favored a conservative policy designed to preserve the status quo. They were willing to support the first two stages in the process but feared the consequences of more coercive measures.

For many Catholics in Germany, a determined Catholicization also implied the domination of the Jesuits, and the papacy, as well as the complete acceptance of Tridentine Catholicism. The latter suggests the third reason for the failure of Catholicization in Speyer: many in the local Church were highly skeptical of reformed Catholicism. As a result, they focused on the restoration of the most traditional institutions, the monasteries. Many churchmen resisted proposals to use monastic incomes for pastoral purposes, fearing this was the first step in an attack on the privileges and incomes of the chapters.

There were other reasons for the failure of Catholicization in general. One was the division of the Catholic party. The various occupying powers of the Palatinate, the Bavarians, Austrians, Spanish, and French all had different policies. None wanted to give the bishop more authority. The bishop of Speyer, Philipp Christoph von Sötern, was not a church reformer and was much more interested in increasing his political power and financial resources. In any case, his interest in Speyer faded after he was elected elector-archbishop of Trier in 1623.

For much of the war, the Bishopric of Speyer was an important campaigning area. The destruction caused by marauding soldiers, the constant forced levies and quartering of troops, and the extensive population loss severely hurt the Church. The economic problems associated with the war, especially in the 1630s and 1640s, forced the authorities to cut the salaries of the parish priests and made it impossible to hire new ones. By the late 1640s there was a severe shortage of priests, even to serve the reduced population. Clearly, this lack was an impediment to continued reform within the Catholic villages as well as to the conversion of Protestant villages.

It is possible, however, to exaggerate the long-term damage done by the war.[4] Although the population loss was enormous, it was also temporary. The recovery of the region in the late 1640s was striking, rapid, and free of major structural disruption. In the Bishopric of Speyer the organization of village life, the economic position of the Church, and the power of the village communes retained their prewar character.

For the Counter-Reformation, the Thirty Years' War provided an opportunity to Catholicize Protestant areas, but it also weakened the Church financially and slowed the internal reform of Catholicism. Significantly for the long-term course of the Counter-Reformation, the failure of Catholicization convinced Catholic authorities that confessional divisions were permanent in this part of Germany. The long and destructive war reinforced the conservative and traditional tendencies of the local clergy, which included a skeptical attitude toward Tridentine reforms and a growing dislike of religious fanaticism. Already by the 1630s, churchmen demonstrated a focus on the institutional survival of the Church and a pragmatism that bordered on religious indifference.

## Impact of the War and the Decline of the Reform Impulse

Most studies of religious reform in Germany end with the Thirty Years' War. This holds true especially for studies of the institutionalization of the Protestant churches and of the Counter-Reformation.[5] Studies of the Counter-Reformation in France have a different chronological perspective; French historians have often argued that the final implementation of Tridentine reforms only came in the seventeenth and even eighteenth centuries.[6] The history of the Counter-Reformation in

4  Günther Franz, *Der dreißigjährige Krieg und das deutsche Volk. Untersuchung zur Bevölkerungs- und Agrargeschichte* (1940; reprint, Stuttgart: Gustav Fischer Verlag, 1979), esp. the introduction and ch. 1.
5  Bernhard Vogler, *La vie religieuse en pays rhénan au siècle de la Réforme (1555–1619)* (Paris: Ophrys, 1976). Studies of the Counter-Reformation that take the long view include R.Po-Chia Hsia, *Social Discipline in the Reformation: Central Europe, 1550–1750* (New York: Routledge and Kegan Paul, 1989) and Franz Ortner, *Reformation, Katholische Reform, und Gegenreformation im Erzstift Salzburg* (Salzburg: Universitätsverlag Anton Pustet, 1981). Ortner's history includes part of the eighteenth century.
6  See especially Philip T. Hoffman, *Church and Community in the Diocese of Lyon, 1500–1789* (New Haven: Yale University Press, 1984); and Louis Châtellier, *Tradition chrétienne et renouveau catholique dans le cadre de l'ancien Diocèse de Strasbourg (1650–1770)* (Paris: Ophrys, 1981).

Germany would also benefit from this longer perspective, since the effort to reform the Church continued both during and after the war. The continuities in Church organization, in the policies of episcopal authorities, and in the responses of the laity to these policies during the whole early modern period were more important than the discontinuities caused by the war. Indeed, the war reinforced some of the most important characteristics of Catholicism in the Bishopric of Speyer, especially the conservatism of the upper clergy and the influence of the communal church.

## Bishop Philipp Christoph von Sötern, 1610–52

The election in 1609 of Philipp Christoph von Sötern as coadjutor and successor to Bishop Eberhard was a sign of the weakness of the reform party in the Cathedral Chapter.[7] Sötern had a deserved reputation as an influential and politically adept churchman, but he had few of the personal qualities of a Tridentine bishop.[8]

Sötern's career followed the pattern of many aristocratic churchmen in the Tridentine German Church. He began his clerical career in the traditionalist Ritterstift (a powerful and semi-independent corporation of noble churchmen) in Bruchsal and by 1600 had accumulated an impressive number of prestigious and well-endowed benefices in the middle Rhine region.[9] Like his opponents, the reform-minded canons, he had received a Jesuit education and was a dedicated Catholic. His interests, however, were above all political, as demonstrated by two reports he sent to the pope (1616 and 1623).[10] The 1616 report discusses the economic problems of the prince-bishopric (Hochstift),

---

7    The coadjutor was an assistant bishop with the right of succession. By 1609, Eberhard had been sick for a long time and the chapter wanted an active bishop.

8    Sötern was not the candidate of the reformers in Speyer and had made enemies in Speyer as early as 1594 by maneuvering his entrance into the Cathedral Chapter in Speyer at the expense of reforming Dean Oberstein's candidate. See Volker Press, "Das Hochstift Speyer in Reich des späten Mittelatters und der frühen Neuzeit-Portrait eines gestlichen Staates," in Volker Press et al., *Barock am Oberrhein* (Karlsruhe: G. Braun, 1985), 266–67.

9    Hermann Weber, *Frankreich, Kurtrier, der Rhein, und das Reich, 1623–1635* (Bonn: Ludwig Röhrscheid Verlag, 1969), 15–16.

10   Ibid., pp. 16–17; Joseph Schmidlin, *Die Kirchlichen Zustände in Deutschland vor dem dreißigiährigen Kriege nach den bischöflichen Diözesanberichten an den heiligen Stuhl*, 3 vols. (Freiburg in Breisgau: Herder, 1908–10). The reports to the pope are in Franz Remling, ed., *Urkundenbuch zur Geschichte der Bischöfe von Speyer*, vol. 2 (Mainz: Franz Kirchheim, 1853), pp. 653–60, 665–70.

the Palatine threat and the political dependence of the bishopric on the emperor, and Sötern's building projects, especially the construction of the fortress at Philippsburg. In addition to these political concerns, he reports on the successes and expansion of the Jesuit and Capuchin orders.[11] In the 1623 report, sent during a period of Catholic victory, Sötern emphasizes the economic problems caused by the war and the possibility of Catholicizing the Palatinate. In both reports, he is self-confident and even self-promoting, but in neither does he concern himself with the internal reform of the Church.

His election in 1623 as elector-archbishop of Trier allowed him to play an important role in imperial politics. He was a strong supporter of militant political Catholicism and an early champion of the Catholic League. As ruler of Trier and Speyer, he also saw himself as the leader of the anti-Habsburg Catholic party. Both in Speyer and in Trier he followed an independent policy.[12] Concern about the expansion of Habsburg power and conflicts with the Spanish led Sötern to conclude an alliance with France in 1632, which brought French troops into the empire, and when imperial forces captured Trier in 1635, earned him twelve years in imperial prisons in Belgium and Austria.[13]

Nationalist German historians have judged Philipp Christoph von Sötern harshly for "playing the French card." Ranke's comment that Sötern "only worked for territorial power and religion, but had no idea what the fatherland was" is anachronistic but not far from the truth.[14] Sötern, like many of the upper clergymen who dominated the Church in seventeenth-century Germany, worked to expand Catholicism. At the same time he was imbued with aristocratic ideals, politically narrow-minded with an essentially regional focus, and traditional enough to exploit the Church for his and his family's financial benefit. The Counter-Reformation did not break the hold of the traditional ecclesiastical establishment on the German Church. Sötern's pro-French and anti-Habsburg policy was a reaction against the centralizing trends of the imperial court as well as a reaction against the growing political power of the emperor.[15]

11    Ludwig Stamer, *Kirchengeschichte der Pfalz*, 3 vols. (Speyer: Pilger-Verlag, 1949–55), pp. 150–1; Remling *VB*, pp. 653–60.
12    Weber, *Frankreich, Kurtrier, der Rhein, und das Reich*, esp. pp. 24–26.
13    Remling II, pp. 490–96.
14    Paraphrased in Weber, *Frankreich, Kurtrier, der Rhein, und das Reich*, pp. 13–14.
15    Robert Bireley, S. J., *Religion and Politics in the Age of the Counterreformation: Emperor Ferdinand II, William Lamormaini, S. J., and the Formation of Imperial Policy* (Chapel Hill: University Press of North Carolina, 1981). Bireley emphasizes the close ties between the most militant Counter-Reformers (especially the Jesuits) and the emperor.

## The war and Catholic reform

The Bishopric of Speyer lay in the middle of an important war zone. The presence of the strategically vital fortress of Philippsburg, the importance of the Rhine river as a line of communications, and the wealth of the region made the Prince-Bishopric a target for marauding armies of both sides. The bishopric suffered two periods of sustained campaigning, the first during the so-called Mansfeld War (1621–3) and the second during the Swedish invasion (1631–2).[16] The French entrance in the war put Speyer and the Palatinate on the front lines, as would be the case throughout the seventeenth century. There were periodic campaigns in the 1630s and 1640s, but most of the destruction in this period was caused by foraging armies of both sides. Neither the loyalty of the Cathedral Chapter to the emperor nor the alliance of Bishop Sötern with the French spared the bishopric the exactions of the various armies.

It is almost impossible to estimate the demographic effect of the war. There is no question that all the inhabitants of some villages fled. This was especially the case on the left (west) bank of the Rhine. Some parts of the Palatinate lost over 75 percent of their inhabitants, and the overall population loss in the Rhine valley has been estimated at 66 percent.[17] The assessment of the bishop's council in 1644 that the population of the Prince-Bishopric had declined during the war from thirteen thousand to one thousand, however, probably overestimates the losses.[18] The population decline was, however, significant. Even on the right bank of the Rhine, which was somewhat less exposed to foraging armies, one group of Catholic villages reported a population loss of over 80 percent.[19]

The effect of the war on the local economy is obvious. As the population declined, agricultural production plunged, as did tax receipts and tithes. Especially between 1635 and 1648, peasants stopped farming marginal land. The collapse of trade particularly reduced the profits

16   Remling II, p. 468. Bishop Philipp Christoph von Sötern estimated that three quarters of the population of the bishopric had fled or been killed during the "Mansfeld War."

17   Günther Franz, *Der dreißigjährige K!ieg und das deutsche Volk: Untersuchung zur Bevölkerungs- und Agrargeschichte* (Jena: G. Fischer, 1940; reprint Stuttgart: G. Fischer, 1979), pp. 46–52.

18   Joseph Baur, "Das Fürstbistum Speyer in den Jahren 1635 bis 1652, "*Mitteilungen des historischen Vereins der Pfalz* 24 (1900): pp. 104–5. Baur accepts these figures, which probably underestimate the population before and after the war.

19   Generallandesarchiv Karlsruhe [hereafter GLAK] 153/149 (1645 figures from 13 villages in Amt Kißlau). The population loss may have been somewhat lower, because the villagers overestimated the prewar population in an effort to show that the villages had been overcrowded before 1620.

from wine production.[20] These developments were extremely damaging to the Catholic Church in Speyer. Most of the income that supported both the rural and the urban clergy came from tithes, interest on loans to the peasantry, and the profits on the wine and grain trade. Income from all these sources collapsed during the war. Just as the population explosion of the period before the Thirty Years' War had enriched the clergy, the war and the drop in population impoverished them.

The Thirty Years' War also caused a setback in the effort to reform the clergy and bring Tridentine Catholicism to the Catholic population of the bishopric. The Church faced difficult choices in the allocation of scarce resources. Those institutions that had been founded during the period of prosperity in the late sixteenth century were the first to suffer as revenues declined. These were precisely the institutions that had been founded to further reform, among them the Jesuit college and the cathedral school, called the Alumnat. Financial difficulties affected the rural clergy as well, cutting incomes and making it impossible to hire new priests. The number and quality of priests and services fell, and the influence of the Church in the countryside weakened.

One consequence of the war was the collapse in 1636 of the Alumnat, which had been training parish priests since the 1560s. In the 1620s, perhaps anticipating a demand for priests in newly Catholicized regions, the Cathedral Chapter admitted several new students to this seminary.[21] At the same time, however, the income of the Alumnat was declining. In 1623, it had a "debt" of three thousand gulden, which meant that it had been operating beyond its own endowment on funds provided by the chapter.[22] The students had to live on very little, and by 1629 this situation began to affect their behavior and discipline. The canons complained that the students were not obeying the rules and suggested that it might be better to close the Alumnat entirely.[23]

The final collapse of the Alumnat in 1635–36 reflects the serious problems that faced the Church during the war. The Alumni had become increasingly disobedient, refusing to attend services in the Cathedral and being insolent to their teacher. The Cathedral Chapter felt that it was too expensive to support the students and decided to close the school. At the same time, however, there was such a shortage of priests in the countryside that the canons decided to send these half-trained

20   Kuno Drollinger, *Kleine Städte Südwestdeutschlands. Studien zur Sozial- und Wirtschaftsgeschichte der Städte im rechtsrheinischen Teil des Hochstifts Speyer bis zur Mitte des 17. Jahrhunderts* (Stuttgart: Kohlhammer Verlag, 1968), 117.
21   GLAK 61/10957, pp. 51–2, 69–70, 249, 290, 319, 361, 446, 541, 787–8.
22   Ibid., p. 60.
23   GLAK 61/10959, p. 206v.

priests out to the parishes to fill vacancies.[24] Not only had the Alumnat (which was originally conceived as a Tridentine seminary) fallen apart, but the wartime situation had forced the Church to lower its standards for rural priests.

The shortage of priests grew more serious as the war progressed. Through the 1620s, it was the physical destruction caused by passing armies that caused the greatest number of problems. The priests reported serious damage to churches and parsonages. The priest in Geinsheim wrote to the Cathedral Chapter that Mansfeld's troops had destroyed an altar, windows, pictures of the Virgin and Saints Peter and Paul, and the pulpit in his church.[25] The destruction forced the patrons to cut the salaries of rural priests in half, at least in the first half of the 1620s.[26] By 1626 conditions had improved. The priest in Geinsheim received 42 malter (c. 63 hectoliters or almost 190 bushels) of grain from the Cathedral Chapter, which was close to his peacetime allotment of 48 malter.[27] Nevertheless, priests found it difficult to survive on reduced resources and kept a lookout for better parishes. The priest in Bauerbach, Vitus Volck, left this poorly endowed parish for Baden in 1628. In 1629, the priest in Geinsheim requested a position in the city of Speyer and, when none was available, asked to be transferred to the town of Landau.[28] This priest was concerned about his physical safety in the countryside as well as about his impoverishment.

After the Swedish invasion of 1631–4, the shortage of priests became acute. Church officials were forced to send monks out from Speyer to hold services in the villages around the city. This was not a new practice. Before the war two parishes had been served by Franciscans, but in the 1630s and 1640s, as many as nine parishes were served by Franciscans, Carmelites, Dominicans, and Capuchins. Because they continued to live in the city and were not trained as parish priests, the quality of service provided by the regulars was poor.

Those parish priests who continued to serve despite invading armies, plague, and food shortages were compelled to handle several parishes. Whereas before the war almost all priests served one parish, by 1640 most priests had two and sometimes three to take care of. Between 1635 and 1650, thirty-two parish priests appear in the records, and these held

24    GLAK 61/10959, p. 570r; GLAK 61/10961, pp. 34v–35r, 91v–92r, 96v.
25    GLAK 61/10957, pp. 93–4.
26    Ibid., pp. 294, 524. Also see Häusser, *Geschichte der rheinischen Pfalz*, 2 vols (Heidelberg: Mohr, 1856; reprint Pirmasens: Buchhandlung Johann Richter, 1970), p. 483. Häusser mistakenly says that Catholic officials reduced only the income of reformed pastors in the Palatinate in an effort to drive them out. In fact, all clergy had to take a pay cut in the 1620s.
27    GLAK 61/10957, pp. 900–1.
28    GLAK 61/10959, pp. 20v, 21r (Bauerbach), pp. 188v, 206v (Geinsheim).

services in fifty-seven different parishes.[29] Those priests who stayed in the villages did not live well. In 1641, Hartmann Stibius, the priest in Deidesheim, commented that he had lived in poverty for more than ten years.[30] Many priests survived by farming. The priest in Königsbach was forced to give up his parish in 1637 because (probably due to age) he was no longer physically able to farm the parish property.[31]

The villagers frequently complained that the priests did a poor job. No doubt this failing was to a great extent the result of serving too many parishes. The shortage of priests also made it unwise for episcopal authorities to discipline neglectful ones. The priest in St. Leon tried to justify his failure to administer the sacraments and say Mass by pointing out that his income was small and he had two parishes to oversee. His parishioners were not sympathetic, and the Cathedral Chapter reminded him that as he was a graduate of the Alumnat they expected better of him.[32]

Many villages had no priest and no services. There were no priests, for example, in the Lauterburg *district* in the late 1630s, an area that had nine before the war.[33] In 1640, the mayor and council of the town of Lauterburg complained that no priest had resided there in three years.[34] The villagers of Langenbrücken withheld the tithe the same year in an effort to get the patrons to appoint a priest. The amount of the tithe was so small (about three gulden) that the patrons, the Gregorian Vicars of the Cathedral Chapter, decided not to press the villagers. No priest was appointed.[35]

The shortage of clergy, the general disorganization of both secular and spiritual administration, and the disruption of rural life led to a serious setback in the efforts of the Church to discipline the laity. Wartime conditions jeopardized even the limited prewar gains of the reformers, especially in Church attendance and respect for Sundays and holidays. Although no records of Church attendance could be kept, there is evidence that villagers increasingly neglected services and worked in the fields instead.[36] The clergy's interest in disciplining the people was limited before 1620. During the war it was nonexistent.

29 These priests are mostly found in the minutes of the Cathedral Chapter and in the Bishop's Council minutes. There were probably others (GLAK 61/10959 to 61/10969, GLAK 61/11499 to 61/11504, GLAK 229).
30 GLAK 61/10963, p. 284r.
31 GLAK 61/10961, p. 345r.
32 Ibid., pp. 285v–286r.
33 GLAK 61/11499, pp. 244v–245r.
34 GLAK 61/10963, p. 86r.
35 Ibid., pp. 143r–143v, 162r, 163r.
36 Ibid., p. 359r; GLAK 61/10965; pp. 139v–140r. These are both examples from the village of Ketsch, where a diligent, but nonresident, priest reported on the *fahrlessigkeit* (neglectfulness) of his parishioners.

Another unmistakable sign of the declining importance of Tridentine reform was the deteriorating relationship between the Jesuits and the Cathedral Chapter during the war. In part problems developed because financial constraints forced the chapter to reduce the support it gave the Jesuits. More important, local churchmen opposed the militant anti-Protestant policy favored by the Jesuits and feared the growing influence of the order in Germany. Like many German Catholics, some in Speyer accused the Jesuits of being over-involved in politics, too powerful at the imperial court, too ambitious, and (perhaps most important) too closely linked to the papacy.[37] In 1644, for example, the cathedral canons lamented the influence the Jesuits wielded in Rome and Vienna. Using this leverage the fathers had acquired the income of the former Cistercian monastery in Klingenmünster, at a time when the bishopric could have used the money.[38] The somewhat imperious tone taken by the rector of the college with church officials did not improve relations between the order and the local Church. Even the general aggressiveness of the Jesuits bothered the canons. In 1636, the fathers asked to take over several damaged and vacant chapels in the Cathedral. The canons hesitated, commenting, "Once they [the Jesuits] are let into the Cathedral Chapter, they will be hard to get out again."[39]

These conflicts and financial difficulties caused the number of Jesuits in the Speyer house to decline as the war progressed. In the early 1620s there were thirty to thirty-five Jesuits living in Speyer (peaking at thirty-six in 1621) whereas in the 1640s the number hovered between twelve and eighteen.[40] In part the numbers of Jesuits declined because of their unpopularity with the French, who increasingly dominated the region. Perhaps more important, however, was the sense among the local clergy, especially in the Cathedral Chapter, that the Jesuits represented outside forces (the papacy and the emperor) and had little interest in the welfare of the local Church. This view was confirmed when Jesuits refused to accept gracefully a reduction in income, at a time when the whole Church was suffering.[41] The Jesuits' attitude gave them a reputation for

---

37   Bireley, *Religion and Politics in the Age of the Counterreformation*, ch. 7. Many Catholics suspected, not without justification, that the Jesuits planned to take over the bulk of the monasteries restored by the Edict of Restitution.

38   GLAK 11501a, p. 21r. The Jesuits also appealed to the emperor to force the Cathedral Chapter to pay what it owed the college in Speyer (GLAK 61/10957, pp. 607–8, 611, 743–4, 754, 792–3).

39   GLAK 61/10961, p. 117r.

40   ARSJ Rh.Inf.48, pp. 226v, 257v; ARSJ Rh.Sup. 29, pp. 118r, 121r, 127r, 133r, 137r, 141r, 146r; ARSJ Rh.Sup. 31, pp. 4r–5r, 32r, 46v, 51r, 178v, 208v.

41   The Jesuits kept careful track of all money, grain, and wine owed them and bombarded the Cathedral Chapter with requests for support. See for example GLAK 61/10959, p. 560, GLAK 61/10961, pp. 187v–188r.

selfishness and arrogance that stayed with them for the whole seventeenth century.

One result of the war, then, was a perceptible weakening of the impetus for reform in the Bishopric of Speyer. In a very practical way, the Thirty Years' War reduced the resources available for the Jesuits, the Alumnat, and the rural clergy. In a broader sense, the political insecurity of the period, especially after the Swedish invasion, reinforced the conservative tendencies of the local churchmen and reduced their enthusiasm for the Counter-Reformation.

### The postwar consequences

Conditions in the postwar period accentuated the traditionalist tone of Catholicism, especially by strengthening the communal church. This strengthening was a consequence of the rapid economic recovery of the region. A French diplomat who passed through the area in both 1646 and 1658 commented at the time of his second visit that the villages and fields were in such good shape that it appeared as if there had never been a war.[42] There are strong indications that those who survived were better off than they had been before the war, for quite simple reasons. In general, villages had been overcrowded in the prewar period, and in the 1650s the population recovered at a lower level. In the late seventeenth century, the villagers of Ostringen reported a population of 180 but claimed that it had been over 300 before the "great war." In the prewar period, they said, the village had been overcrowded, with several families living in each house. Every village in the two districts (*Ämter*) of Rotenburg and Kisslau reported similar figures and informed the bishop's officials that they did not want a return to the conditions of the early part of the century.[43]

This was a prosperous region, and the postwar recovery made the survivors comfortable. The smaller population did away with the overcrowding, the farming of marginal lands, and the impoverishment of some segments of the rural population that had existed between the

42 Häusser, *Geschichte der rheinischen Pfalz*, p. 588. Production began to increase in the 1640s. In 1646, for example, the Cathedral Chapter collected a tithe of 85 malter of grain from the town of Landau. In 1649 the Landauer paid 120 malter. On a smaller scale, the peasants in Rödersheim, which in the mid-1630s was completely abandoned, paid one malter in 1646, five malter in 1649 (GLAK 61/10967, pp. 165–81, 933–66; GLAK 61/10961, p. 57v). Towns recovered rapidly as well. See Kuno Drollinger, *Kleine Städte Südwestdeutschlands: Studien zur Sozial- und Wirtschaftsgeschichte der Städte in rechtsrheinischen Teil des Hochstifts Speyer bis zur Mitte des 17. Jahrhunderts* (Stuttgart: Kohlhmmer, 1968), pp. 114–21.
43 GLAK 153/157. See above, note 19.

1590s and the 1620s. After 1650, previously landless peasants acquired property, while the shortage of landless laborers forced wealthy peasants to plant less land. There was a decline in social differences within villages and a resultant easing of social tensions. This situation, combined with the disorganization of secular and spiritual authority, strengthened village unity and local communal institutions.[44]

As a result, village communes continued to have an important role in local Church affairs and even expanded their influence in the late 1640s. The residents of Lauterburg, for example, appealed several times to the Church authorities in Speyer for a resident priest. In 1649, not having obtained satisfaction through the proper channels, the townsmen, working with local officials, appointed their own.[45]

In 1648, the commune of Edesheim wrote to the Cathedral Chapter that the parish was vacant and that the chapter could not appoint a new priest "without allowing the commune, as tradition and practice prescribe, to confirm him."[46] The chapter was quite hostile to this idea, commenting that "the Cathedral Chapter as patron . . . should examine the qualities of the priests, and not (against all laws) the commune."[47] The canons also suspected that the outgoing priest, Jost Gerber, was responsible for this letter, which they found "passionate," impertinent, and criminal. They did not, however, punish Gerber or the villagers. A priest was hired from a neighboring village, but it is not clear if he was the choice of the Cathedral Chapter, the villagers, or both.[48] In any event, the commune had openly claimed extensive rights over the local church.

A long-running feud between Johan Lammit, priest in Neipsheim, and his parishioners further illustrates the villagers' power over the clergy. In the summer of 1648, Lammit and the Cathedral Chapter's agent in Neipsheim personally collected the tithe in the fields – a clear break with tradition, since the Cathedral Chapter had always negotiated with the commune and collected the tithe through the village representatives. The priest and his helper apparently followed the example of Protestant clergy in neighboring villages, a clear indication that

---

44  There is no evidence of a weakening of communal institutions or of the loyalty of the villagers to the commune, either before or after the war, as Robisheaux has found for Hohenlohe and Rebel for Upper Austria. Thomas Robisheaux, *Rural Society and the Search for Order in Early Modern Germany* (Cambridge: Cambridge University Press, 1989), esp. ch. 3; Hermann Rebel, *Peasant Classes: The Bureaucratization of Property and Family Relations under Early Habsburg Absolutism, 1511–1636* (Princeton: Princeton University Press, 1983), esp. ch. 5. See also Heide Wunder, *Die bäuerliche Gemeinde in Deutschland* (Göttingen: Vandenhoeck and Ruprecht, 1986), ch. 5.
45  GLAK 61/10967, p. 1020.
46  Ibid., p. 546.
47  Ibid., p. 547.
48  Ibid., p. 558.

Catholic communes traditionally had a greater role in Church affairs than their Protestant neighbors. The bishop's council, while conceding that the Cathedral Chapter had a right to collect tithes as it wished, argued that the method used by Lammit only served to alienate the villagers from the Church.[49] The council further lamented the failure of the vicar general to adjudicate the dispute, fearing that the conflict would cause the villagers to boycott services and endanger their souls.[50]

In 1649, the bishop's officials expressed even greater disgust with Lammit's behavior. The priest had, in effect, excommunicated the village mayor and his wife. He had taken this drastic step after a confrontation with the mayor's wife, who tore out some of the priest's hair. Lammit announced to the villagers in church that "any lay person who strikes a priest or cleric is damned to hell."[51] The bishop's council once again blamed the priest for his "scandalous and very dangerous actions" and suggested that the vicar general treat him severely.[52]

The incident in Neipsheim indicates several subtle but important effects of the war on the relationship between the communes and the Church. The self-assurance of the villagers in their conflict with the priest is evidence of their strength. The disruption of war had forced them to rely on local initiative for everything from poor relief to military defense. Furthermore, the sympathy for the villagers shown by the bishop's officials suggests that the elites in the bishopric were not unified. Perhaps in an effort to attract immigrants, officials tried to tone down the activities of overzealous priests. Finally, the heavy-handed behavior of Lammit is a sign that the quality of the rural clergy had declined during the war.

### Catholicization: The Monasteries and the Palatinate

The Thirty Years' War forced Catholics in the Bishopric of Speyer to face the issue of Catholicization. Whereas before the war Catholics had political authority over few Protestants, the defeat of the Protestant Palatinate in the early 1620s made the restoration of Catholicism in large areas of the region a possibility.

Some Catholic powers in the Empire moved quickly to Catholicize thoroughly areas brought under their control. In the 1620s the Austrians cleared Bohemia of Protestants efficiently and brutally. Bavarian

49  GLAK 61/11503a, pp. 148r–148v.
50  Ibid., p. 219r.
51  GLAK 61/11503b, p. 43r: "Der seye in abgrundt der höllen verdambt."
52  Ibid., p. 44r.

policy in the Upper Palatinate was similarly effective in making the formerly Palatine province completely Catholic. Both powers used military means and property confiscations to convert or drive out Protestant elites and forced Catholic practice on the populations, often by sending soldiers into the villages.

Catholic authorities in Speyer did not share the enthusiasm of their colleagues in Vienna and Munich for such a ruthless policy. After seventy-five years as the minority and politically weaker religion in the middle Rhine valley, the local Church had difficulty grasping the consequences of Catholic victory. Having based their political and financial security on the religious peace of 1555, many of the Catholic elite in Speyer hesitated to seize the possibly short-lived fruits of victory. During the war, the Swedish invasion in the early 1630s confirmed this view. Rather than attempt a thorough Catholicization of the bishopric, the local Church sought more limited gains for Catholics, especially hoping to restore certain legal and financial rights "usurped" by the Palatinate.

When examining the process of Catholicization in the Bishopric of Speyer, one must consider the restitution of the monasteries and the Catholicization of the Palatinate. Because the Palatinate had taken over the monasteries after the Peace of Augsburg, their incorporation into the Electorate had always been of dubious legality. As early as 1622, Bishop Sötern attempted to gain control of the income of the monasteries.[53] The Catholicization of the Palatinate as a whole was now possible because the emperor stripped Elector Frederick V of his principality and assumed direct imperial control. Without such legal justification, however, Catholic authorities in Speyer did not attempt to Catholicize other Protestant areas in the bishopric, such as the Principality of Zweibrücken, the Margravate of Baden-Durlach, or the Imperial City of Speyer.

Catholicization proceeded very haphazardly. Financial and political problems caused by the war made expediency more important than long-term policy. There were serious divisions among the various Catholic powers (the Austrians, Bavarians, and Spanish) occupying the Palatinate, as well as between these powers and the episcopal authorities. Bishop Sötern and the Cathedral Chapter were rarely in agreement, especially after the bishop's French alliance and subsequent imprisonment. Ultimately, it was the reluctance of the local Church to undertake a major Catholicization program that determined Catholic policy. By the 1650s it was apparent that the war had done little to change the confessional geography of the region. Although a few Catholic minorities

---

53    Stamer III/1, p. 160; Remling II, pp. 471–2.

could be found in Palatine territory, religious divisions closely resembled those of 1620.

## The restitution of the monasteries

Some German Catholics did believe that Protestantism could be eradicated in the empire. Emperor Ferdinand's Jesuit confessor, William Lamormaini, even wrote to the pope, "Perhaps even all of Germany may be led back to the old faith."[54] Catholic militants considered the restoration of Church lands that had been taken by Protestants since the Peace of Augsburg an essential first step in this process. Robert Bireley has argued that some leading Catholics, especially in Bavaria and Vienna, considered the Edict of Restitution as only the beginning of a Catholicization of all of Protestant Germany.[55] The precise practical connection between the restitution of Church property and the conversion of Protestant populations was never clearly formulated. It seems that the Jesuits in particular hoped that the recovered property would be used to support more Jesuit colleges and missions as well as other Counter-Reformation measures, such as the education of Catholic clergy. These measures in turn would facilitate the conversion of Protestant populations.

Bishop Sötern did not view the restitution of the monasteries as part of an attempt to restore the Church to its pre-Reformation condition or even to the situation in 1552, before the secularization of the monasteries. He hoped above all to gain episcopal control of monastic rights and incomes. Although he favored using some of the monastic revenues for a new episcopal seminary, most of the new income was to be used to support his ambitious political plans as prince-bishop of Speyer and elector-archbishop of Trier.

As soon as Catholic armies conquered the Palatinate, Sötern attempted to take possession of the monasteries. In November 1622, Pope Gregory XV gave the bishop his support for this plan, but the opposition of Emperor Ferdinand delayed the project.[56] A year later the bishop asked Gregory's successor, Urban VIII, to assign the incomes of the monasteries of Limburg, Eußerthal, and Seebach directly to the

54   Quoted in Geoffrey Parker et al., *The Thirty Years' War* (London: Routledge and Kegan Paul, 1984), 94.
55   Robert Bireley, SJ, *Maximilian von Bayern, Adam Contzen S.J. und die Gegenreformation in Deutschland 1624–35* (Göttingen, Vandenhoeck und Ruprecht, 1975); idem, *Religion and Politics in the Age of the Counterreformation.*
56   Stamer III/1, p. 160; Remling II, pp. 471–2.

bishop of Speyer. The new pope turned down this request, instead giving most of the Palatine monasteries to Archduke Leopold of Austria for two years. Sötern gained possession only of the small former Augustinian chapter in Hördt.[57] In the early 1620s, as one historian has emphasized, "what was urgent for the Emperor . . . and for the Bishop of Speyer was not so much the Recatholicization of the conquered land, as the restitution of the clerical foundations."[58] In other words, financial and political concerns outweighed religious ones.

The Edict of Restitution (March 1629) accelerated the process of recovering the monasteries for the Catholic Church, greatly increased the number of institutions involved, and caused serious conflicts within the Catholic party. The edict provided (among other things) that all ecclesiastical institutions incorporated by Protestant authorities since 1552 be returned to the Church. Within the Bishopric of Speyer, in addition to the Palatine monasteries, the Catholics now claimed five monasteries and chapters in Württemberg, two in Baden-Durlach, and one in Zweibrücken.[59] Who was to control the monasteries and their considerable incomes and how these resources were to be used remained in dispute.

One program was to use the newly acquired resources to promote Catholic reform measures and the conversion of Protestants. This may have been the policy favored by Emperor Ferdinand II when he promulgated the edict, and it also had supporters in Speyer.[60] Sötern himself used the income of the chapter in Hördt to help support a small seminary in Philippsburg. He even hoped to use the revenue of some of the monasteries to fund a large episcopal seminary in Speyer. The bishop also wrote to Rome proposing the transfer of various rural monasteries and chapters to places where their resources could be used for pastoral purposes.[61] It is perhaps possible to dismiss these plans as window dressing devised by a bishop who ultimately wanted the resources of the

57   Stamer III/1, pp. 160–1; Remling II, pp. 472–3, 477. Remling points out that Sötern also took benefices of the bishopric for his own use, including the primissary in Schifferstadt. This was an attempt to channel church resources to political and military uses.
58   Karl Lutz, "Fürstbischöfliche und kaiserliche, österreichische und französische Rekatholisierung im südlichen Speiergau, 1622–1632, und ihre reichs- und kirchenrechtlichen Begründungen," *Archiv für mittelrheinische Kirchengeschichte* 20 (1968): 281.
59   Stamer III/1, pp. 161–2.
60   Bireley, *Religion and Politics in the Age of the Counterreformation*, chs 4 and 5.
61   Stamer III/1, p. 165. Sötern proposed the monastery of Limburg be moved to Deidesheim, Hornbach to Lauterburg, Hördt to Philippsburg, and Klingenmünster to Landau. These were all safer locations and put the monasteries close to the seat of episcopal government in Philippsburg. See also Remling II, pp. 477–8; Remling *UB*, pp. 668–9.

monasteries for military and political purposes. In any case, the Swedish invasion and wartime dislocations put an end to these plans.

The Jesuits benefited from the Edict of Restitution, although not to the extent they might have anticipated. Between 1623 and 1646 two Jesuits resided in the former Cistercian convent of Heilsbruck. The fathers not only managed the convent's property but used Heilsbruck as a base for missions to convert the local population. In 1646, however, the Jesuits lost a long court battle with the Cistercians and had to turn the convent over to the nuns.[62]

The conflict over Heilsbruck was similar to those fought all over Germany between the Jesuits and the old orders. In 1630 the Jesuits presented a plan in Vienna, calling for the establishment of ninety new Jesuit colleges. Many of these were to be missionary outposts dedicated to the conversion of Protestants, and all were to be supported by the resources of the monasteries. The Society argued that especially the income of female houses should go to the Jesuits, for the nuns did no pastoral work. These ambitious plans were quashed by a strong anti-Jesuit reaction within the Church. Ultimately, it was monks from the old orders who took possession of the monasteries.[63]

In the Bishopric of Speyer the Benedictines returned to Hornbach and Limburg, the Cistercians to Eußerthal, and the Augustinians to Hördt. In each case the old orders were able to send only a couple of monks to establish their possession of the monasteries. None of these orders had the manpower or initiative to establish a strong presence in the countryside.[64] The monks of the old orders did nothing to support the Counter-Reformation or help Catholicize Protestant areas. In fact, peasants of all religions were traditionally quite hostile to the monks, whom they considered parasites. Where they were active, the Jesuits and Capuchins developed better relations with the rural population.

Finally, the Catholic powers who occupied the Palatinate were eager to use the resources of the monasteries to help defray the costs of the war. The Austrians gained control of several monasteries in the 1620s for this purpose. The Spanish were very reluctant to allow the bishop or the orders to administer clerical property in their zone of influence.[65] In the 1630s, the episcopal authorities had a drawn-out dispute with the Bavarians over control of the small chapter in Sinsheim.[66] All these conflicts only underscore the divisions within the Catholic party that

62  Stamer III/1, p. 163; Duhr II/1, p. 170; St. A. MZ, 15/400, 1637.
63  Bireley, *Religion and Politics in the Age of the Counterreformation*, ch. 7, esp. pp. 134–6.
64  Stamer III/1, pp. 162–5.
65  GLAK 61/11497/II, p. 363v.
66  GLAK 61/10961, pp. 8v–9r, 17r–17v, 69v, 193v.

turned out to be especially significant for the failure to Catholicize the Electoral Palatinate.

### Catholicization in the countryside

The campaign to Catholicize Protestant villages, especially in the Palatinate (*Kurpfalz*), was unsuccessful over the long term for three reasons. The divisions among the Catholic powers meant that Catholicization proceeded haphazardly and without clear direction. The episcopal authorities in Speyer had little prewar experience in converting Protestant regions, nor indeed much confidence in the success of such an endeavor, and therefore did not press Catholicization very energetically. And finally, the disruption of war and the shortage of trained priests meant that neither the funds nor the manpower was available to accomplish the task in any case.

The local Catholic authorities had some prewar experience trying to convert Protestant villagers, and this experience gave them little reason to expect the easy success of Catholicization during the war. Between about 1580 and 1620, Catholic officials moved to convert the people of two regions on the edges of the prince-bishopric with large Protestant populations. The first was the region of five large villages under the nominal secular rule of the Ritterstift in Bruchsal. The second was the lordship of Dahn, an episcopal fief that returned to the possession of the bishop at the extinction of the von Dahn family in 1603. This holding included six villages that had been Protestant for many decades.[67]

The Catholicization of these regions proved very difficult. Catholic authorities instituted the first two steps in this process, establishing legal authority in ecclesiastical affairs and installing new clerics in the parishes. There followed an effort to persuade or convert the population of the benefits of Catholicism. This, however, was the extent of it. The third, more coercive stage of Catholicization was not undertaken. No restrictions were successfully placed on the Protestant inhabitants of these village, and no effort was made to evict non-Catholics. This moderate policy toward Protestant villagers dovetailed with the relatively restrained policy of the Church toward Catholic popular religion and popular culture.

Above all, however, the villagers themselves prevented the Catholicization of these regions. The Protestant inhabitants of Dahn and the Ritterstift villages exploited the moderation of the local Counter-Reformation, used the political support of the Palatinate, and main-

67    For Dahn see Stamer III/1, p. 218.

tained their strong traditions of local political autonomy and communal control of the Church. Lengthy lawsuits and even armed resistance
restricted the impact of Catholicization. In the long run, all these
methods allowed the Protestant villagers to practice their religion inside
the Catholic prince-bishopric.[68]

During the war, local Catholic authorities applied this experience to
the attempt to Catholicize the Palatinate. The process was quite straight-
forward. Catholic priests were in short supply, but when possible Protestant clergymen were removed from the parishes. The religious orders,
especially the Jesuits, supported the secular clergy with missions and
pastoral work. By 1625, episcopal authorities had decided that they
would pay the remaining Protestant pastors in the conquered territory
half of their salary (Catholic priests were no better paid) and that
pastors illegally serving parishes would not be paid at all. The parish
patrons were not to fill vacancies unless the villagers wanted a Catholic
priest.[69] The Cathedral Chapter, as patron of a number of parishes in
Palatine territory, appointed about eight priests to serve in Protestant
villages in the 1620s. The secular authorities also appointed priests to
serve in the villages. In 1626, the Habsburg archduke Leopold, who governed the area around Germersheim, ordered all Protestant clerics out
of the area and moved to hire Catholic priests.[70] The Spanish government, based in Kreuznach, began to install Catholic clergy in the
parishes in 1625, albeit slowly. By 1627 there were twenty-two priests
working in the areas under Spanish rule, although few of them within
the Bishopric of Speyer.[71] The Bavarian government in Heidelberg also
installed priests in the villages on the right side of the Rhine, especially
after 1625.[72]

Not surprisingly, the Jesuits actively supported the Catholicization
of the Palatinate. The fathers set up several small establishments in
Palatine territory, in Germersheim (1628–31), Bretten (from 1625),

---

68    For the Ritterstift villages see Leopold Feigenbatz, *Kurzer Abriß der Geschichte
von Odenheim und seiner Benedictinerabtei, dem nachmaligen Ritterstift Odenheim im
Kreichgau* (Bühl: Konkordia, 1886), p. 21. See also GLAK 94/392, GLAK 61/5341,
pp. 41–46, 48–59, 777–78; GLAK 61/5342, p. 117v; for Landshausen see GLAK
229/57523, 229/57524; for Odenheim see 229/79246, 229/79260; ARSJ Rh.Inf.
48, p. 104v. For Dahn see Stamer III/1, p. 218; LASp. D2/348; ARSJ Rh.Inf. 48, p.
160v.
69    GLAK 61/10957, pp. 536–7; Stamer III/1, p. 166.
70    Karl Lutz, "Fürstbischöfliche und kaiserliche, österreichische und französische
Rekatholisierung," pp. 282–3.
71    Anna Egler, *Die Spanier in der linksrheinischen Pfalz, 1620–1632. Invasion, Ver-
waltung, Rekatholisierung* (Mainz: Selbstverlag der Gesellschaft für mittelrheinische
Kirchengeschichte, 1971), 126–44, 154.
72    Häusser, *Geschichte der rheinischen Pfalz*, pp. 481–4.

and Neustadt (1625–32, 1638–50). In all three locations, the Jesuits held services, worked to convert the residents of the three towns, and did pastoral work in neighboring villages. The Jesuits supplemented the work of these "standing missions" with irregular missions to Protestant areas. As always, they claimed considerable success, especially in the area around Neustadt, once an important Calvinist stronghold.[73] Undoubtedly Jesuit influence in the Bishopric of Speyer peaked in the 1620s, especially in the countryside, where they were more active than ever before.

All the Catholic powers in the Palatinate installed Catholic priests in the villages and supported the efforts of the Jesuits and other orders to convert Protestants. There was no unanimity, however, on the extent to which harsh, coercive measures should be used to force the population to attend Catholic services. Anna Egler, in her study of the Spanish occupation of the Palatinate, has shown that Spanish policymakers were primarily interested in safeguarding their political and military position in the area. Fearing a mass emigration of the Protestant population, Spanish authorities refrained from instituting harsh anti-Protestant ordinances, especially in the 1640s, when the population loss was severe and eventual Catholic victory doubtful.[74] The Spanish had no long-term interest in governing this part of the Palatinate and considered the occupation temporary. For this reason they avoided strong Counter-Reformation measures that risked antagonizing the population.

The Bavarian authorities had more extensive goals than the Spanish. As a reward for his service to the Catholic cause, Duke Maximilian of Bavaria received the Palatine Electoral dignity as well as large pieces of Palatine territory. Maximilian hoped to make these gains permanent. Partly in order to break the loyalty of the inhabitants of the Palatinate to their Calvinist rulers (now in exile in Holland), Maximilian favored an aggressive anti-Protestant policy. Maximilian's strong Catholic faith, the influence of the Jesuits at his court, and his personal antipathy to Calvinists, whom he blamed for the war, further contributed to this policy.[75] In 1625 the Bavarians banished all Protestant clergy, and in

73    Duhr II/1, pp. 171–4; St.A.MZ 15/400, 1636–8, 1640, 1641. See also ARSJ Rh.Sup. 31, p. 5r. Over five hundred people took communion in the Jesuit church in Neustadt in 1646. According to the fathers, this was a large number given the size of the Catholic population. See also Meinrad Schaab, "Die Wiederherstellung des Katholizismus in der Kurpfalz im 17. und 18. Jahrhundert," *Zeitschrift für Geschichte des Oberrheins* 114 (1966): 170–1.

74    Egler, *Die Spanier in der linksrheinischen Pfalz*, esp. p. 154; Schaab, "Die Wiederher stellung des Katholizismus," p. 154.

75    Bireley, *Maximilian von Bayern* (Göttingen, 1974), esp. pp. 7–8 and ch. 4.

1628 they ordered all citizens to convert. These measures could be enforced only in the towns, but the 1628 ordinance caused an exodus of a number of prominent citizens, especially from Heidelberg.[76]

The Bavarians also hoped to use the resources of the University of Heidelberg to support a secondary school, a seminary for the education of priests, and a Jesuit college. The bishops of Worms, Würzburg, and Speyer, whose dioceses all included Palatine territory, considered this an effort to create a Bavarian territorial Church in the Palatinate. The bishops also hesitated to give the Jesuits further influence and distrusted their close ties to Maximilian. As Volker Press has pointed out, the three bishops feared Bavarian domination and "were not ready to sacrifice their fundamental claims [to ecclesiastical jurisdictions and properties] in exchange for the renewal of Catholicism in the Palatinate."[77]

The Swedish invasion in 1631 shattered the confidence of the Catholics in the middle Rhine region, especially the episcopal authorities in Speyer. The new situation caused the Cathedral Chapter to work throughout the 1630s and 1640s to protect the prince-bishopric from outside powers of all religions. The canons realized that a return to the prewar religious division of the region was likely and, taking the long view, pursued a moderate policy vis-à-vis Protestant areas. With the postwar situation in mind, local Catholics focused on strengthening the legal and financial rights of the Church in Protestant territories and ignored opportunities to spread Catholicism.[78]

Even the Bavarians followed a more moderate policy after the Swedish invasion. In 1641, the governor in Heidelberg wrote to Maximilian that it was no longer expedient to force people to go to Catholic services.[79] The French, who occupied most of the left bank of the Rhine, installed Catholic priests where they could, but the shortage of priests greatly hindered any consistent policy of Catholicization in the war-torn region. In the 1640s, depopulation, poverty, and general war-weariness all diminished interest in Catholicization. For local officials and church-

76  Häusser, *Geschichte der rheinischen Pfalz*, pp. 481–4.

77  Volker Press, "Kurfürst Maximilian I von Bayern, die Jesuiten und die Universität Heidelberg im dreißigjährigen Krieg 1622–1649," in *Semper Apertus, Sechshundert Jahre Ruprecht-Karls-Universität Heidelberg 1386–1986* (Berlin: Springer Verlag, 1986), 338–41; Schaab, "Die Wiederherstellung des Katholizismus," p. 173.

78  Some examples: the Cathedral Chapter neglected its right of patronage in Barbelroth (GLAK 61/10963, pp. 333r) and its alternate right of patronage in Lußheim (GLAK 61/10961, p. 135v). In 1636, the Cathedral Chapter wrote to the emperor about political and jurisdictional issues, but not about Catholicization (GLAK 61/10961, pp. 131v–132r).

79  Häusser, *Geschichte der rheinischen Pfalz*, p. 565.

men, the war had proved the danger of the ambitious, independent policies of Bishop Sötern and the uselessness of the endeavor to restore the monasteries and Catholicize the Palatinate.

The attempt to uproot Protestantism and restore Catholic unity during the Thirty Years' War was undoubtedly disorganized and chaotic. The reasons for this chaos – the disruption of war, financial limitations, and divisions within the Catholic party – are also clear. Of perhaps greater importance, however, was the context of traditional confessional relations in the Bishopric of Speyer. The local Catholic elite, in the chapters and in the bishop's administration, were not prepared to exploit Catholic dominance. Accustomed to a policy based on the defense of specific rights (such as territorial rights, patronage of parishes, and legal exemptions), these men were unable and unwilling to attempt anything more ambitious.

Did the Catholicization, however haphazard it may have been, have any long-term effect on Protestant-Catholic relations in the bishopric? It is difficult to determine the percentage of Catholics in the *Kurpfalz* at the end of the war. In the most aggressively Catholicized part of the Palatinate, the part governed by Bavaria, Catholic officials estimated that in 1640, "barely one third [of the population] are truly in their hearts Catholic."[80] The Austrian government in Germersheim reported in 1626 that the local people were "soft" (*weich*) in their religious beliefs and attended Catholic services as ordered.[81] They appear to have returned just as quickly to Protestant services. In other places, however, there was resistance, both passive and active, to Catholicization. After the Peace of Westphalia (1648) the Palatinate returned to the Elector Karl Ludwig, son of Frederick V. Karl Ludwig placed Calvinist clergy in the parishes but also tolerated religious minorities, including Catholics. The wartime Catholicization, the postwar immigration of Catholics to the devastated but fertile Palatinate, and religious toleration all contributed to the establishment of a small but significant Catholic minority in the Palatinate.[82]

Yet the Palatinate remained predominantly Protestant and did not tolerate public Catholic services. The confessional geography of the middle Rhine valley did not change significantly as a result of the Thirty Years' War. In the 1650s, the Catholics were once again the minority religion and the politically weaker confession.

80  Schaab, "Die Wiederherstellung des Katholizismus," pp. 153–4.
81  Stamer III/1, pp. 168–9.
82  Schaab, "Die Wiederherstellung des Katholizismus," pp. 154–5; Stamer III/1, p. 170.

## Catholicization in the Villages: Oberöwisheim

The history of the village of Oberöwisheim between 1623 and the mid-1650s illustrates the process of Catholicization and the resistance faced by Catholic authorities within Protestant villages during the Thirty Years' War. Just as elsewhere in the Bishopric of Speyer, neither Catholic military and political domination nor the presence of Catholic priests achieved the conversion of the Protestant population of this village in the Kraichgau region. During the war the villagers passively resisted authorities by refusing to attend Catholic services and secretly holding Protestant ones. As soon as the war ended, the villagers frustrated Catholic claims more actively, pressing lawsuits, withholding the tithe to force the support of a Protestant pastor, and appealing to Protestant powers for assistance.

Authority in Oberöwisheim was extremely fragmented. Secular power was shared by the Cathedral Chapter in Speyer and two free imperial knights, Herr von Helmstatt and Herr von Sternenfels. Each lord held approximately one-third of the villagers as serfs (*Leibeigene*). The three lords, or their representatives, held regular court sessions together. The Cathedral Chapter possessed the patronage of the village parish. The net effect of this division of power was of allow the villagers extraordinary influence in local government and to leave power over religious matters to the politically dominant confession.

Before the Thirty Years' War, both von Helmstatt and von Sternenfels, like most of the Kraichgau nobility, were Lutherans. Because of the power of the Palatinate and the residence of von Helmstatt in Oberöwisheim, the Cathedral Chapter appointed and paid a Protestant pastor. In fact, no Catholic services had been held in the village since the 1520s or 1530s, and the villagers were firmly Protestant. The war, however, changed the political situation and made it possible for the Cathedral Chapter to install a Catholic priest and attempt to Catholicize the village. The fragmentation of authority, while it made Catholicization possible, also restrained it. The ability of the chapter to enforce its policy depended on the cooperation of the other two lords of the village; for obvious reasons such cooperation was not often forthcoming.

The ebb and flow of the war also hindered Catholicization in Oberöwisheim. Catholic armies dominated the area around the village from 1621 to 1631 and again after 1636. But, between 1631 and 1636, the Swedish invasion allowed the Protestants to reestablish Lutheran services. During the 1640s, because of the decline in population, the reluctance of the villagers to pay the tithe, and the inability of the Cathedral Chapter to enforce its claims, no clergyman (of any religion) lived in Oberöwisheim. Consequently, most of the people attended Protestant services in neighboring villages.

Catholicization in Oberöwisheim, as elsewhere in the Bishopric of Speyer, failed because of the fragmentation of authority, the problems of war, and the resistance of the villagers. It also failed because of the limited program of the Cathedral Chapter. Like episcopal officials in the Palatinate, the canons viewed the Catholic domination as a chance to assert and strengthen their juridical rights in Oberöwisheim, especially that of patronage. These rights, of course, carried financial benefits. Only between 1628 and 1631, however, was there any attempt to encourage Catholic practice in Oberöwisheim. Otherwise, the canons were mainly intent on acquiring and maintaining "possession" of the parish. After a series of postwar conflicts, the Catholics did succeed in attaining this limited goal, but they were never able to change the religious practice of the villagers.

## Methods of Protestant resistance

The Catholicization of Oberöwisheim went through very clear stages. Between 1623 and 1628, the Cathedral Chapter, as patron of the parish, installed a Catholic priest and tried to maintain him against the hostility of the villagers. Beginning in 1628, the chapter tried to force Catholic practice on the villagers. After the Swedish invasion, the Cathedral Chapter returned to a limited policy of asserting its juridical rights in Oberöwisheim. Finally, after the Peace of Westphalia in 1648, the Catholics worked to keep these juridical rights and tried to prevent the return of Protestant pastors.

If the Catholic bid to convert the villagers of Oberöwisheim was implemented inconsistently, the local Protestants, for their part, resisted Catholicization with single-minded tenacity. Once again, the tradition of local autonomy and communal control of the village church provided the villagers with an effective defense against outside authorities. Furthermore, the villagers aptly played each lord off against the others, leaving the gemeinde as the only institution uniting the village. Protestant opposition to Catholicization was led by the gemeinde, by the two Protestant noblemen, von Helmstatt and von Sternenfels, and by the Protestant pastor. Although the Protestants had to keep a low profile during much of the war, at the end they still controlled village institutions and stood united to restore open, public Lutheran worship.

Catholicization began in 1623 when the Cathedral Chapter, asserting its right as patron of the parish, refused to appoint a new Lutheran pastor and ordered the priest from the bishop's village of Zeuthern to perform services in Oberöwisheim. This priest had a difficult time in Oberöwisheim, especially with Marquard von Helmstatt. Imperial law protected von Helmstatt's personal religious practice because he was a free imperial knight. As one of the lords of Oberöwisheim, he also had a certain immunity in his dealings with the Cathedral Chapter. In 1623, he prevented visiting Catholic priests from using the church, arguing that the Cathedral Chapter could not appoint Catholics to the parish. Apparently disregarding the presence of Catholics armies in the area, von Helmstatt gave the schoolteacher's benefice to a Protestant pastor and demanded that the Cathedral Chapter pay him. These efforts, however, failed to end Catholic services, and the Cathedral Chapter appointed a resident priest to maintain a presence in the village. Von Helmstatt, however, did make it possible for a Lutheran pastor openly to hold Protestant services until at least 1625.[83]

From 1623 to 1628, both Catholic and Protestant services took place in Oberöwisheim. In August 1623, the Catholic priest, Johan Beuerlin, reported that he was diligently doing his services, but that a Protestant preacher came regularly to preach, baptize children, and visit the sick. By November, von Helmstatt was no longer harassing Beuerlin, but the nobleman had appointed a Protestant pastor as resident school-teacher.[84] The Cathedral Chapter accepted this division of the benefices in Oberöwisheim, albeit somewhat reluctantly, because it gave the chapter "possession" of the parish.

If the Catholics had possession of the parish, it was almost purely a legal position. In 1649, when an imperial commission was investigating conditions in Oberöwisheim during the war, the villagers reported that in January 1624 "the Catholic priest's sermons were heard by no person in the community, as a result he preached to no one except the walls, chairs, and benches . . . [there was] no Catholic practice . . . by the sub-jects of the village."[85] There is little evidence to contradict this report. In 1649, the Catholics argued that services did not require an audience to be considered *Exercitium* under the provisions of the peace treaty, implicitly conceding that there were few, if any, practicing Catholics in Oberöwisheim in 1624.[86]

It seems that the Cathedral Chapter hoped to encourage at least its own serfs to convert to Catholicism. To this end the canons tried to

83   GLAK 61/10957, pp. 34, 68–9, 85, 99–100, 102–4, 108, 287–8, 301, 111–12.
84   Ibid., pp. 141, 185, 190, 259.
85   GLAK 229/82623, October 26 1649 ("Restitutions Sachen"): "Er (hat) Niemand anderst alss den wänden, Stühlen und bänckhen gepredigt."
86   GLAK 229/82623, October 26 1649 ("Protokolle der Commission, Bönnigheim").

protect them from the depredations of the Bavarian troops in the area. The practical benefits of being Catholic may have led to some conversions. In 1625, the canons protested to von Helmstatt that the Lutheran pastor had insulted the Catholic religion in general and those in the village who went to Mass in particular. Von Helmstatt, recognizing the power of the Catholics, forced the pastor to apologize for calling the Mass "the devil's work."[87] By all indications, however, the vast majority of the villagers remained Protestant. Throughout the war they attended services in neighboring Protestant villages when necessary and regularly found a pastor to bless weddings, perform burials, and baptize children. These methods allowed the villagers to avoid direct confrontation with the Catholics and prevented the suppression of Protestant practice.

In early 1628, the Catholics instituted a more aggressive policy. Interestingly, it was a newly appointed priest, Bartolomeus Vogt, who pushed for a more extensive Catholicization of Oberöwisheim. Vogt presented a detailed proposal to the Cathedral Chapter. His first goal was to get rid of the Protestant pastor. Vogt argued that the pastor's presence was illegal, since the noblemen had installed him after the religious peace of 1555. Although Vogt's chronology was inaccurate and his evidence shaky, he went on to argue (somewhat inarticulately) a more persuasive point.

> As my lords [the canons of the Cathedral Chapter] are the patrons . . . it would now be the best time, since the imperial soldiers are in the region and this is a good opportunity that otherwise might be lost, . . . and he would like, with great eagerness, to build up something good. [Having] studied and done other things unfortunately without result, he would like also to teach school and the catechism at no extra cost and stay a while, until slowly the numbers [of Catholics? or people?] grow.[88]

Vogt expressly argued that the political and military situation provided an opportunity that should not be neglected. His proposal for a more active policy in Oberöwisheim received the support of the canons, although with some hesitation. The canons warned Vogt above all to respect the rights of the two noblemen to hold Protestant services in their homes. When Vogt complained that the villagers did not show him proper respect, the canons responded: "The priest's enthusiasm in religious matters is to be commended, but he should be reminded to behave somewhat more modestly with the people. Heretics are converted by

87   GLAK 61/10957, pp. 367, 441, 541, 543, 564–5, 596.
88   GLAK 61/10959, pp. 14r–14v.

good example, not by bloodshed."[89] The chapter suspected that Vogt's aggressive style was the cause of his disputes with the villagers.

Notwithstanding their hesitation, Catholic authorities barred the Protestant pastor from the church and ordered the villagers to attend Catholic services and stop going to neighboring villages to baptize their children.[90] In an attempt to enforce these regulations, the Cathedral Chapter refused to intercede on behalf of Oberöwisheim with the Bavarians. The canons would not prevent further quartering of troops unless the villagers were "more reasonable" toward the Catholic religion. At least seven times between 1628 and 1631 the canons threatened to have troops sent to Oberöwisheim if the villagers did not put an end to their stubbornness in regard to religion. Using the carrot as well as the stick, the canons also promised to reduce taxes and levies if the villagers became Catholic.[91] These threats and promises had little effect on the villagers; they probably realized that the canons in Speyer had little influence with the Bavarians, who were likely to tax and force levies on the villagers no matter what religion they practiced.

The Swedish occupation ended this period of vigorous Catholicization. From 1632 to 1635 there was a resident Lutheran pastor in Oberöwisheim, and no Catholic services were held.[92] Beginning in 1636, the Catholics sent a neighboring priest to perform services "so that we stay in religious possession." But attendance was low, and the Cathedral Chapter complained that "few peasants come to church, only a few women."[93] No clergyman, Protestant or Catholic, lived in Oberöwisheim in the 1640s, making it easier for the villagers to attend services elsewhere. Most continued to go to Protestant villages, especially for baptisms. The disruption caused by the war in this period also made any consistent policy of Catholicization difficult. Many villagers died or fled Oberöwisheim, and those who stayed could not support a priest or pastor. The Cathedral Chapter was unable to find a priest for the village and the priests in neighboring areas refused to conduct services there without being paid.

Catholic policy during all but three years of the Thirty Years' War was limited to restoring and maintaining the Cathedral Chapter's patronage of the village parish. The canons most likely understood this policy as a way to increase the financial resources of the chapter, especially by collecting the priest's income when the parish was vacant. Yet they also

89   Ibid., pp. 36r–36v.
90   Ibid., pp. 18r–18v, 22v–23v.
91   Ibid., pp. 22v–23r, 28r, 64r–64v, 76r–76v, 91v, 216v–217r, 380r.
92   GLAK 229/82623, October 26 1649 (Oberöwisheim).
93   GLAK 61/10061, p. 127r.

appeared to believe that if Catholic services took place in Oberöwisheim, the villagers might eventually be converted to Catholicism. The Peace of Westphalia did not change this goal. In fact the peace treaty, by setting January 1, 1624, as the "normative date" for religious matters, legalized the presence of a Catholic priest in Oberöwisheim.[94]

The imperial commission that investigated the religious situation in Oberöwisheim in October 1649 concluded:

> Because the Protestants were also there in 1624, they should stay . . . both the Protestants and the Catholics should have their services, and neither [religion] should hurt the other, but instead [they should] live peacefully together. Neither should publicly or privately attack the other in religious matters . . . and both should have their services in the church.[95]

The commission (made up of the bishop of Constance and the duke of Württemberg) ordered the creation of a biconfessional village. This plan caused new problems because after the war the Protestants wanted a full restoration of the *status quo ante* – a difficult matter since the religious peace protected the Catholic priest. Furthermore, the political balance within Oberöwisheim had changed: in 1641 a Catholic branch of the von Helmstatt family came into possession of the family's rights in Oberöwisheim.[96] The Protestants were not pleased with the decision of the imperial commission of 1649, but they accepted it and were determined to make the Cathedral Chapter obey it as well.

The most problematic part of the commission's decision related to the payment of the two clergymen. The commission required that the Cathedral Chapter, which held the tithe, pay both the Catholic priest and the Lutheran minister. Not surprisingly, the chapter was reluctant to comply, recognizing that splitting the tithe lowered the income so much that it might be impossible to fill the post. To prevent this eventuality, the chapter could have cut its own take from the tithe, but this solution did not appeal to the canons. Furthermore, the commission did not spell out how the tithe was to be collected and then disbursed. Under the pretext of this confusion, the Cathedral Chapter refused to support the

---

94  Geoffrey Parker et al. *The Thirty Years' War* (London: Routledge and Kegan Paul, 1984), p. 182. The "normative date" of January 1 1624 generally benefited the Protestants. In the Palatinate, where the Catholics had begun Catholicizing in the early 1620s, it helped the Catholics, although not in the Electoral Palatinate itself, where the son of Elector Frederick V was fully restored to power.

95  GLAK 229/82623 ("Protokolle der Commission"): "Keiner dem andern in Religions Sachen publice vel privatim nach reden."

96  GLAK 61/10963, p. 335v.

Protestant pastor, and, in retaliation, the villagers refused to pay the tithe.

The village council organized the withholding of the tithe in 1649, 1650, 1651, and 1652. The goal was clear. In October 1650, for example, the villagers forcefully took the tithe wine from the Cathedral Chapter's local agent and delivered it to the Lutheran pastor.[97] In August 1651 the villagers defied a second imperial commission, which ordered them to pay the tithe to the Cathedral Chapter, and delivered the grain directly to the pastor. Soon after, they closed the church to the Catholic priest.[98]

The villagers of Oberöwisheim continued to withhold the tithe despite the orders of an imperial commission, a mandate from the Imperial Chamber Court and the periodic application of military force by the Cathedral Chapter. The most serious confrontation took place in July 1652, when a Cathedral canon and twenty musketeers arrived in Oberöwisheim to collect the tithe. A crowd of peasants gathered in front of the barn where the grain was stored. The canon, Herr von Frenz, was on horseback and tried to force a passage to the barn. A villager challenged the canon and von Frenz clubbed him over the head with his pistol, apparently killing him. The troops then took away the tithe and arrested two peasants.[99]

A second method of resistance was to appeal to neighboring Protestant powers. One villager said in 1649, "[The canons] will have soldiers take our property, now they deprive us of our salvation too. We should make sure that the Cathedral Chapter will have not only the entire nobility of the Kraichgau on its back, but also the military might of the Duke of Württemberg."[100] The support of these Protestant powers, especially Württemberg, was very important for the villagers and discouraged the Cathedral Chapter from severely punishing the organizers of the various "tithe strikes" in the 1650s.

By 1655, in fact, the disputes over the tithe had become routine. In July the Cathedral Chapter's agent in Oberöwisheim refused to pay the Protestant pastor, citing the religious peace. The peasants then took the tithe from him and gave it to the pastor. The chapter protested, commenting that there was little else it could do.[101] These disputes continued without resolution into the 1660s. In practice, however, conditions closely resembled what the imperial commission had ordered in 1649. Both religions had a resident clergyman in Oberöwisheim, the

97   GLAK 61/10969, p. 435.
98   GLAK 61/10971, pp. 83–4, 166.
99   Ibid., pp. 274–5.
100   GLAK 61/10967, p. 866.
101   GLAK 61/10971, pp. 587–8.

schoolteacher was a Protestant, both religions used the church, the whole community used the "old calendar" (as the Protestants did), and the Protestants held all the positions on the village council.[102]

Protestant resistance had succeeded. Even though two of the three lords of the village were Catholic after 1641, Protestant villagers continued to control the village. In Oberöwisheim as elsewhere it was not possible to force Catholicism on a Protestant population without a massive application of force. Such a policy was never contemplated by churchmen in Speyer and was, in any case, beyond their powers.

### The murder of Peter Kranz, priest of Oberöwisheim

On May 8, 1653, Christopher Saposius, the Lutheran pastor of Oberöwisheim, sent his maid, Anna, to a kitchen garden to gather some vegetables for supper. As she worked in the garden, Anna was confronted by the Cathedral Chapter's agent in the village, the keller, who told her the pastor had no right to use the garden. The keller struck Anna, knocking her down.[103]

This episode was part of a long dispute between the keller and the pastor. The keller claimed the garden belonged to the Cathedral Chapter, while the pastor argued it belonged to the parish. Upon hearing Anna's story, Saposius grabbed his newly purchased pistol and, ignoring his wife's pleas to seek help from the mayor and other members of the village council, rushed to the garden. There he confronted the keller: "You rogue (*Schelm*), why did you knock my maid down? I will shoot you!" The keller responded, "Go right ahead, I am standing on my lords' property."[104]

A brawl broke out, with the keller getting the upper hand. Onlookers attempted to break up the fight, telling the keller that he had done enough. Both combatants were on the ground when Peter Kranz, the Catholic priest, attempted to pry the two men apart. Suddenly the pastor's gun went off and Kranz fell to the ground dead. The keller, apparently unaware someone had been hit, continued to pound the pastor until someone cried, "O lord Jesus, stop it, the priest has been shot."[105]

---

102    GLAK 229/82623, November 8–19 1649. (Oberöwisheim).
103    The story of the murder of Kranz comes from two sources: GLAK 229/82734, pp. 8–11, which includes the evidence of five witnesses to the events of May 9; and GLAK 61/10971, pp. 373–80, which is the report received by the Cathedral Chapter.
104    GLAK 229/82734.
105    Ibid.: "O herr Jesu, Amptman hörst doch auff der Probst ist geschossen."

All the witnesses to the event testified that the shooting had been an accident. The priest and the pastor had a civil, if distant, relationship. It was the Cathedral Chapter's keller and the pastor who had repeatedly battled over property and religious issues. Saposius, however, did not wait to see if the courts would find Kranz's death accidental. The night after the shooting he and his family fled, leaving most of their property behind.

The shooting itself, which demonstrates the level of tensions within the village in the 1650s, is not as interesting as the aftermath. First of all, the corpse of the priest behaved strangely. Catherine Holtz, a widow, had helped to wash it. An excitable witness, she was unable to recall the events of the shooting due to "fear," but she discussed the behavior of the corpse in gory detail. First the body sweated through the bullet hole, then it started bleeding again the next day. Two days after the shooting the corpse started sweating from the mouth and nose to such an extent that Catherine Holtz could not clean it. Clearly there was something unusual, perhaps supernatural, about the body of the dead priest.

The Cathedral Chapter was determined to exploit the shooting to the fullest. The canons discussed the burial and decided "that a funeral sermon [should] be given, using the opportunity to admonish the subjects as to the effects of rebellion and disobedience."[106] The funeral itself was an attempt to demonstrate the special status of the priest. The funeral procession included three neighboring parish priests, two sacristans, a Dominican friar, and an Augustinian father from Speyer. All arrived in Oberöwisheim in full clerical regalia and followed the coffin into the church singing.

This was no ordinary funeral. Not only was there a large and impressive clerical presence, but all the villagers attended as well as many from neighboring villages. Representatives of all three lords were present. Herr Zacharias Meyer, the priest in Odenheim, gave such a good sermon that everyone stayed to the end. Finally, six Protestant members of the village council served as pallbearers for the priest, a clear attempt to defuse confessional conflict.

If the funeral was in part an attempt to calm the tensions within Oberöwisheim, it succeeded. Reports from late 1653 indicate that the villagers had solved their religious disputes "among themselves."[107] But the Cathedral Chapter and the Catholics also had a second goal. The carefully organized attendance of Catholic clergy from neighboring villages and from Speyer served to remind the Oberöwisheim Catholics that they were part of a wider community, not just a minority within their

106    GLAK 61/10971, p. 376.
107    GLAK 229/82734, p. 12v.

village. Of course the Church was also not averse to exploiting the propaganda victory afforded it by the murder of an innocent man. Finally, it did not hurt to demonstrate the power and beauty of Church services to the villagers.

The funeral of parson Kranz is also indicative of the growing confidence of Catholics in the middle Rhine valley after the Thirty Years' War. This confidence was warranted in Oberöwisheim. Although the villagers who survived the war were almost all Protestants, many of the postwar immigrants to Oberöwisheim were Catholics. By 1652, sixteen Catholics had settled in the village.[108] In 1660 Herr von Helmstatt claimed there were one hundred Catholics in Oberöwisheim.[109] The Catholic community grew because two of the three lords of the village were now Catholic and did not allow the immigration of non-Catholics. As the seventeenth century progressed, the population of Oberöwisheim became increasingly Catholic.

Ultimately, then, the modest gains of the Catholics in Oberöwisheim during the Thirty Years' War were significant. By establishing Catholic services and maintaining a priest in the village, the Cathedral Chapter made the later formation of a Catholic community possible. Because one of the lords remained Protestant, however, and because Protestant practice was also protected, the village remained biconfessional. It is somewhat ironic that the effort to force Catholic unity in the village in fact created religious diversity.

The attempt to Catholicize Protestant areas was never the central thrust of the Counter-Reformation in the Bishopric of Speyer. Efforts before the war to convert the Ritterstift villages and the villages of Dahn were circumscribed. The Church establishment was unwilling to go beyond the initial steps of solidifying its juridical position and installing a Catholic priest in the villages.

The Catholic victories in the early years of the Thirty Years' War changed the political context but did little to change the policies of the local Church. Pressured by other Catholic powers and seeking new financial resources, Speyer officials participated in the attempt to Catholicize the Palatinate and recover the monasteries for the Church. Protestant resistance at the village level, wartime dislocation, and the resulting financial problems and shortage of priests all frustrated this effort.

The war, which crippled the bishopric's finances and destroyed the region economically, was more of a setback than a boost for the Counter-

108    GLAK 61/10971, p. 241.
109    GLAK 61/10973, p. 394.

Reformation. Indeed, it threatened to remove many of the gains of the years from 1580 to 1620 – a more educated and celibate rural clergy, a reform-minded upper clergy, and better Church attendance in the villages. Rural communes were able to maintain and even increase their control of local churches, reversing the prewar period's tentative trend toward centralization.

Ultimately, the surprisingly rapid recovery of the region after the war restored the economic health of the bishopric. Economic recovery, the restoration of the Palatinate to Protestant control, and the election in 1652 of a reformer, Lothar Friederich von Metternich, as bishop, all contributed to a return to prewar conditions. The Counter-Reformation in the Bishopric of Speyer was characterized by considerable temporizing and hesitancy to use force, despite the opportunities the war offered, at the outset at least, to replicate the successes of the Bavarian and Austrian Catholics elsewhere in the Empire. However lacking in apparent coherence, was this not a policy of the art of the possible?

# 9

# "The Heart Has Its Reasons": Predicaments of Missionary Christianity in Early Colonial Peru

*Sabine MacCormack*

Originally appeared as MacCormack, Sabine, "'The Heart Has Its Reasons': Predicaments of Missionary Christianity in Early Colonial Peru," *Hispanic American Historical Review* 65 (1985): 433–46.

*Editor's Introduction*

Beyond Europe, the Counter-Reformation coincided with campaigns to convert the newly subjugated native peoples of Mexico, Peru, and the Caribbean. In her essay on Catholic missionary activity among the Incas, Sabine MacCormack describes how the cultural and political circumstances of colonial Peru combined to harden the missionaries' ideas about conversion. Initially, many advocated conversion by persuasion, not force, within a framework of indigenous Quechua language and culture. Owing to their inability to understand Andean culture on its own terms, however, most missionaries became convinced that persuasion alone was inadequate without coercion, a view that was supported by the Viceroys of Peru, who saw conversion as a means to strengthen their rule. By 1600, the colonial church had withdrawn its earlier concessions and shifted to a belligerent policy of religious extirpation. The dynamics of forcible conversion, in turn, elicited multiple responses among the Inca: Some reformulated traditional values to resist conversion more effectively, others adapted Christianity to native outlooks and needs. In MacCormack's view, this shift to force was not inevitable, and the story of conversion is therefore one of lost opportunities. Her analysis also reveals a complex process of mutual, if unequal, cultural exchange with profound consequences for all sides. Doctrinal rigidity in matters of conversion, for example, was an *outcome* of encounter, not its only precondition. In the manner of "confessionalization," moreover, conversion by force was the by-product of an alliance between the church and state.

# "The Heart Has Its Reasons": Predicaments of Missionary Christianity in Early Colonial Peru

*Sabine MacCormack*

From New Testament times, Christian thinking about what is entailed in conversion to Christianity has followed divergent patterns. On the one hand, it was thought, conversion occurs according to an inner understanding within the individual, in which the missionary is merely a helper. Thus, Paul, in his address to the Athenians, suggested to his listeners that the god whom he preached was in some way already known to them, as witness their altar to the "unknown god."[1] All that he would add was a more specific understanding of a truth already familiar. This model of conversion had many advocates in early Christianity. Clement of Alexandria, Origen, and Eusebius, among others, argued that pagan religion and philosophy enshrined much of what was to be learned more concretely in Christianity, and that potential converts should study their own non-Christian philosophers as an introduction to specifically Christian teaching.[2] In the early fifth century, Augustine took up and elaborated this argument in the *City of God*. On the other hand, Paul asked in the second letter to the Corinthians, "what is there in common between justice and injustice?"[3] and Tertullian echoed the question in his, "what is there in common between Athens and Jerusalem?"[4] According to this model, more is required in conversion than a mere reminder of what a person already knows to be true. Early Christian

---

1 *Acts*, 17, 23, quoted and discussed as applicable to Peruvian Indians by Jeronimo Ore, *Symbolo católico indiano* (Lima, 1598), section 9.

2 See Werner W. Jaeger, *Early Christianity and Greek Paideia* (Cambridge, Mass., 1961); A. D. Nock, *Conversion. The Old and the New in Religion from Alexander the Great to Augustine of Hippo* (London, 1933). Some further landmarks: H. I. Marrou, *Saint Augustin et la fin de la culture antique* (Paris, 1938, 1949); A. D. Nock, "Hellenistic Mysteries and Christian Sacraments," in his *Essays on Religion and the Ancient World*, 2 vols. (Oxford, 1972), II, 791–820; T. Klauser, *Gesammelte Arbeiten zur Liturgiegeschichte, Kirchengeschichte, und christlichen Archäologie* (Münster, 1974); A. Diehle, *The Theory of the Will in Classical Antiquity* (Berkeley, 1982); for the sixteenth century, see E. Campion, "Defences of Classical Learning in Saint Augustine's *De doctrina Christiana* and Erasmus' *Antibarbari*," *History of European Ideas* (Oxford), 4 (1983), 467–72.

3 2 Corinthians 6:15.

4 See J. C. Fredouille, *Tertullien et la conversion de la culture antique* (Paris, 1972), pp. 317–18.

advocates of this model therefore argued that little in non-Christian religion could be salvaged, and that conversion to Christianity entailed a rejection of earlier ways of worship and of thought.

This dichotomy in views of conversion refers not only to the social and cultural identity of potential converts, but to the working of the human mind. For, is Christianity to be embraced as a result of a person's being convinced by propositions such as can be proved by argument, as was suggested by Tertullian, and in a different context, by Ambrose;[5] or is a deeper, more imponderable assent required – an assent, however, which can be given because the conception of the Christian god is innate in the human mind – seeing that it could be said, as by Augustine in his work on *The Trinity*, that God is sought by humans thanks to a patterning of the human mind which corresponds, however distantly, to the three persons and one substance of the Trinity?[6]

At another level, throughout Christian history, the question of what is implied by an assent to Christian teaching, and thus, by conversion, has been framed, on the one hand, in terms of an acquiescence, based on faith, to the authority of scripture and of the tradition of the church; on the other hand, there is posited an assent based on reason and argument. This tension between faith – or authority – and reason,[7] one of which cannot exist without the other, is captured in Pascal's saying: *Le coeur a ses raisons, que la raison ne connaît point.*[8]

A further dimension entered into this debate between faith or authority, and reason, whenever the message of Christianity was backed, on different grounds, by the legislative and coercive power of the state. Thus, Augustine arguing against the pagans of the Roman empire in the *City of God*, a work written to one side of legislative endeavors at achieving conversions, employs a very different language from the Augustine who writes against pagans and Donatists while bearing in mind that these opponents could be coerced by the state.[9] This dichotomy in Augustine's thought, sustained as it was in the New Testa-

---

5   Ambrose, *Letters*, 17; 18; 57, trans. by Sister Mary Melchior Beyenka, O P, vol. 26 of *The Fathers of the Church* (New York, 1954); see J. Wytzes, *Der letzte Kampf des Heidentums in Rom* (Leiden, 1977).

6   Augustine, *The Trinity*, ix; x, trans. by S. McKenna, vol. 45 of *The Fathers of the Church* (Washington, D.C., 1963); M. Schmaus, *Die psychologische Trinitätslehre des hl. Augustinus* (Münster, 1927), pp. 210–416.

7   J. F. Quinn, C.S.B., "Certitude of Reason and Faith in St. Bonaventure and St. Thomas," in *St. Thomas Aquinas, 1274–1974: Commemorative Studies*, 2 vols. (Toronto, 1974), II. 105–40.

8   Pascal, *Pensées*, edition Brunschvicg 277.

9   See Peter Brown, "Religious Dissent in the Later Roman Empire. The Case of North Africa," in his *Religion and Society in the Age of Saint Augustine* (London, 1972), pp. 237–59; and "St. Augustine's Attitude to Religious Coercion," in ibid., pp. 260–78. On the practical feasibility of religious coercion as a factor contributing to its theological justification, see E. Lamirande, *Church, State and Toleration: An Intrigu-*

ment itself, has persisted in much of Christian history, and is echoed in the first council of Lima, the decrees of which, like other ecclesiastical legislation, were enforceable by the secular government. One constitution thus insists that the Indians of Peru must not be subjected to forced baptism, that assent to Christianity should be voluntary.[10] What was envisaged here was a conversion to Christianity resulting from persuasion. Elsewhere, however, the council laid down that the Indians must be forced to listen to Christian teaching regularly,[11] and here, the idea of voluntary conversion is circumscribed by the use of constraint.

The position of converts and potential converts to Christianity in early colonial Peru had been anticipated in the later Roman empire. There, also, Christian argument was enforced by secular legislation.[12] But in Peru, a further difficulty existed. As a result of centuries of coexistence around the shores of the Mediterranean, the inhabitants of the Roman empire shared certain modes of experience and expression on which Christian argument and persuasion could and did build. This was not the case in subsequent centuries of Christian expansion, least of all in Peru. In Peru, missionaries arrived in the wake of the conquest, and in the wake of the partial collapse of indigenous institutions.[13] At the same time, missionaries in Peru, unlike their intellectual ancestors of the late Roman empire, knew next to nothing about those who were to

*ing Change of Mind in Augustine* (The Saint Augustine Lecture) (Villanova, 1975), pp. 51ff on the *locus classicus* in Scripture, Luke, 14:23, "compel them to enter"; further, see n. 72 below.

10  R. Vargas Ugarte, ed., *Concilios Limeños (1551–1772)*, 3 vols. (Lima, 1951–4), Lima I, naturales 7. The First Council of Lima (1551–2), promulgated in Spanish, consists of two discrete sets of constitutions for "naturales" and "españoles." The Second Council of Lima (1567–8), promulgated in Latin, also has separate constitutions for Spaniards and Indians (Indi), summarized in Spanish as parts I and II of the council, respectively. I cite these two councils as follows: number of council, group being legislated for, number of constitution. The Third Council of Lima (1582–3), in Latin with Spanish translation, is in five *actiones*, each with numbered chapters, and is cited accordingly. On voluntary conversion, see further, Bartolomé de Las Casas, *Del único modo de atraer a todos los pueblos a la verdadera religión*, ed. by A. Millares Carlo and Lewis Hanke (Mexico City, 1975).

11  Lima I, naturales 26, 27.

12  *Codex Theodosianus*, ed. by T. Mommsen (Berlin, 1905), p. xvi; *Codex Iustinianus*, ed. by P. Krueger (Dublin, 1967), I, 1, 5–7, 9–11.

13  A revealing episode: Pedro de Cieza de León, *Crónica del Perú* (Biblioteca de Autores Españoles, published in Madrid between 1856 and the present, hereinafter BAE), XXVI, 117. On the conquest from the Andean point of view, *Tragedia del fin de Atahualpa*, in T. L. Meneses, ed., *Teatro quechua colonial* (Lima, 1983); J. M. Arguedas, "El mito de Inkarrí y las tres humanidades," in J. M. Ossio A., comp., *Ideología mesiánica del mundo andino: Antología de Juan M. Ossio A.* (Lima, 1973), pp. 379–91; Frank Salomon, "Chronicles of the Impossible: Notes on Three Peruvian Indigenous Historians," in R. Adorno, ed., *From Oral to Written Expression: Native Andean Chronicles of the Early Colonial Period* (Syracuse, 1982), pp. 9–40. On the interdependence

hear their message. From the beginning, it was thus obvious that the history, the customs, and the languages of the Indians had to be studied if the Christian message were to be communicated in any meaningful fashion. And indeed, much of our information about all aspects of Andean history before the conquest was collected and recorded by missionaries. At the same time, however, this information is often very limited, so that what contemporary scholars seek to understand about the Andes has to be extrapolated from the sources fragment by fragment.[14] The issue here is, first, that a modern investigator asks different questions from his sixteenth-century predecessor. But second, the missionaries themselves, like other early writers on matters Andean, simply failed to understand the phenomena they encountered, and they did this, so I suggest, because in the perennial Christian tension between faith, or authority, and reason, the missionaries came to opt for authority, and with this, for religious coercion, conversion, that is, not so much by persuasion as by force. This happened because the missionaries came to think that Andean cultures could not sustain an understanding of Christianity which came from within those cultures and from within their individual representatives. These cultures were therefore not found worthy of systematic investigation.

I will accordingly argue that during the early decades of evangelization in the Andes the model of conversion by persuasion was implemented by some missionaries, in particular by the friend and follower of Las Casas, Domingo de Santo Tomás.[15] Subsequently, however, this model was supplanted by an ever-increasing insistence on the authority, not only of Christianity, but of European concepts of culture, to the exclusion of their Andean equivalents. Conversion to Christianity thus came to entail, not only the acceptance of a set of beliefs and religious observances, but also a broad acceptance of alien customs and values. Indians were therefore faced with a double system of constraints: on the one hand, the economic and political constraints imposed by the secular state, and on the other, the spiritual and cultural constraints of Christ-

of conquest and evangelization, and the different phases of missionary strategy, see A. Tibesar, *Franciscan Beginnings in Colonial Peru* (Washington, D.C., 1953).

14　An example of just how much information has been lost because, although available, it was recorded only cursorily, is provided by the current discussion of the Inca dynasty or dyarchy that was initiated by R. T. Zuidema, in *The Ceque System of Cuzco: The Social Organization of the Capital of the Inca* (Leiden, 1964); P. Duviols, "La dinastía de los Incas: ¿Monarquía o diarquía?," *Journal de la Société des Américanistes*, 66 (1979), 67–83.

15　The two Dominicans jointly wrote against the perpetuity of encomiendas on behalf of the Indians of Peru; see J. Pérez de Tudela Bueso, ed., *Obras escogidas de Fray Bartolomé de Las Casas*, V, BAE CX, 465–8; further, M. Mahn-Lot, *Bartolomé de Las Casas et le droit des indiens* (Paris, 1982), pp. 197ff, 215–41.

ian mission. Las Casas described the conquest as the "destruction of the Indies."[16] I here argue that this term can be applied as much to the spiritual as to the secular and political conquest of Peru. Given the different models of the functioning of conversion to Christianity outlined at the start, however, I also argue that this outcome was not altogether inevitable, and that therefore the story of missionary Christianity in Peru is a story of lost opportunities, the significance of which reaches far beyond the original purposes of the missionaries and of the Catholic church, because it spells out a general European failure to describe and understand non-European cultures during the early modern period.[17]

One of the first issues encountered by missionaries in Peru was the problem of language. Should Christianity be preached in Spanish, or in the indigenous languages? The issue had been anticipated in the earlier Spanish debate about the nature of European vernacular languages. Were these vernacular languages, in particular Spanish, ordered structures that could be described and analyzed like Latin, the language of scholarship and Holy Writ? The publication, in 1492, of Nebrija's *Gramática castellana* was a landmark in this debate, because it demonstrated that the vernacular languages were structured according to rules of grammar and syntax[18] analogous to those operating in Latin. The categories Nebrija used to analyze, or, as it was expressed in the sixteenth century, to "reduce" the Spanish language to the order of parts of speech, declensions, and conjugations were the same categories that he also applied to Latin in his Latin grammar. The publication of Nebrija's Spanish grammar converged with research on the text of the Bible. In 1516, Erasmus published his Greek edition with Latin translation of the New Testament, and in 1517 appeared the Alcalá polyglot

16   The much discussed treatise of Las Casas, *Brevíssima relación de la destruyción de las Indias*, was published without license in Seville in 1552; reprinted in Pérez de Tudela Bueso, ed., *Obras escogidas*, V, 134–81.

17   B. Bucher, *Icon and Conquest: A Structural Analysis of the Illustrations of de Bry's Great Voyages* (Chicago, 1981). J. H. Elliott, *The Old World and the New, 1492–1650* (Cambridge, 1970), and Anthony Pagden, *The Fall of Natural Man: The American Indian and the Origins of Comparative Ethnology* (Cambridge, 1982), takes a more positive view of early modern ethnography. See further, X. Albo, "Jesuitas y culturas indígenas," *América Indígena*, 26 (1966), 249–308, 395–445.

18   Antonio de Nebrija, *Gramática de la lengua castellana* (Salamanca, 1492), ed. by A. Quilis (Madrid, 1980). This work was apparently unknown to Juan de Valdés when, at least a generation later, he wrote the *Diálogo de la lengua*, ed. by Lope Blanch (Mexico City, 1966), where he maintains that "las lenguas vulgares de ninguna manera se pueden reduzir a reglas de tal suerte que por ellas se puedan aprender"; p. 32; compare 4, 24. See further, M. Bataillon, *Erasmo y España: Estudios sobre la historia espiritual del siglo xvi* (Mexico City, 1966), in particular, pp. 694–8; E. Asensio, "El erasmismo y las corrientes espirituales afines," *Revista de Filología Española*, 36 (1952), 31–99.

Bible, which had been prepared by a team of scholars assembled by Cardinal Ximénez, Nebrija among them. The immediate issue raised by these editions and translations was indeed the theological viability of new Latin translations of the Bible, seeing that Jerome's Vulgate had been canonized by the usage of more than a millennium; but behind such new Latin translations stood the possibility of translations into the vernacular.[19]

This issue affected not only Spain, but also the New World. For, insofar as Nebrija's *Gramática castellana* validated the language of Spanish daily life, it at the same time helped to validate the indigenous languages – also languages of daily life – of the New World as vehicles of communication beyond bare necessities. The Dominican friar Domingo de Santo Tomás, one of the first missionaries to work in Peru, spelled out the implications not only for missionary Christianity in Peru, but also for an understanding of Andean and Inca civilization in general.[20] His Quechua lexicon and grammar were published in Valladolid in 1560.[21] In the dedication of the grammar to Philip II he says:

> How easy and sweet is the pronunciation of Quechua, which is ordered and adorned with the regularity of declension and the other properties of the noun, and with the moods, tenses, and persons of the verb. In short, in many respects and ways of expression, it conforms to Latin and Spanish. . . . The language is civilized and abundant, regular and ordered by the same rules and precepts as Latin, as is proved by this grammar.

In his preface to the reader, accordingly, Santo Tomás explicitly echoes the preface to the third edition of Nebrija's Latin grammar, thus juxtaposing as analogous the composition of a Latin grammar and that of a vernacular language such as Spanish, and now Quechua.

The issue raised here was not merely linguistic. Rather, both the culture and the human capacity of the Indians were at stake, as Santo Tomás points out:

19   Bataillon, *Erasmo y España*, pp. 1–51; also, J. H. Bentley, *Humanists and Holy Writ. New Testament Scholarship in the Renaissance* (Princeton, 1983) and A. Guy, *La pensée de fray Luis de León. Contribution à l'étude de la philosophie espagnole au xvi<sup>e</sup> siècle* (Paris, 1943), pp. 184–257.

20   M. Mahn-Lot, "Transculturation et evangélisation dans le Pérou du xvi<sup>e</sup> siècle. Notes sur Domingo de Santo Tomás, disciple de Las Casas," *Mélanges en honneur de Fernand Braudel. II: Méthodologie de l'histoire et des sciences humaines* (Toulouse, 1973), pp. 353–65; Fr. José María Vargas, O P, *La primera gramática quichua por Fr. Domingo de Santo Tomás, O.P.* (Quito, 1947), reprints the text of this work with a useful introduction.

21   Domingo de Santo Tomás, *Lexicon o vocabulario de la lengua general del Perú* (Valladolid, 1560), and idem, *Grammática o arte de la lengua general de los indios de los Reynos del Perú* (Valladolid, 1560), both reprinted by Raúl Porras Barrenechea (Lima, 1951).

My principal intention in offering this small work to Your Majesty has been that Your Majesty should see clearly and manifestly how false is the position of which many have sought to convince your Majesty, that the people of Peru are barbarians and unworthy of being treated with the same gentleness and liberty as Your Majesty's other subjects.

And farther on:

Let Your Majesty understand that the people of those great kingdoms of Peru live in a most civilized and ordered way and lack nothing except that Your Majesty should know this, and should understand that those who persuade Your Majesty to the contrary seek to mislead because they attend only to their own personal advantage.[22]

Santo Tomás here alludes to a statement in Aristotle's *Politics*, which had also been expounded by Aquinas,[23] according to which it is language that distinguishes man from the other animals and qualifies him for a social life, life in a state. Languages, however, vary, and the sophistication, or lack of it, of any given language is an indicator of the sophistication, the social and political order of those who speak it.[24]

According to Domingo de Santo Tomás, therefore, the order and regularity of the Quechua language demonstrated that the Incas and their subjects were civilized people, and had, before the conquest, lived in a rightfully constituted state. This argument gave a quite new turn to the highly abstract and theoretical debate among Spanish intellectuals and bureaucrats about the humanity, the intellectual and political capacity of the Indians, because it contributed to this debate a concrete piece of evidence. This is clear, for instance, from the Quechua vocabulary of Fray Domingo, where Christian terms, such as "soul," "baptize," "confession," for which later the church introduced Latin or Spanish terms into Quechua,[25] are expressed by already existing Quechua terms. The grammar and vocabulary, written explicitly for missionaries, show

22   Domingo de Santo Tomás, *Arte*, pp. 10, 16, 11–12, respectively.
23   Aristotle, *Politics*, trans. by H. Rackham (Cambridge, Mass., 1944), pp. 1, 10–12; Aquinas, *In libros politicorum Aristotelis expositio* (Rome, 1951), lectio 1, 23.
24   See Juan de Valdés, *Diálogo de la lengua*, p. 20.
25   Antonio Ricardo, *Vocabulario y phrasis en la lengua general de los indios del Perú, llamada quichua, y en la lengua española* (Lima, 1586, repr. 1951); here, some Quechua terms survived in Christian usage; e.g., "baptizar, baptizani sutiani, sutiacuni" (i.e., to give a name in public); Diego de Torres Rubio, SJ, *Arte de la lengua quichua* (Lima, 1619). On the "capacities" of the Indians, see Lewis Hanke, *Aristotle and the American Indians: A Study in Race Prejudice in the Modern World* (Chicago, 1959); M. Bataillon, "Les 'Douze Questions' péruviennes résolues par Las Casas," in his *Etudes sur Bartolomé de Las Casas* (Paris, 1965), pp. 258–72; Pagden, *Fall of Natural Man*.

that conversion to Christianity, in the mind of the author, did not have to entail either the use of force, or a conversion to a European or Spanish way of life, such as was envisioned by many representatives of the secular government.[26] Indeed, the grammar and lexicon met with considerable success, in that they were the first among many similar works on Peruvian languages, and in that early attempts to teach Christianity in Spanish[27] were supplanted by the practice of teaching it in the indigenous languages.[28]

Acceptance of Andean languages by the missionaries, however, did not in the outcome entail any analogous acceptance of Andean religious institutions as equally capable of adaptation by Christianity. Andean religion before the conquest had known a series of institutions that, according to some observers, resembled those of Catholic Christianity. Among these were fasting and confession of sins, followed by atonement and restitution.[29] Some of the early missionaries accordingly concluded that the way had providentially been prepared for Christianity. Subsequent experience, however, showed that in many *doctrinas* ("missionary parishes") fasting and confession within the Andean religious framework, together with pilgrimages to and worship of Andean holy places, had survived alongside their Christian counterparts.[30] This

26 Letters by Domingo de Santo Tomás to Philip II, Archivo General de Indias (Seville), Lima 313. The argument for preserving Andean customs was still made by José de Acosta, *Historia natural y moral de las Indias* (Seville, 1590; repr. Mexico City, 1962), VI, 1, 7. But in Acosta's day, real continuity between Inca and Spanish public life in Peru, as distinct from salvaging a residue of Andean customs, was no longer at stake. Even so, seeing that church councils were capable of legislating that holy lights in churches must be fed from bees' wax and olive oil imported from Spain (Lima II, Españoles 38), rather than from any combustibles produced locally, and that the use of tables and beds like those of Europe was essential for Christian "pulicia" (Lima II, Indi 112, Lima III, actio 5, ch. 4), Acosta's comments may sound liberal.

27 Lima I, Naturales 1; for an overview of the issues, see E. J. Burrus, SJ, "The Language Problem in Spain's Overseas Dominions," *Neue Zeitschrift für Missionswissenschaft*, 35 (1979), 161–70.

28 Juan de Matienzo, *Gobierno del Perú (1567)*, ed. by G. Lohmann Villena (Paris, 1967), I, 36; Lima II, Indi 3; Lima III, actio 2, chs 3, 6; the Indians are not to be taught prayers and catechism in Latin; Francisco Mateos, SJ, ed., *Historia general de la Compañía de Jesús en la Provincia del Perú*, 2 vols. (Madrid, 1944), II, 17; the Indians have learned prayers in Latin and Spanish, "like parrots." Antonio de la Calancha, *Corónica moralizada del Orden de San Agustín en el Perú, con sucesos ejemplares vistas en esta monarquía* (Barcelona, 1639), pp. 1, 20, 2, observed that teaching Christianity in Latin in the early days was as useless as it would have been teaching it in Greek.

29 Acosta, *Historia natural y moral*, V, 25 and n. 31 below.

30 On Andean conceptualizations of the holy as mountain, steam, stone, or cave, see Jorge L. Urioste, trans. *Hijos de Pariya Qaqa: La tradición oral de Waru Chiri* (Syracuse, 1983), e.g., pp. 69ff, 90ff, 95ff, and so forth; L. Huertas Vallejos, *La religión en una sociedad rural andina, siglo xvii* (Ayacucho, 1981), pp. 77ff; María Rostworowski

brought about a shift in missionary thinking. Where some early missionaries, both in Mexico and Peru, had thought that conversion was an organic process which could take place within an indigenous social and cultural framework, more prolonged familiarity with concrete circumstances led to the conclusion that, so far from there having occurred a *praeparatio evangelica* in the Andes, Andean religious institutions were incapable of being transformed into any Christian equivalents. Concurrently, the missionaries came to conclude that conversion by persuasion without use of force would not work. Missionaries and indigenous priests thus confronted each other in an explicit combat for the allegiance of the Indians. A telling example comes from a report, dated 1560, of the first Augustinian mission to Guamachuco.[31]

> The manner of their confession was that they told their *ochas*, which is to say sins . . . And I was informed of a notable thing, that after the devil [*demonio*] sees how the Indians already do what the [Christian] Fathers tell them, . . . he commands them, since they are now Christians, not to be Christians voluntarily, and not to do anything that the Fathers tell them with respect to being a Christian and going to church and being taught, but only to do it by force; and this we observe to be the case with some [Indians] who by pure force are taken to catechism class and to mass, and they flee. Thus, I have also been told that the sorcerers [*hechiceros*] make them confess if they went to catechism class . . . of their own free will.

We have here not only a report – one from among many more – of an Andean response to evangelization, but also a telling indication of how this response was viewed by many missionaries.

According to them, the devil or the demons were ubiquitous in the Andes. Like some of their European contemporaries,[32] they followed the Christian apologists of the early church and the church fathers in attributing all non-Judaic and non-Christian religious practices to initiatives of demons, that is, of fallen angels who had usurped the place of God in human life by attracting worship to themselves. So, with

de Diez Canseco, *Estructuras andinas del poper: Ideología religiosa y política* (Lima, 1983), pp. 61ff.

31  *Colección de documentos inéditos relativos al descubrimiento, conquista, y organización de las antiguas posesiones españolas en América y Oceania, sacados de los archivos del reino y muy especialmente del de Indias*, 42 vols. (Madrid, 1864–84), III, 44–6.

32  E.g., Jerónimo Román y Zamora, *Repúblicas del mundo, divididas en xxvii libros* (Medina del Campo, 1575), libro 7 de la república gentílica, c. 14, on the origin of magic. For discussion of the rationale of resorting to the existence of the devil to explain religious phenomena being rejected, see *Saeculum. Jahrbuch für Universalgeschichte*, 34 (1983), Sonderheft on the theme, *Dämonen und Gegengötter. Antagonistische und antinomische Strukturen in der Götterwelt*.

respect to confession in the Andes, the demons had anticipated the pure rites of the church by moving the Indians to make confession of their sins: this confession, however, was a travesty of true Christian confession, because it was addressed to the *huacas*, which, the missionaries thought, were the equivalent of Greco-Roman idols: and these, in their day, like the *huacas* in Peru, were inhabited by demonic spirits. In addition, the demons of the Andes were thought to inspire their human ministers, that is, those who heard confessions and administered the cults, whom the missionaries invariably called *hechiceros* or sorcerers.[33]

Most missionaries thus convinced themselves that the demons held an almost invincible command over the Indians, a command that could ultimately be broken only by religious coercion. Coercion was further justified in their minds because they thought of the Indians as simple people,[34] who were all too easily deceived by the cunning of the demons. Accordingly, no qualms were felt by those who in the second council of Lima decreed that *hechiceros*, Indians who heard confessions and supervised the cult of *huacas*, should be taken out of their communities and be forced to live in seclusion and perpetual confinement in a house apart.[35] Such a policy seemed appropriate because many Spaniards thought that the Indians lacked the capacity for a full understanding of

33   Cf. S. MacCormack, "Calderón's La aurora en Copacabana," *Journal of Theological Studies*, 33 (1982), pp. 451ff.

34   See, for example, Lima I, naturales 1; Lima II, Indi 75, on extreme unction: the Indians, although easily persuaded to return to their old religion by "idolorum ministri et venefici," should be given extreme unction because they are "timidi, inopes ingenii"; cf. Lima III, actio 2, ch. 17; Lima III, actio 3, ch. 3 makes grim reading, being a mixture of humanitarian concern and feelings of cultural superiority. As a result, Indians were not at the outset considered fit to receive the Eucharist (Lima I, naturales 14, repealed by Lima II, Indi 58) and until modern times, they could not become priests (Lima II, Indi 74); José de Acosta, *De procuranda Indorum salute (Predicación del evangelio en las Indias)*, trans. by Francisco Mateos, S J (Madrid, 1952), Book VI, p. 19. On this issue Felipe Guaman Poma de Ayala, *El primer nueva corónica y buen gobierno*, ed. by John V. Murra and Rolena Adorno; trans. by Jorge L. Urioste (Mexico City, 1980), p. 4. (This work is hereinafter cited as Guaman Poma. I follow the revised pagination of the editors.) The position in Mexico was similar; Robert Ricard, *The Spiritual Conquest of Mexico* (Berkeley, 1966), pp. 122ff, 308. Historians of missionary Christianity who accept its rhetoric at face value tend to overlook the fundamental importance of this question; e.g., F. de Armas Medina, *Cristianización del Perú (1532–1600)* (Seville, 1953), pp. 364ff; and even more so, Pedro Borges, O.F.M., *Métodos misionales en la cristianización de América, siglo xvi* (Madrid, 1960), pp. 536ff.

35   Lima II, Indi 107; Lima III, actio 2, ch. 42. Domingo de Santo Tomás, who was present at the Second Council of Lima, opposed this policy: W. Espinosa Soriano, F. P. Gutiérrez Flores, and John V. Murra, eds, *Visita hecha a la provincia de Chucuito por Garci Diez de San Miguel en el año 1567* (Lima, 1964), p. 235; Juan de Matienzo, *Gobierno del Perú*, ed. by G. Lohmann Villena (Lima, 1967), pp. 1, 36.

Christianity. They could therefore only be taught the rudiments of the faith. Just how rudimentary such teaching could be emerges from a report dated 1580, by the Viceroy Toledo to the crown. The viceroy comments on the negligence of the Dominicans in instructing the Indians of Chucuito and continues:

> I arranged that the Indians . . . be gathered in the courtyards of the priests' houses and in the squares in front of the churches and forbade them to leave before they knew the prayers and the other [teachings] which are required for baptism, and that they should meanwhile be fed on the resources of the community. This was done, and in very few days they knew [the prayers] and understood [the teachings] and were baptized.[36]

One reason for Toledo's commitment to a policy of evangelization was that Christianity, or rather the organization by the church of the Indians into parishes, could be a means of strengthening the hold of government over the vast territory of the Viceroyalty of Peru. A case in point were the *reducciones*, resettlements in villages of Indians who had formerly lived in scattered communities. Most government officials regarded the *reducciones* as a necessity, because they were the means of integrating the Indians into a non-Andean government and a non-Andean structure of landholding and taxation, which were all superimposed, along with Christianity, on what endured of preconquest religion and economic and social organization.[37] At the same time, the *reducciones* were advantageous to the church, because one priest could oversee a sizeable community without interminable travel. In addition, moving the Indians to new homes, amounted to moving them away from their ancestral *huacas*: ancestral in every sense, because not only did the *huacas* receive a long established cult, but also, many of them were thought of as the place of origin of Indian communities and nations.[38] Leaving one's home therefore brought with it not only

36 *Colección de documentos inéditos para la historia de España*, 112 vols. (Madrid, 1842– ), XCIV, 496.

37 One of many examples: Marcos Jiménez de la Espada, ed., *Relaciones geográficas de Indias – Perú*, BAE CLXXIII, "Descripción . . . de la provincia de los Yauyos" . . . por Diego Dávila Brizeño, corregidor de Guarocheri, who, in over thirteen years of service, "reduced" more than 400 villages to 39. On ecclesiastical attitudes, Lima II, Indi 80; cf. Lima I, naturales 30, on the advantages of streets for evangelization, seeing that streets make people accessible to an administrative network, whether this is the administration of the sacraments (as in the constitution here cited) or the administration of measures taken by the secular government.

38 P. Duviols, "Un inédit de Cristóbal de Albornoz: La instrucción para descubrir todas las Guacas del Pirú y sus Camayos y haziendas," *Journal de la Société des Américanistes*, 56 (1967), 20: "Hay . . . el principal genero de guacas que antes que fuesen

material, but also spiritual, upheaval and confusion. Christianity taught in such circumstances could not foster that patterning of the human mind which, Augustine thought, naturally led to belief in the Christian god, and therefore to a lasting conviction of the Christian truth. Relapses to the old religion were frequent.

This outcome was in part the product of the missionaries' involvement with the state. In one sense – as in the case of the *reducciones* – their work was eased by the needs of the state. In another sense, however, the needs of the state determined missionary policy. For the viceregal government tended to favor rapid evangelization and, if need be, forced conversion, whereas the church adhered, in principle, if not in daily practice, to the idea that baptism must be voluntary.[39] A series of decisions, quite apart from decisions imposed by government, however, impelled the missionaries toward religious coercion. The most important of these arose from the conviction that Inca and Andean religion had been inspired by demons, that nothing therefore could be salvaged for Christianity from among existing beliefs and religious practices. The opening of most missionary campaigns accordingly consisted of first discovering what were the holy places and holy objects of any given region, and of then destroying them. Like Martin of Tours and others in the fourth century,[40] the missionaries hoped to demonstrate in this way that the idols could not help themselves, let alone anyone else. The next stage was to organize catechism classes, attendance at which, with the assistance of the secular government, was made compulsory; the classes would be followed by baptism and more detailed instruction.[41] Missionary campaigns which began without the destruction of holy objects, if they happened, must have been rare indeed. Mostly, they commenced with acts of violence,

subjetos al ynga tenian, que llaman pacariscas, que quieren dezir creadoras de sus naturalezas"; Pablo José de Arriaga, *Extirpación de la idolatría en el Perú*, in Francisco Esteve Barba, comp., *Crónicas peruanas de interés indígena*, BAE CCIX, pp. 219–20; Archivo Arzobispal, Lima, Idolatrías IV, 18, AD 1615, Cauri near Guánuco, fols. 1ff: the people revere a rock from which came their originator Yanaraman.

39   On military expeditions to the frontiers, where soldiers were accompanied by missionaries, see Lima I, naturales 36; Lima III, actio 2, ch. 7; Fr. Diego de Córdoba y Salinas, O.F.M., *Crónica franciscana de las provincias del Perú*, ed. by Lino Gómez Canedo, O.F.M. (Washington, D.C., 1957), pp. 449ff, describes expeditions of this kind. Further, J. M. García Recio, "La iglesia en Santa Cruz de la Sierra," *Missionalia Hispánica* (Madrid), 40 (1983), 258–313. Issues relating to missionary policy and government generated much tension between church and state; on the case of the Jesuit Luis López, see *Colección de documentos inéditos para la historia de España*, XCIV, 473.

40   Sulpicius Severus, *La vie de Saint Martin*, ed. by J. Fontaine (Paris, 1961–9), pp. 13–14, 22.

41   Lima I, naturales 2–13, outlines the running of a recently established *doctrina*.

and thus, with coercion, even when, overtly, coercion was employed only to bring about abandonment of old beliefs, not the adoption of Christianity.[42]

The real and lasting difficulty, however, was that violence and coercion did not end there. Rather, the first destruction of *huacas* was only the start of an ever-accelerating momentum of violence which it proved impossible to arrest. For, first, the Indians often successfully concealed their *huacas* during an initial campaign of extirpation, leaving these to be discovered on subsequent occasions – a fact which led to mutual distrust and enmity between Indians and their *curas*.[43] And, second, the holy was ubiquitous in the ancient countryside of the Andes, and it could not be separated from the sights and doings of everyday life. We are dealing here not merely with tenacious ancient usages adhered to generation after generation, usages such as missionaries had also found in the countryside of the late antique Mediterranean and beyond. For in the Andes, these customs were part and parcel of the deeply rooted resistance to the conquest and its outcomes.[44] This resistance brought forward its own leadership and pitted itself not only against physical violence, the violence involved in campaigns of extirpation of idols and in resettlement in *reducciones*, but also against spiritual violence and its result, spiritual impoverishment.

42   Lima I, naturales 26, 27; note Lima II, Indi 115, "vana esset lex illa seu praeceptum quod non haberet vim aliquam coercivam et compulsivam," reiterated in Lima III, actio 4, ch. 7. The distinction between abandoning old beliefs and adopting new ones is made in missionary literature so as to save consciences. In general, the deliberate desecration of indigenous holy places quite spontaneously went hand in hand with seizing their treasures and arguing for the superiority of the Christian god. The earliest example of this conglomeration of themes in Peru occurs in the account by Miguel de Estete of Hernando Pizarro's expedition to Pachacamac in 1532, which is inserted in Francisco de Jerez, *Conquista del Perú*, BAE XXVI, pp. 338–43. See also n. 68 below.
43   Archivo Arzobispal, Lima, Idolatrías II, 12, AD 1659. The Indians of Acas (Cajatambo) against their cura Bernardo de Noboa; note fols 210rff, where the huacas Guaman Camac and Cargua Tcilla Urau are consulted and revered for protection against cura and corregidor. Idolatrías IV, 42, Santo Domingo de Atunyauyos, AD 1680, fols 1ff: the Indians apostasize and plan to murder their cura. See also Lima II, Indi 98.
44   Duviols, "La instrucción," pp. 35ff. Luis Millones, ed., *Las informaciones de Cristóbal de Albornoz: Documentos para el estudio del Taki Onqoy* (Cuernavaca, 1971), see pp. 1, 36–7; Todas las guacas del reino quantas avian quemado los cristianos e destruido avian rresuscitado y estavan rrepartidas en dos partes las unas con la guaca Pachacama y las otras con la guaca Titicaca, que heran los dos principales e questas se avian juntado para dar batalla a Dios Nuestro Senor. M. Curatola, "Posesión y chamanismo en el culto de crisis del Taqui Ongo," *III Congreso Peruano. El Hombre y la Cultura Andina 1977. Actas y Trabajos*. Segunda serie, III (Lima 1980), pp. 43–64.

Spiritual violence was the inevitable outcome of physical violence. It can be documented in the aggressively simplistic arguments with which some missionaries propounded to the Indians the truth of Christian monotheism and the falsity of Andean religion.[45] Thus, the catechisms, manuals for confession, and sermons for Indians, as well as the teaching of the first three councils of Lima, make dry and depressing reading. Again and again it is reiterated that the Indians must learn by heart the Lord's Prayer, the Hail Mary, and the Creed, and that they must understand the Ten Commandments, the works of mercy, and the articles of the faith.[46] Repeatedly the leaders of the church emphasize that Christian instruction must be simple and consistent, because otherwise the Indians will not grasp it.[47]

In the framework of missionary work, this argument had a profoundly negative effect. For it allowed the missionaries to repeat, without much self-questioning, that the Indians were an easy prey for demons and had to be nursed away from their inadequate religious ideas by the most simplistic of methods. Furthermore, it led the missionaries to reduce Christianity as addressed to Indians to the bare bones. This reduced Christianity did receive some form of assent, because almost everyone accepted baptism. Such teaching, however, anchored almost exclusively in the exercise of authority and force, precluded such inner assent as is postulated by the necessary coexistence of faith and reason in Christian thought.

By the late sixteenth century, missionary Christianity had thus crystallized into a rigid and self-contained body of doctrine impermeable to any influence from Andean religion. Quechua terminology used to describe Christian concepts had been carefully eliminated from dictionaries, catechisms, and manuals of preaching to Indians, and the same purist attitude defined all other aspects of Christian life in the Andes. In the wake of the Council of Trent, which regulated the appearance of

45    The central tenet that early modern Europe and early modern Christianity addressed to the world at large concerned unitary causation: whether this was with respect to creation (see n. 38 above), the functioning of the universe (Acosta, *Historia natural y moral*, I, 1ff), or monotheistic theology. One of the more remarkable theological attainments of the Incas was thus – according to a somewhat fanciful echo of the theory of the unmoved mover – thought to be the realization that the sun could not be divine since it always moved: there must be a more universal cause beyond the sun; see Garcilaso, *The Royal Commentaries of the Incas and General History of Peru*, trans. by H. V. Livermore (Austin, 1966), I, 8, 8 (citation from Blas Valera).
46    Lima I, naturales 1, 38–9; Lima II, Indi Prologue; Indi Constitutions 2, 32–5, 88; Lima III, actio 2, chs 3–4; see also the priest's manual for hearing confessions in Torres Rubio, SJ, *Arte*.
47    Lima I, naturales 1; Lima II, Indi 2.

holy images,[48] Indian sculptors and painters of such images had to conform their work to European iconographies and aesthetic norms – as was made clear to don Francisco Tito Yupanqui, the sculptor of the image of Our Lady of Copacabana, when he first requested a license to make religious images from the Bishop of La Plata. He had presented the bishop with a painting of the Virgin and received the following response: "I do not want to give you a license to be a painter, or that you should make paintings or statues of the Virgin, and if you want to be a painter, paint the monkey with its tail. . . . And if you make images of the Virgin, I shall punish you very thoroughly."[49]

Where, therefore, in 1560, the Augustinian missionaries in Guamachuco could still consider the possibility of using Andean textiles to adorn Christian buildings and images, so validating one part at least of Andean culture and thereby acculturating Spanish Christian notions of beauty to the Andes, by the end of the century any such adaptation of Christianity to its new environment had been rejected.[50]

A similar result emerges when we examine missionaries' attitudes to Andean social structure. The recognition or nonrecognition of non-Christian marriages was a perennial problem in the missionary churches of the early modern period, the Andes not excluded. But no clear understanding of the rules of Andean marriage and of the kinship system that underlay it, can be gained from ecclesiastical legislation. It follows that the rules of the church governing marriage and exemptions from them,

---

48   Council of Trent, Session XXV (S. Binius), *Conciliorum omnium generalium et provincialium collectio regia*, XXXV (Paris, 1644), pp. 602–5.

49   Alonso Ramos Gavilán, *Historia de Nuestra Señora de Copacabana* (Lima, 1621, repr. La Paz, 1976), II, 6, p. 125. The bishop's response was to be expected after the formal reception of the decrees of the Council of Trent in Peru, in 1567; on images, see Lima II, Indi 87. R. Lebroc, "Proyección tridentina en América," *Missionalia Hispánica* (Madrid) 26: 77 (1969), 129–207; S. Aparicio, "Influjo de Trento en los Concilios Limenses," *Missionalia Hispánica*, 29: 86 (1972), 215–39. For the American missions, the Council of Trent came at the wrong time: cf. Ricard, *Conquest*, p. 35. On Copacabana, see S. MacCormack, "From the Sun of the Incas to the Virgin of Copacabana," *Representations* (Berkeley), 8 (1984), 30–60.

50   Andean textiles in Christian cult: "Religiosos Agustinos" in *Colección de documentos inéditos relativos al descubrimiento, conquista y colonización de las posesiones españolas en América y Oceania*, III, 26, "de la ropa [of a destroyed huaca] hicieron frontales y doseles para las iglesias"; see also pp. 27, 30. T. Gisbert, *Iconografía y mitos indígenas en el arte* (La Paz, 1980), chs 1 and 2, makes a convincing case for the continued use of pre-Columbian religious motifs in early colonial ecclesiastical art; but the fact remains that such survivals are the exception, not the rule. For an analogous imposition of European norms on African Christians, see W. Buhlmann, "L'autre face de l'histoire des missions," *Neue Zeitschrift für Missionswissenschaft*, 38 (1982), 124–35.

promulgated for Indians by Pope Paul III, were usually applied blind-fold.[51] This fits into a wider picture of almost universal ecclesiastical incomprehension of preconquest Andean law and society. If we are to set aside information derived from *Visitas*,[52] the main purpose of which was to assess Indians for taxation, there is only one known author who set out, in a systematic fashion, to describe the Andean interdependence of law, social structure, and religion. This was the lawyer Juan Polo de Ondegardo. His principal purpose was indeed to provide information needed to create an equitable tax structure; but, unlike many others, he thought that this could not be done without an understanding of the workings of the Inca state and of Andean customary law. Polo's views were independently confirmed by a late contemporary, the Jesuit Luis López,[53] who thought that lawyers could be dispensed with in Peru, because the land should be administered according to the law, the *fueros*, of the Incas. By this time, however, thanks to thirteen years of relentless government by the Viceroy Toledo, the conquerors' grip on the viceroy-alty had tightened sufficiently for any thought of adapting viceregal gov-ernment and law to the earlier government and law of the Incas to be dismissed. One of the reasons for this outcome is to be found in the fact that the missionaries, who were widely regarded as experts on matters Indian, were never able to translate Christianity into Andean terms: that is, to separate Christianity from its European cultural, sociological, and even political framework. In short, most of them failed to reach an autonomous grasp of Andean culture.

When in 1580 Toledo returned to Spain, the early and enthusiastic, if violent, years of founding the church of Peru were over. The founders of the viceregal polity, both secular and ecclesiastical, were old or had died, and the controversies and encounters of the first fifty years which have occupied us so far, were continued in a more sober strain by a new generation of missionaries and servants of the Spanish crown. These men experienced the reality of the fall of the Incas less radically, less vio-lently, and less exuberantly than had the previous generation. Their clearly perceived task was to preserve what had been gained for the crown of Spain and for themselves.

51   The exemptions, Lima I, naturales 18; uncertainties about the validity of Andean marriage, Lima I, naturales 16, 17, 19, 27; Lima II, Indi 60–73. See also R. T. Zuidema, "The Inca Kinship System: A New Theoretical View," in R. Bolton and E. Mayer, eds, *Andean Kinship and Marriage* (Washington, D.C., 1977), pp. 240–92, where date from missionary literature are used and evaluated.
52   Franklin Pease G. Y., "Las visitas como testimonio andino," in *Historia, prob-lema y promesa. Homenaje a Jorge Basadre* (Lima, 1978), pp. 437–53.
53   See above n. 39. On Polo, see John V. Murra, "Las investigaciones en etnohis-toria andina y sus posibilidades en el futuro," in his *Formaciones económicas y políti-cas del mundo andino* (Lima, 1975), pp. 306ff.

The gulf between Indians and newcomers accordingly deepened. For while Spaniards in Peru inevitably viewed the conquest as the key event in their past, many Indians, notwithstanding decades of governmental and ecclesiastical activity designed to incorporate them into a state constituted on a European model and a church to match, looked back to the Incas. At about the time when Don Quixote rode the tracks of La Mancha, two gentlemen of Lima, of Spanish extraction, but born in Peru, engaged in a polite and erudite conversation, in which the one gentleman told the other the following story.

> In the valley of Xauxa, I met on the road an old Indian carrying a bundle of *quipus*, which he tried to hide. When challenged, he explained that these *quipus* were the account he had to give to the Inca when he returned from the other world, of all that had happened in the valley in his absence. In the account were included all the Spaniards who had traveled on that royal road, what they had wanted and bought, and all they had done, both the good and the bad. The *corregidor* with whom I was traveling took and burned these accounts and punished the Indian.[54]

The speaker used the story as evidence to prove that, despite their limited capacity, the Indians believed in an afterlife, in the existence of the soul, and even in the resurrection of the body. All these were ideas which the missionaries had worked hard to inculcate – yet the story illustrates, not as much the narrator's point, as how far apart were the two civilizations of postconquest Peru, the *república de indios* and the *república de españoles*.

The early seventeenth century witnessed a new missionary strategy, in the form of systematically organized ecclesiastical campaigns designed to extirpate idolatry among the Indians, and to destroy what was left of the old religion. These campaigns revealed that in many places, the old religion, so far from having been dislodged from the minds of the Indians, had become a vehicle to resist not only Christianity, but all other forms of absorption into Spanish ways. The practice of removing the bodies of the dead from the Christian cemetery and of reburying them next to their pagan ancestors in the ancient sites for burial was almost ubiquitous, and was the means of reaffirming non-Christian

---

54  Diego Avalos y Figueroa, *Miscelánea austral* (Lima, 1602), p. 151r; cf. Garcilaso's famous passage on memories of the Incas in Cuzco, *Royal Commentaries*, I, 1, 15. But it was not only in the central parts of the empire that the Incas were remembered. A Franciscan missionary in Pantaguas listened to a cacique's "canto triste, en que nombró los Ingas del Peru y la muerte que los Españoles dieron al rey Atahualpa Inga": Fr. Diego de Córdova Salinas, O.F.M., *Crónica*, p. 222. Quipus were prohibited by the church as a source of superstition, Lima III, actio 3, ch. 37; on the immortality of the soul, Lima II, actio 3, ch. 113.

values and beliefs.[55] Christianization had amounted to a reorganization of space, in that life in the *reducciones* centered on the public square and the church with its cemetery, which were a feature of the Toledan and other *reducciones*. To re-bury the bodies of the dead in the old burial grounds outside the village meant that this reorganization of space, and the Christian beliefs to which it gave expression, were deliberately rejected by the Indians. Simultaneously, reburial amounted to a careful reformulation of the old religion and of non-Hispanic values.

This reformulation began with material culture. Before reburial, the bodies of the dead were dressed and adorned with indigenous textiles, and received the traditional offerings of llamas, guinea pigs, maize, and coca: no Hispanic products were ever offered to them. The old burial grounds were usually situated near the villages and settlements, which the Indians had been forced to abandon when the *reducciones* were formed.[56] Continued use of these burial grounds thus reemphasized a pre-colonial sacred topography, which also comprised other places – such as streams, mountains, rocks – which had been sanctified by myth and custom. Reburial was arranged according to kin group (*ayllu*).[57] so that the world of the living was mirrored in the world of the dead, and both were anchored in a rigorously non-Christian perception of the countryside.

Reburial, and the cult of the dead which followed it, were part and parcel of an overall restatement of non-Christian belief and practice, and of integrating and reformulating the hostile impact of Christianity, which by now was quite impossible to ignore. In this way, for instance, the Indians would fast during Lent, but they would do so according to their own non-Christian definition of fasting.[58] Similarly, since in many places it was impossible to circumvent attendance at church, non-

55    This is the issue that most regularly unleashed enquiries designed to uncover idolatrous practices; see P. Duviols, *La lutte contre les religions autochtones dans le Pérou colonial: "L'extirpation de s'idolâtries," entre 1532 et 1660* (Lima, 1971), pp. 147ff *passim*. On reaffirmation of Andean values, Irene Silverblatt, "Andean Women under Spanish Rule," in M. Etienne and E. Leacock, eds, *Women and Colonization: Anthropological Perspectives* (New York, 1980), pp. 149–85.
56    Corpses dressed in indigenous textiles receive offerings of Andean products: Archivo Arzobispal, Lima, Idolatrías (hereinafter Idolatrías), II, 12, doctrina de Acas, provincia de Cajatambo (1659), fol. 206; IV, 18, San Francisco de Cajamarquilla (1656), fols 4ff, 9ff; reburial in burial grounds near abandoned villages, Idolatrías, II, 12 fols 176, 177, 185, 187; IV, 18 fol. 12. Cf. Idolatrías IV, 2, Cauri (1615), fols 9ff during an outbreak of smallpox, Christian images, crosses, and other holy objects of non-Andean origin are removed in the hope of recovering from the disease.
57    Idolatrías, II, 12, fol. 220; IV, 18, fol. 10.
58    Idolatrías, II, 12, fol. 176, en la quaresma aiunaban su aiuno gentilico no comiendo sal ni aji, no durmiendo los casados con sus mujeres ni los solteros con sus amigas; fol. 197, AD 1659.

Christian holy objects were often integrated into the structure of the church, or concealed near it, and Andean festivals were celebrated under the guise of Christian ones.[59]

Christianity thus did make an impact, but often it was far from the impact that the missionaries had intended, as for instance in a tale that circulated among the Indians during the volcanic eruption that devastated Arequipa in 1600. It was related that the two volcanoes near Arequipa, one named Omate, and the other, like the city, Arequipa, had a disagreement. Omate wanted Arequipa to join with him in an eruption so as to destroy the Spaniards. Arequipa, however, refused, saying that he was now called San Francisco and was a Christian. Whereupon Omate erupted on his own.[60]

By this time, Christianity and Spaniards had penetrated all but the remotest parts of Peru, with the result that not only Andean storytelling, but also some strands of Andean myth acquired a Christian coloring. In 1550, Cieza de León at Tiahuanaco was shown an ancient statue of a personage alleged to have been an apostle, most probably Thomas, who was thought to have preached to the Indians before the arrival of the Spaniards. Cieza expressed disbelief, but later the story proliferated, and the apostle was widely identified with Viracocha or Tunupa, both of whom come from an Andean supernatural universe.[61]

The *Nueva corónica y buen gobierno* of Felipe Guaman Poma de Ayala, an Indian noble of Guamanga, forges many analogous connections between Andean religion and Christianity, and between Andean and European history. The book, completed in 1612–13, documents Andean life and the Andean past as understood by a man who, for all his considerable Christian knowledge,[62] could not and did not abandon his own people's way of thought. The *Corónica* begins with two distinct

59   Pagan objects hidden in or near the church, Idolatrías, II, 12, fol. 220; IV, 18, fol. 6; cf. IV, 4, Santo Domingo de Ocros (1615), renouncing baptismal names. Celebration of pagan under the guise of Christian festivals: Idolatrías, II, 12, fol. 176 (Christmas, Corpus Christi); 211; IV, 42, Santo Domingo de Atunyauyos (1680), fol. 1ff (Holy Name of Jesus); IV, 18, fol. 3, 7 (Nativity of St. Mary); fol. 4, 17ff (Corpus Christi, All Saints). Garcilaso has a characteristic story on this topic, *Royal Commentaries*, I, 8, 1.

60   Mateos, SJ, ed., *Historia general de la Compañía de Jesús en la provincia del Perú*, II. 220–1; for an analogous story of a dispute involving an issue relating to human sacrifice that also appears to point to some Christian influence, between the mountains of Pariacaca and Guallallo, both revered by the people of Huarochiri, see *Relaciones geográficas*, BAE CLXXXIII, II, 161.

61   Pedro de Cieza de León. *El señorío de los Incas, Segunda parte de la Crónica del Perú*, ed. by C. Araníbar (Lima, 1967), 5, p. 11. Franklin Pease G. Y., *El Dios creador andino* (Lima, 1973), pp. 27ff; T. Gisbert, *Iconografía y mitos indígenas en el arte* (La Paz, 1980), pp. 35–46.

62   See R. Adorno, "Las otras fuentes de Guaman Poma: Sus lecturas castellanas," *Histórica* (Lima), 2: 2 (1978), 137–58.

chronologies, the first Biblical and Christian, going in five ages from Creation to Noah, to Abraham, to David, to Christ, to the present time; and the second Andean, going in four ages from the origin of man in the Andes to the Conquest. The fifth Andean age is the period after the Conquest.[63] The two chronologies are linked through the Incarnation, which occurred in the fourth Andean age, under the second Inca Sinchi Roca. It was at the time of this Inca, according to Guaman Poma, that the apostle Bartholomew taught the Indians Christianity, and left them, among other mementos of his message, the cross of Carabuco. The shadowy figure of the apostle whose statue Cieza was told he had seen thus became a tangible reality, a pivotal point in relation to which the connection between the Indies and Spain could be considered and understood.

Guaman Poma accepted Christianity and its Spanish representatives with some qualifications, and in this acceptance one can see reflected the attitudes, dilemmas, and failures of missionaries that have been described. Thus, Guaman Poma mentions Domingo de Santo Tomás, whose *Vocabulario* he knew, as one of those "santos dotores, alumbrado por el Espíritu Santo que le dió gracia."[64] Even Cristóbal de Albornoz, the extirpator of the Taqui Onkoy, a religious movement whose adherents hoped to supplant Christianity by a reformulation of Andean ideas, is mentioned with respect as a Christian judge, who punished all alike, whether humble or exalted.[65] On the other hand, Guaman Poma did not fail to notice what is also apparent from Albornoz's own writing, that this man was, like so many others, caught between the spiritual interests of the missionary church, and his own and the civeroyalty's material interests.[66]

Campaigns to terminate the cult of *huacas* had a double focus. They consisted in the first place of destroying the *huaca* itself, and in the second place of disposing of its property, half of which in theory was to pass to the crown.[67] The destruction of *huacas* could thus never be a purely spiritual exercise, performed for religious reasons alone. Furthermore, as Guaman Poma also noticed, the destruction of *huacas* was all too often undertaken for reasons of personal greed. With this topic,

63   See N. Wachtel, "Pensée sauvage et acculturation. L'espace et le temps chez Felipe Guaman Poma de Ayala et l'Inca Garcilaso de la Vega," *Annales. ESC*, 26: 3–4 (1971), 793–840, reprinted in Spanish in his *Sociedad e ideología* (Lima, 1973), pp. 163–228.
64   Guaman Poma, pp. 912, 1079.
65   Guaman Poma, pp. 280, 283.
66   Guaman Poma, p. 690; Duviols, *Lutte*, pp. 317ff.
67   Juan de Solórzano y Pereira, *Política indiana*, BAE CCLV, VI, 5, note section 24, quoting Theodosian Code, 16, 10, 20, dated AD 415, is a telling indicator of governmental contempt for Andean institutions.

we touch on the corruption of the early colonial church, legislated against in every church council of the period,[68] and documented in grim detail by Guaman Poma himself. In this context, Guaman Poma reiterates a statement which runs throughout his work: *mundo al rrevés*, world upside down.

The statement refers not only to the gulf between Christian teaching and Christian practice as experienced by many Indians, but also to the reversal of Andean values and the Andean social order which was brought about as much by the success of the missionaries in penetrating every aspect of Andean life as it was by the conquest. For where the viceregal state sought to restructure and reevaluate the outer, public world of Andean people by imposing an alien social, economic, and political order on them, the missionaries endeavored to restructure their private, inner world by imposing an alien supernatural order, and an alien definition of human nature.[69] This endeavor of the missionaries went hand in hand with their general failure to understand Andean life in such a way as to achieve the conversion of the Indians from within their own system of values. Just how negative the result could be was spelled out by an old man from Chancay who was imprisoned and interrogated during a campaign of extirpation of idolatries in 1677.

> Asked what concept he had of the mysteries of our holy faith, he answered that he did not believe in them, and that the saints were *conopas*, that is, gods of the Spaniards. But later, because five of his sons had died . . . he said in his heart, perhaps the god of the Spaniards would be better, I would like to convert myself to him. And he went to an Indian . . . who was master of the chapel, so that he might teach him to pray and say the rosary . . . and he lived in this way for a few days, but afterwards he returned to his idolatries as before, and believed with firmness neither in his *Guacas* nor in the mysteries of our holy faith.[70]

One of the arguments addressed to pagans that Christians of the early church and of late antiquity frequently reiterated ran, in the words of Augustine in the *City of God*:[71]

---

68   Lima I, naturales 33, 35; Lima II, Indi 6–10, 17; Lima III, actio 3, ch. 4; Lima V (AD 1601), decree 4; also see n. 42 above.

69   See Daniel Defert, "The Collection of the World: Accounts of Voyages from the Sixteenth to the Eighteenth Centuries," *Dialectical Anthropology* (Amsterdam), 7 (1982), 11–20, esp. 19.

70   Lima, Idolatrías, 5, 15, f. 3r with 35v; on the images of the saints as "conopas of Spaniards," cf. Idolatrías IV, 4, Santo Domingo de Ocros (1615), fol. 38: Como los cristianos tienen imagines ellos pueden tener los idolos que quisieren. A similar story: Guaman Poma, p. 1122.

71   Augustine, *The City of God*, trans. by H. Bettenson (London, 1972), VIII, 9.

> There are [pagan] philosophers who have conceived of God, the supreme
> and true God, as the author of all created things, the light of knowledge,
> the final good of all activity, and who have recognized him as being for us
> the origin of existence, the truth of doctrine and the blessedness of life.
> ... There may be others to be found who perceived and taught this truth
> among those who were esteemed as sages or philosophers in other
> nations: Libyans of Atlas, Egyptians, Indians, Persians, Scythians, Gauls,
> Spaniards. Whoever they may have been, we rank such thinkers above all
> others.

In this way, as we saw at the outset, many apologists of the early church
anchored their appeal for conversion in an explicit acceptance of values
which, although held dearly by their pagan audience, might be integrated in Christianity, rather than in an outright rejection of these
values. With some exceptions, this was not the theological strategy of
the missionaries in Peru. Instead, if the comparison with the early Christian and late antique Mediterranean is to be continued, missionaries
applied to their situation the ideas of post-Constantinian Christianity,
when the legislative authority of the state, that is, religious coercion,
could be invoked to reinforce persuasion. In late antiquity the precept
"compel them to enter" acquired theological potential at just the time
when it could also be executed in practice.[72] It was this same precept,
which, as we have seen, came to prevail in the Peruvian church.

In Peru, as in the Roman empire, religious coercion was the by-
product of the church's involvement with the state. At the same time,
in Peru, as in the Roman empire, the church's involvement with the
state could bring about this outcome only because the tension between
faith and reason, and the accompanying polarity between persuasion
and coercion is innate to the Christian view of the nature of truth, a
view that postulates both the authority of scripture and the endeavor of
human thought and speculation as necessary to the attainment of
truth. I have here argued that the possibility of concluding that the
Indians were capable of this thought and speculation was countenanced
in the sixteenth century. I have also shown that this possibility was set
to one side. The same pattern of theological reasoning anchored in circumstances that set in motion religious coercion in the fourth century
thus reemerged in Peru in the sixteenth. Nonetheless, religious coercion,

---

72   See n. 9 above. For the interdependence of Christian conceptual systems, on
the one hand, and social and political practice, on the other, in late antiquity, see E.
A. Judge, "Christian Innovation and its Contemporary Observers," in Brian Croke
and A. M. Emmett, eds, *History and Historians in Late Antiquity* (Elmsford, N.Y.,
1983), pp. 13–29. An analogous interdependence was at work in early colonial
Peru.

and the accompanying concept of religious conversion, were not the same in Peru as in Rome, because in Peru there existed the additional complication of cultural difference. In late antique Rome, the debate about conversion and persecution could raise the question of the possibility of religious tolerance because the participants in the debate shared the same culture. In Peru, they did not. The question of religious tolerance could not arise in Peru because it can only be discussed among people who view each other as equal in some respect. Those who pleaded the cause of the Indians therefore concentrated on proving that in various ways they were equal to Spaniards. This had been the issue which Domingo de Santo Tomás addressed in this work on the Quechua language, and the same issue was still at the center of debate two generations later.

At this time, when Guaman Poma was gathering material for his *Corónica*, Garcilaso de la Vega the Inca was writing his *Royal Commentaries of the Incas* in Córdoba. A significant chapter in this work[73] argues that the Incas and their subjects knew of a creator God who foreshadowed, and in effect was, the Christian God. This is Pachacamac, "Creator of the World." Hence, Garcilaso says, this name Pachacamac should be used by the missionaries when they talk of God, but it is not. For,

> the Indians do not understand or dare tell these things with the true interpretation and meaning of the words. They see that the Christian Spaniards abominate them all as works of the devil, and the Spaniards do not trouble to ask for clear information about them, but rather dismiss them as diabolical, as they imagine.

Garcilaso also explains how Pachacamac was conceived of as not a material, but as a spiritual, being, omnipotent and eternal.

In attributing such a divinity to the Incas, he possibly had in mind passages such as the one from the *City of God* cited earlier. For, Garcilaso wrote to explain Peru, its culture, politics, and religion, to Spaniards within an intellectual framework such as Spaniards could understand and accept. He in effect adopted a Spanish, even a European framework, but, like Domingo de Santo Tomás, he did this in such a way as to change the framework and expand it. Guaman Poma, on the other hand, did not adopt a Spanish framework for what he wanted to say, but retained the conceptual categories of the Andes.

From within these categories, however, Guaman Poma also articulated a response to the missionaries, which joins hands with Garcilaso's response. Near the beginning of his *Corónica*, Guaman Poma lists the

73  *Royal Commentaries*, I. 2, 2.

twelve months of the year along with descriptions and drawings of the festivals which in each month the Incas used to celebrate.[74] The conclusion of the *Corónica* consists of another list of the twelve months, this time with drawings depicting the agricultural tasks to be performed month by month.[75] The countryside has been converted to Christianity: it is not, as in Inca times, inhabited by *huacas* or their Christian equivalent, the demons. For, where Guaman Poma for the Inca months depicted in his drawings the old sacrifices and rituals made intelligible to a Spanish and Christian audience by the presence of demons, for the Spanish and Christian months at the end of the *Corónica*, he merely depicted, in the idiom of the European Middle Ages, the labors of the months: breaking the earth, sowing, harvesting. These Christian drawings of the months are matched by a Christian calendar, which lists the saints of each day according to the Tridentine missal. The land has been swept clean of demons. But, unlike the countryside of the Catholic Mediterranean, Guaman Poma's countryside was not repopulated by the saints, those "*conopas* of Spaniards," as some Indians would have said. In this way, as every Andean anthropologist knows, the countryside remained pagan.[76]

However, in his description of the Christian month November, Guaman Poma records a Quechua prayer, which, he says, in former times was addressed to God for water. In this prayer, God, *runa camac*, creator of man, is also addressed by the Spanish word Dios: *Dios runa camac*.[77] Guaman Poma here makes a point that he spells out at length elsewhere in the *Corónica*: the Indians knew of the Christian god long before the Spaniards ever came to the New World, for, not only did the Apostle Bartholomew preach to them, but also, during the first four ages of Indian chronology, that is, during the ages before the Incarnation, and before the Incas, the Indians followed a pure worship, a worship without idols or *huacas*. For Guaman Poma, therefore, conversion to

74   Guaman Poma, pp. 236–59.
75   Guaman Poma, pp. 1141–75. These two sets of calendar drawings, with their contrasting perception of the organization of time according to both natural and socially agreed rhythms, spell out the polarities between Andean religion and Christianity. See W. Bermann, "Der römische Kalender. Zur sozialen Konstruktion der Zeitrechnung." *Saeculum. Jahrbuch für Universalgeschichte*, 35 (1984), 1–16.
76   Gary Urton, *At the Crossroads of the Earth and the Sky: An Andean Cosmology* (Austin, 1981). By contrast, M. Marzal, *La transformación religiosa peruana* (Lima, 1983), argues that during the seventeenth century, the missionaries did succeed in "transforming the Andean supernatural universe. But it is only by significantly shifting the categories that most missionaries applied during the period here discussed that one can call the result Christian in any sense.
77   Guaman Poma, p. 1161. On these and related prayers in Guaman Poma, see J. Szeminski, "Las generaciones del mundo según don Felipe Guaman Poma de Ayala." *Histórica* (Lima), 7: 1 (1983), 69–109.

Christianity, so far from requiring the wholesale destruction of earlier beliefs and observances, consisted of nothing other than an organic transition. Guaman Poma thus articulated a model for a religious evolution from Andean religion to Christianity which matches the model that had earlier been posited by Domingo de Santo Tomás and men of a similar persuasion.

By the time Guaman Poma wrote, however, this model had lost the practical significance which it had during the first generation after the conquest. As a result, the state in which Guaman Poma lived was a state in which he and his people were not and could not be accommodated or understood. It was in this *mundo al rrevés* that Guaman Poma looked for a god both of Indians and of Spaniards, a god who transcended both conversion and persecution, the arm of the church and the arm of the state. Hence, when writing of the first age of the Indians, Guaman Poma attributes to these Indians a prayer which echoes the psalm *de profundis*: Señor, hasta cuándo clamaré y no me oyrás, y daré bozes, y no me rresponderás?[78] And he repeats these words in Quechua. In the second age, the Indians prayed more urgently.

> Lord, where are you? In the heavens, or in the earth, or at the ends of the earth, or in the nether world [*infierno*]? Where are you? Hear me, maker of the world and of man. Hear me, oh God.[79]

This prayer, formulated in terms familiar both to readers of the Psalms and to students of Andean religion[80] bridges that gap of cultural and political as well as religious difference which the Peruvian church of the sixteenth and seventeenth centuries ultimately failed to bridge.

One deep calleth another.

## Acknowledgment

Part of the research here presented was funded by the American Philosophical Society and the Pew Foundation at Stanford University. To both I extend my thanks for support of my work.

---

78   Guaman Poa, p. 50; see on the fourth age, p. 78. The prayer is repeated as spoken by Guaman Poma himself p. 922, where it expresses the author's despair over the time he lives in.
79   Guaman Poma, p. 54; *Psalm*, 129, 1.
80   See Cristóbal de Molina el Cuzqueño, *Fábulas y ritos de los Incas*, in *Las crónicas de los Molinas* (Lima, 1943), p. 38; prayer to the Creator during Citua.

# Index